Spinoza on Learning to Live Together

SUSAN JAMES

OXFORD
UNIVERSITY PRESS

OXFORD
UNIVERSITY PRESS

Great Clarendon Street, Oxford, OX2 6DP,
United Kingdom

Oxford University Press is a department of the University of Oxford.
It furthers the University's objective of excellence in research, scholarship,
and education by publishing worldwide. Oxford is a registered trade mark of
Oxford University Press in the UK and in certain other countries

© Susan James 2020

The moral rights of the author have been asserted

First Edition published in 2020

Impression: 3

Published in the United States of America by Oxford University Press
198 Madison Avenue, New York, NY 10016, United States of America

British Library Cataloguing in Publication Data
Data available

Library of Congress Control Number: 2020945703

ISBN 978-0-19-871307-4

Printed and bound in Great Britain by
Clays Ltd, Elcograf S.p.A.

Contents

Acknowledgements

The essays in this volume were written over a number of years, and I am deeply grateful to the institutions, colleagues, students, and friends who have made them possible. My greatest institutional debt is to Birkbeck College. I offer my warmest thanks to my colleagues in the Philosophy Department for their constructive comments on my contributions to our Work in Progress seminar, and my gratitude to the Department's students for their probing questions about early-modern philosophy. I am also deeply conscious of how much I have learned from discussions at the London Spinoza Circle (based at Birkbeck), and from my Ph.D. students, whose work has helped me to develop some of the ideas presented here.

I am further indebted to the Birkbeck Philosophy Department for several periods of research leave. I wrote the first draft of Chapter 3 as a fellow of the Wissenschaftskolleg zu Berlin in 2003–4. Chapter 4 was written when I was John Findlay Visiting Professor in the Philosophy Department of Boston University in 2008. Chapter 7 was drafted in 2013 while I was a Laurance S. Rockefeller Visiting Fellow at the Center for Human Values at Princeton University. In 2017 I was fortunate to be able to present versions of Chapters 12 and 13 at the University of Chicago, where I was Kohut Visiting Professor of Social Thought in the Committee of Social Thought, and a visiting fellow of the Neubauer Collegium. Finally, some of the talks I gave between 2015 and 2018 as an associate member of the Humanities Center (now the Department of Comparative Literature) at Johns Hopkins University went into the Introduction and Chapters 11, 12, and 13.

Each of these experiences taught me about different ways of approaching the history of philosophy and the work of Spinoza in particular. I am grateful to Dieter Grimm for inviting me to the Wissenschaftskolleg, and to the group of scholars I met there; to Charles Griswold and Aaron Garrett for inviting me to Boston University and to my colleagues and students in the BU Philosophy Department; to Alan Patten for inviting me to the Center for Human Values, and to the Center's lively faculty members and visitors; to Robert Pippin for arranging my visit to the Chicago Committee of Social Thought, to Jonathan Lear for inviting me to be a Visiting Fellow of the Neubauer Collegium, and to the colleagues and students at the University of Chicago who took my seminar on Spinoza; and finally to Hent de Vries, Yitzhak Melamed, and their colleagues at Johns Hopkins University for the opportunity to visit them over three years and engage in extended conversation.

In all these visiting positions I was fortunate to be able to exchange ideas with outstanding students and colleagues whose ideas are reflected in this book, and who form part of the broader community of scholars who have helped me to try to understand Spinoza. At the beginning of each essay I thank particular individuals for their comments and suggestions; but I am also more generally indebted to the colleagues who have given me opportunities to present my ideas, the audiences who have heard me out, the questioners who have been kind enough to respond, and the people with whom I have had conversations about the problems of learning to live together. For inspiration, solidarity and friendship I am grateful to Aurelia Armstrong, Jane Bennett, Kum-Kum Bhavnani, Deborah Brown, Clare Carlisle, Emanuele Costa, Michael Della Rocca, Alexander Douglas, Sabrina Ebbersmeyer, Cynthia Farrar, Dan Garber, Aaron Garrett, Moira Gatens, Francis Gilbert, Paul Ginsborg, Charles Griswold, Jen Guttenplan, Sam Guttenplan, Timothy Harrison, John Heyderman, Mogens Laerke, Jacqueline Lagrée, Jonathan Lear, Melissa Lane, Hallvard Lillehammer, Beth Lord, Steph Marston, Jo McDonagh, Victoria McGeer, Yitzhak Melamed, Lyvia Morgan, Stephen Nadler, Yi-Ping Ong, Martine Péchermann, Philip Pettit, Robert Pippin, Andrea Ray, Gabriel Richardson Lear, Sandy Reiter, Ursula Renz, Beate Roessler, Michael Rosenthal, Martin Saar, Laurencia Saenz Benavides, Ayse Saraçgil, Eric Schliesser, Lisa Shapiro, Angela Smith, Nigel Smith, Piet Steenbakkers, Robert Stern, Theo Verbeek, and Catherine Wilson.

Some of the essays included here have been published before, and where this is so I thank the original publisher at the beginning of the chapter. For help with preparing the manuscript I am indebted to Emanuele Costa and Noemi Magnani, who between them have saved me from delay and a host of editorial errors, and I am grateful to Jenny King, Martin Noble, and Markcus Sandanraj who have seen the book through the press. Peter Momtchiloff, Philosophy Editor at Oxford University Press, has as always exercised just the right combination of patience and impatience, and it is a special pleasure to thank him for his encouragement and trust.

As Spinoza urges us to recognize, a way of life in which one can exchange philosophical ideas and write books depends on a multitude of factors. Perhaps the most vital of these, in my case, is the support of my family, above all of my husband, Quentin Skinner. As well as correcting the manuscript from start to finish, he has commented insightfully and knowledgeably on each of the essays in this volume and given me every kind of encouragement. I am boundlessly grateful for his empowering presence.

Note about References

All references to, and quotations from, Spinoza's works and correspondence are taken from the two volumes of *The Collected Works of Spinoza* edited and translated by Edwin Curley. In citing passages from individual texts I follow the usual conventions. I refer first to Curley's edition, then to the volume and page number of the Latin *Opera* edited by Carl Gebhardt.

Titles are abbreviated as follows:

Treatise on the Emendation of the Intellect	TIE
Short Treatise on God, Man and his Wellbeing	ST
Ethics	E
Theological-Political Treatise	TTP
Political Treatise	TP

Introduction

Philosophy as the Art of Living Together

Human lives can go better or worse. They may be dominated by the miseries and frustrations that Spinoza describes as sadness, or enriched by the satisfactions that he classifies as forms of joy. The emotional tenor of a life may be consistently cheerful or anxious and unsettled. Spinoza's opinion as to which kind of life is preferable never wavers; we all do what we can to live joyfully and avoid sadness. But success does not come easily. To work out what will make us most joyful and put our knowledge into practice we need many skills and insights, and these can only be effectively cultivated in propitious circumstances. Learning how to harness and strengthen our power to live in the ways that are most deeply empowering and satisfying is therefore a ramifying and always unfinished project. Above all, however, it is a collective one. Learning to live joyfully is a matter of learning to live together.

Spinoza's commitment to this view is evident throughout his mature philosophical works. The *Political Treatise* considers how states need to be organized if their members are to live peacefully and securely. Tackling the problem of disagreement within the state, *The Theological-Political Treatise* explains how people with conflicting beliefs and aspirations can nevertheless share mutually empowering and satisfying ways of life. Working on a much larger scale, the *Ethics* situates these insights within a more comprehensive conception of living together that extends beyond our relationships with one another to our relationship with nature as a whole. The more we are able to align our ways of life with the workings of the totality that Spinoza describes as God or nature, the more profoundly and securely joyful we become.

Learning how to make the transition from a way of life narrowly focused on our immediate individual desires to an existence aligned with the whole of nature is, in Spinoza's view, the defining project of philosophy. This is what true philosophers achieve, and the joyfulness that their knowledge engenders is what makes philosophizing supremely valuable. But philosophy also has practical manifestations. Because we get better at living together as our rational understanding grows, our capacity to sustain harmonious ways of life is the surest expression of our philosophical insight. At its fullest, understanding is as motivating as it is illuminating. As well as giving us access to truths about the benefits of cooperative ways of life, it strengthens our commitment to act on them, so that a community

Spinoza on Learning to Live Together. Susan James, Oxford University Press (2020). © Susan James.
DOI: 10.1093/oso/9780198713074.001.0001

whose members share an exceptionally high level of understanding will be over-whelmingly motivated to put their knowledge to work. They will appreciate, for instance, that individuals find it easier to cooperate when they are sure they will be treated fairly, and will also act on this insight by giving as much weight to the good of others as to their own.

Realizing this exemplary ideal may be more than we can achieve. Nevertheless, even a comparatively limited philosophical understanding will strengthen our capacity to sustain mutually satisfying social ties, and will enable us to enter into a degree of cooperation with further features of our environment. As we come to understand how we are situated in nature as a whole, we get a clearer view of what we do and do not have the power to bring about, and learn to act accordingly. The project of learning to live together therefore encompasses every aspect of our knowledge and is reflected in every aspect of our lives.

Spinoza's insistence on the simultaneously theoretical and practical quality of our understanding echoes a classical conception of philosophy as the art of living.[1] Seneca, for example, characterizes philosophy as a comprehensive *ars vivendi* that unifies doctrines about life as a whole with precepts about how to act on them. Philosophy, he affirms, 'is both theoretical and practical; it con-templates and at the same time acts'.[2] Sketching the theoretical doctrines on which our knowledge of how to act is grounded, Seneca goes on to claim that if we aspire to practise philosophy 'we must set before our eyes the goal of the supreme good towards which we may strive, and to which all our acts and words may have reference—just as sailors guide their course according to a certain star'.[3] Since the supreme good lies in knowing God, our first task is to understand him so that we can learn how to worship him.[4] Our next problem is to learn to deal with humans, and here we need to recognize that we are part of nature. 'All that you behold, that which comprises both god and man, is one—we are the parts of one great body.'[5] Spinoza is sympathetic to many aspects of this Stoic outlook; for him, too, the philosopher's supreme good lies in understanding a God who is identified with the whole of nature and in which all individual things exist; and for him, too, understanding is both theoretical and practical. Nevertheless, it is important to stress the extent to which philosophizing as Spinoza portrays it is at the same time a collective project—an art of living together.

Spinoza's conviction that we have no real alternative to learning to live together is rooted in a view that runs through every aspect of his philosophy: that indi-vidual things are not free-standing or autonomous, but on the contrary are deeply interdependent. This outlook is evident from the very beginning of the *Ethics*, where Spinoza deprives individuals of the independence traditionally

[1] Perhaps the greatest historian and exponent of this tradition is Pierre Hadot. See Hadot 1995.
[2] Seneca 1971, Letter 95.10.   [3] Seneca 1971, Letter 95, 45.
[4] Seneca 1971, Letter 95, 47–8.   [5] Seneca 1971, Letter 95, 51–2.

accorded to substances. A star in the firmament, a worm in the blood or a woman in the street are not substances, he claims, but merely modes of the one all-encompassing substance that he calls God or nature. Explicating this form of ontological dependence, Spinoza goes on to ask what distinguishes one mode from another. The essence of an individual thing, he argues, is its power to persevere in its being. Here we seem to have hit upon a sense in which individuals are independent of other things—each has its own power to persevere in its being. But again, Spinoza is cautious. The power of an individual mode, he argues, is dependent on the all-encompassing power of God or nature, without which the mode could not exist. 'Nothing can be or be conceived without God, but all things are in God.' Individuals therefore depend for their existence and essence on nature as a whole, and their power to persevere in their being is determined by its overall operations.

At a less exalted ontological level, individuals are also dependent on the things around them. As Spinoza often reminds us, they can only survive when conditions are right—a change in temperature may melt a glacier, destroy animal food sources and flood a town. Equally, individuals require certain conditions in order to flourish. Spinoza is adamant, for example, that humans are disempowered by solitude and can only live joyfully in community with other people. In general then, an individual's power to exist and go on existing depends on how external things affect it and how it is able to affect them.

The dependences we have so far traced apply to individuals of all kinds; any individual mode is dependent on substance or nature and on the modes around it. As human modes, however, we strive to persevere in our being by living joyfully, and our experience of affecting and being affected by external things is manifested in joy and sadness. As we have begun to see, it takes many relationships with many kinds of things to sustain our joyfulness; but Spinoza accords a special place to our relationships with other people, or as he prefers to put it, with things that are like us. The crucial sense in which people are alike is that their relationships with external things, and indeed with one another, are coloured by the same joyful and saddening affects. Like us, other people fear danger and are pleased by the happiness of their friends, and commonalities such as these play a part in shaping our mutual relationships.

There is no guarantee that these affective exchanges will make our lives more joyful; they incline us, Spinoza says, to vengefulness as much as to love. But they nevertheless make space for a form of empowerment that only arises from our relationships with other humans. While a mountain, for example, is incapable of responding to the awe it arouses in us, the ways in which we answer one another's affects can increase our joyfulness and change what we are able to do. When two friends consistently and lovingly adapt to one another's desires, they create a cooperative relationship that brings with it novel satisfactions and new ways of opposing sadness. Together, they acquire powers to live joyfully that neither possesses on their own. One may wonder whether we are also capable of mutual affective exchange with at least some non-human individuals, but Spinoza passes over this line of thought. Learning to live joyfully, as he construes it, is first and foremost a matter of learning to live cooperatively with other people, and our responsiveness to their affects is crucial to this process. By binding ourselves together in mutually satisfying relationships, we make our lives more joyful and establish conditions that are conducive to the growth of understanding.

To make the most of the benefits that flow from cooperation, Spinoza argues that we need to face up to our physical and emotional vulnerability. Instead of ignoring the extent of our dependence on other individuals, the precariousness of our relationship with our natural environment, or the restraints imposed by our place in the overall operation of nature, we need to keep these forms of dependence clearly in view and develop ways of living joyfully within the space they provide. Once we take this stance, Spinoza suggests, various things become clear. First of all, we have no viable alternative to learning to live together—our individual power is just too slight. More than this, learning to live together is a process of finding ways to address the forms of dependence that make us vulnerable to sadness, and transform them as far as we can into elements of progressively more empowering ways of life.

Since we are always striving to persevere in our being, there is a sense in which this process is already underway. In his own fashion, a tyrant who routinely murders his rivals is striving to make himself less vulnerable, and a patriarch who rules his family with a rod of iron may be bent on upholding a harmonious domestic life. What both men fail to understand is that the fears and resentments they arouse in those around them not only sadden particular individuals, but also weaken the forms of life they are trying to sustain. The fact that the patriarch's children hate him, for example, stunts the family's joyfulness and threatens its stability. It makes the family more vulnerable to internal conflict and reduces its resilience in the face of external threats. Although we are always trying to compensate for our individual and collective vulnerability, our efforts often fail or backfire, so that a first condition of making our lives more deeply and securely joyful must be to learn to overcome these limitations. We ourselves are the initial focus of the project of learning to live joyfully, and the satisfactions that most concern us are the ones we derive from our relationships with each other. In the ordinary course of things, experience teaches us quite a bit about the advantages of cooperation and sets us on the path of understanding. But for Spinoza, as for Seneca, it is only as our understanding grows, and we acquire a relatively systematic grasp of how to oppose sadness, that our power to live harmoniously becomes secure. While philosophy grows out of experience, it also introduces us to distinctive forms of joy.

Spinoza's project of learning to live together is nothing if not ambitious and it is not always easy to see what his prescriptions involve. How exactly are we supposed to counteract the debilitating forms of dependence that he itemizes, and what sort of philosophically informed life are we aiming for? While these questions can fruitfully be raised about every aspect of Spinoza's system, the essays collected in this volume concentrate on three overlapping areas in which they arise—in his epistemology, his political philosophy, and his conception of philosophy itself.

In Part I, I explore the epistemological demands of learning to live together. I consider what kinds of understanding we need to cultivate and how they enhance our power to live cooperatively. Spinoza distinguishes three kinds of knowledge or *cognitio*, imagining, reasoning, and intuition. Each has a role to play in the project of sustaining joyful ways of life, and the contribution of one complements that of the others. Chapters 1 to 5 focus on the relationship between imagining and reasoning, and aim to show how these two forms of *cognitio* support and blend into one another. Imaginative practices, I argue, already embody many of the epistemological skills and norms associated with reasoning. Equally, reasoning relies on our capacity to imagine diverse forms of cooperation and different ways of life. To learn how to live together, we therefore have to work out how to combine our rational and imaginative powers in such a way that each tempers and enhances the other.

Since Spinoza's most detailed illustrations of this mutual dependence concentrate on the relationship between philosophy and revealed religion, the essays in Part I draw on this example. Chapter 2 uncovers continuities between an imaginative religious outlook and a rational philosophical one. Chapter 3 examines the grounds on which Spinoza distinguishes an empowering religious life from a degraded superstitious one, and suggests how even superstitious practices can help us live together. Chapter 4 considers the extent to which our rational understanding of how to live together appeals to imaginative narratives. How far, it asks, does reasoning make use of fictions? The same issue is taken up in Chapter 5, where I appeal to Spinoza to give fictions a place in a rational way of life.

Taken together, the essays in Part I aim to illuminate Spinoza's view that, in order to live as empoweringly and joyfully as we can, we have to learn how to harmonize our imaginative and rational insights. The way we understand our powers of imagining and reasoning affects our ability to use them and has consequences for how we are able to live. We need each of these two loosely distinguishable ways of thinking in order to understand the forms of dependence of which any successful effort to build a cooperative way of life must take account; and each of them helps us to put our understanding to work in the particular circumstances in which we find ourselves. To live as joyfully as we can, we have to resist the temptation to conceive of philosophy as a purely rational practice and take advantage of its imaginative dimensions.

Blending imagination and reason into an empowering philosophical practice, and expressing it in a cooperative way of life, requires a range of skills that can only be acquired and exercised in certain conditions, many of which are political. In a state of nature where nothing prevents individuals from doing anything in their power, opportunities for cooperation are limited, and it is only within the state that our understanding can get a firm grip on the way we live. Politics is therefore central to Spinoza's project. Taking up a range of familiar issues, he considers, for example, how sovereigns can best maintain peace, what gives them legitimacy, and what forms of government are most conducive to freedom. Underlying these discussions, however, there is a deeper preoccupation. To count as successful, a state must sustain a cooperative ethos that protects its members from the kinds of sadness that come with tyranny, poverty, war, or religious conflict. But states also confront the task of enhancing their own resilience by providing conditions in which understanding can grow. Rather than merely upholding the status quo, states empower themselves by encouraging philosophical understanding and putting it to work, and the nature of this process is examined in Part II.

The essays in this section explore some of the pervasive misunderstandings that habitually obstruct our efforts to create successful political communities. Instead of facing up to our dependence on nature and acknowledging the painful truth that it is indifferent to our desires, we tend to imagine it as more hospitable and controllable than it is and, in doing so, misconstrue the problems that politics has to solve. Indeed, some of our most influential political doctrines exemplify this error. We commonly think of ourselves, for example, as subject to natural laws that guarantee certain moral rights and duties and limit what sovereigns and subjects can rightfully do. According to Spinoza, however, no such laws exist. Positing them may comfort and reassure us; but it gives us a misleading picture of our relationship with nature and distorts our understanding. By setting us on the wrong path, it obstructs our efforts to devise laws of our own that will strengthen our capacity to cooperate and enable us to live more harmoniously.

While I address this theme most explicitly in Chapters 6, 7, and 10, it also runs through the discussion of freedom in Chapters 8 and 9. Freedom, as Spinoza conceives of it, is the antidote to dependence. At one level it is the supreme political value; the very point of the state, Spinoza explains, is to enable us to live freely. If we look through a wider lens, however, political freedom is revealed as one element in a philosophical form of liberty that transforms the kinds of dependence from which we started out. Political freedom is a fine and relatively rare collective achievement; but it also serves as a model for the yet greater freedom that philosophical understanding secures.

Spinoza's discussions of politics focus primarily on states, their institutions and their subjects. Learning to live together, in its political dimension, is a matter of discovering how to create secure and peaceful communities within which people are able to develop and live by their philosophical understanding. The philosophically informed can therefore be expected to set great store by the state's power to protect them and do everything they can to ensure that it is not threatened. They will be on the lookout for ways of strengthening the state's cohesiveness and ready to adjust their ways of life to their growing knowledge. As they will also appreciate, however, political power has its limits. Like other individual things, states are dependent on the overall workings of nature and are vulnerable to individuals whose power exceeds their own. The project of learning to live joyfully therefore cannot stop at the boundaries of the state, or even at the boundaries of a state system, but must also look outward to the rest of nature.

This further aspect of Spinoza's vision is the subject of Part III. Chapter 11 returns to the topic of Chapter 9 and explores a further aspect of the transition from political to philosophical freedom. The greatest liberation of which we are capable shifts our attention away from specifically human ways of life and in doing so changes our sense of what we are. We come to see ourselves, not so much as one human being among others or as members of one state among others, but as one mode of God or nature. This transformation is, however, hard to imagine, and in my final chapters I begin to explore what it might be like. Chapter 12 is a reflection on Spinoza's claim that, as we learn to live in the light of our understanding, our increasing joy is not diminished by any affective loss. Here I draw on literary sources to question his confidence. I end, in Chapter 13 by offering an interpretation of the virtue of fortitude, one of the constitutive conditions of learning to live together. Without fortitude, Spinoza suggests, we cannot develop our understanding or put it to work. But what exactly is it? What qualities do we most need in order to make philosophical progress?

Spinoza's conception of what philosophy is and what it can do, along with his sense of what an empowering way of life involves, are shaped by his experience. They reflect the philosophical and cultural preoccupations of his era, and are sensitive to the philosophical, religious, and political struggles with which he engaged. No attempt to understand his ideas and aspirations can ignore these contexts, and the essays in this book aim to take them into account. One cannot, for example, weigh Spinoza's view of the relationship between religion and philosophy without acknowledging the fierce struggles between theologians and philosophers by which he was surrounded. Nor can one capture the intended force of his view that philosophy is the key to learning to live together without bearing in mind how this commitment threatened the Dutch theological and political establishments. Spinoza's world is not ours, and many features of his work are liable to strike us as implausible or alien. Few of us regard the prophetic narratives of the Bible as a vital source of political insight; few professional philosophers nowadays conceive philosophy as an art of living; most of us are increasingly sceptical of Spinoza's view that we can treat animals as we please; and few of us share his conviction that philosophy can yield a universal and transformative understanding of nature. But despite these radical discontinuities, there are many ways in which Spinoza continues to speak to us. The essays collected here were written with contemporary philosophical issues in mind, and aim to show how

Spinoza's ideas illuminate them. By conceiving philosophy in practical terms as the project of learning to live together, I suggest, we can shift our epistemological and political outlooks, opening up new problems and making space for new solutions. At the same time, Spinoza encourages us to turn to the practice of philosophy itself and look afresh at what it can achieve and what virtues it calls for. Spinoza's worldview may be strange, but it is by no means irrelevant. By jolting some of our everyday presuppositions and reminding us of others, it can help us learn to live together.

PART I

LEARNING TO LIVE TOGETHER

1

Creating Rational Understanding

Spinoza as a Social Epistemologist

Spinoza's *Ethics* maps a path from an everyday way of life burdened by passion and error to an elevated form of existence in which the philosophically initiated are empowered by their love of God to live together justly and honourably (E IV App. XV; II/270).[1] The transformation he describes has many dimensions, ethical, affective, metaphysical, and psychological, but it partly consists in an epistemological progression through three stages of *cognitio* or knowledge. Starting with knowledge of the first kind, which belongs to the kind of thinking known as imagination, we 'perceive many things and form universal notions' from signs, and from sensory perceptions 'represented to us in a manner that is mutilated, confused, and without order for the intellect'. Building on this foundation, we move to what Spinoza describes as reasoning or knowledge of the second kind, which operates with adequate ideas of the properties of things. Finally, we ascend to *scientia intuitiva* or knowledge of the third kind, a type of *cognitio* that derives adequate knowledge of the essence of things from an adequate idea of the formal essence of certain attributes of God (E IIp40s2; II/122).

Some excellent work has recently been done on Spinoza's account of the transition from reasoning to intuitive science,[2] but less has been said about the prior shift from imagining to reasoning.[3] This omission is not altogether surprising. In the *Ethics* imagination is represented in largely negative terms as a persistent but flawed mode of cognition that has to be transcended in order for philosophical inquiry to get a hold. It is the background, so to speak, against which the drama of philosophy is staged, and it is examined from the vantage point of thinkers who are already in a position to provide a rational account of it, informed by their adequate ideas of its operations and deficiencies. Seen from the perspective of knowledge of the second kind, imagining becomes part of the subject matter of philosophy, and many commentators have treated it in this fashion. In doing so,

[1] Originally published in *The Aristotelian Society Supplementary Volume*, vol. 85:1 (2011), 181–99. Reprinted with permission of the Aristotelian Society and Oxford University Press. I am particularly grateful to Jennifer Hornsby, Pieter Pekelharing, and Eric Schliesser for their helpful comments on earlier presentations of this essay. See Schliesser (2011).
[2] See Carr (1987), Malinowski-Charles (2003), Garrett (2009a, 2009b).
[3] For notable exceptions see De Deugd (1966), Curley (1973a), Gatens and Lloyd (1999), Vinciguerra (2005), Gatens (2009a).

Spinoza on Learning to Live Together. Susan James, Oxford University Press (2020). © Susan James.
DOI: 10.1093/oso/9780198713074.001.0001

however, they have tended to overlook an issue by which Spinoza is deeply pre-occupied: the question of how a community where people mainly think and live on the basis of imagination can make reasoning a part of its way of life, and reap the benefits of the second kind of knowledge. Unusually among seventeenth-century philosophers, Spinoza not only explores the kinds of self-discipline and education that allow selected individuals to acquire adequate ideas;[4] he also treats reasoning as a collective undertaking that depends on social as well as cognitive conditions, and can in principle transform not just the way we think but the way we live. The transition from knowledge of the first to the second kind is in part a social one, and it is this aspect of it that I plan to explore.

Imagining, as it is portrayed in the *Ethics*, yields a kind of *cognitio* that is con-fused in several familiar ways. Whereas reasoning operates with clear and distinct ideas that in turn yield an adequate conception of the difference between truth and falsehood, the ideas we form on the basis of sensory perceptions or signs are grounded on our fortuitous encounters with things and reflect the limitations of our experience (E IIp29s; II/114). If my knowledge of the sun is based on my perception of it, I shall have a confused or inadequate idea of its distance from the earth; if my idea of a horse was acquired from reading *Orlando Furioso*, it will be mutilated or inaccurate (E IIp35s; II/117). Deficiencies such as these are exacer-bated by some of the psychological laws to which humans are subject. Because our imagined ideas lead us to conceive of things as existing, they often fail to track change and give us an erroneous picture of what the world is like. To adapt one of Spinoza's examples, if I saw my friend Melinda last year and am unaware that she has since died, I shall persist in imagining her as existing and falsely believe that she is still alive (E IIp17c; II/105–6).[5] Equally, our disposition to asso-ciate ideas leads us to misinterpret situations and misunderstand causal connec-tions. 'A soldier, having seen traces of a horse in the sand, will immediately pass from the thought of a horse to the thought of a horseman, and from that to the thought of war' while a farmer will connect the idea of a horse with that of a plough and a field (E IIp18s; II/107). But such trains of thought can lead the sol-dier or the farmer astray, as when the soldier jumps to the erroneous conclusion that horses are essentially for military use, or the farmer infers that a particular field must have been ploughed by a horse.

Underlying all these dispositions is the principle that Spinoza calls the *conatus*— the striving to persevere in its being that constitutes the essence of an individual thing (E IIIp6, p7; II/146). Like other individuals, humans manifest their *conatus* in every aspect of their existence, expressing it in languages, artifacts, forms of enquiry, and social institutions. People whose thinking is predominantly imaginative

---

[4] See for example TIE.
[5] Imagining, Spinoza writes, encompasses 'the fictitious, the false, the doubtful, and absolutely all those [ideas] which depend only on the memory' (Letter 37).

therefore strive to persevere in their being on the basis of their perceptions and encounters with signs, and this generates its own cognitive limitations. In an effort to assert itself, the mind puts a particular gloss on its experience by striving to imagine 'only what affirms or posits its power of acting' (EIIIp54; II/182), and failing to register things that diminish its own power or that of the body (EIIIp13c; II/151). An affective disposition to resist disempowerment makes us insensitive to the more discouraging features of our experience. When we imagine, ideas that are in fact partial and distorted conceal their own privation and represent themselves to us as whole and true, so that their limitations are reflected in the conceptions of truth and falsity we derive from them. As well as misleading us about particular states of affairs, they encourage us to settle for an epistemological second best, and to negotiate the world on the basis of norms that fall short of clear and distinct understanding (E IIp41; II/123).

Despite its failings, however, imagining is far from useless. It is the mode of cognition we normally employ, and the epistemological basis of our everyday forms of life. While Spinoza allows that some features of imagining stand in the way of reasoning and impede our ability to acquire knowledge of the second kind, he also assigns it a productive part in promoting our capacity to reason. Our imaginative striving to persevere in our being can be harnessed to the philosophical project of thinking with adequate ideas and used to encourage the development of a philosophical way of life. One of the ways in which human beings use their imaginative capacities, Spinoza observes, is to develop bodies of knowledge that will empower them. People with an interest in particular areas of human experience such as cosmology, psychology, history, religion, or politics set themselves to achieve investigative ends that will contribute to some aspect of this overall goal, and develop standards of truth and falsity adapted to the particular ends in question.

To exemplify what Spinoza has in mind, we can extrapolate from the account of history that he offers in the *Theological-Political Treatise*. A narrative historian who aims to provide an account of the history of Rome needs to employ appropriate norms for distinguishing true from false historical testimony, for assessing interpretations of archaeological data, and so forth (TTP VII.19–25; III/101–2). When these norms are themselves derived from confused or inadequate perceptions and signs, they will not meet the requirement of clarity and distinctness that reasoning requires, and will remain open to refutation by further imaginative inquiry. As Spinoza puts it, they will not generate mathematically certain conclusions (TTP II.6–7; III/30–1). But they may nevertheless be well suited to their purpose and provide a basis for acquiring knowledge that satisfies a standard of moral certainty. The claims made by a competent narrative historian, for instance, will be regarded as true when she operates with norms agreed to be sufficient for the specific purpose of providing a reliable account of the past, and avoids standards generally regarded as slack or excessively pedantic. Her conclusions will then count as morally certain.

The goals of imaginative enquiries also shape the extent of their concern with truth. There are, for instance, certain facts that our historian needs to get right, and certain stylistic limits that she needs to observe, if her work is to claim authority. (Were she to assert that Cicero was a Greek, or present her information in an arbitrary order, she would not succeed in narrating the history of Rome.) But other features of her project are more open. (It would not be hopelessly vitiated if some of its peripheral claims were held to be wrong, nor would it be undermined by an unusual though recognizable narrative technique.) A shared conception of what a narrative history, or indeed any form of imaginative inquiry, is meant to achieve therefore determines what range of truths are most relevant to guaranteeing its moral certainty.

A community whose way of life is grounded on imagining can generate standards of truth and falsity that, although inadequate, are sufficient for particular ends, and can use these standards to build up bodies of morally certain knowledge of the first kind. Moreover, as Spinoza repeatedly points out, this sort of knowledge is so vital to ordinary life that it would be ludicrous to condemn it because it fails to meet the norm of mathematical certainty to which philosophy aspires (TTP XV.37; III/187). For many purposes, moral certainty is all we need and all we can achieve. On the one hand, then, imaginatively based forms of inquiry can provide us with useful though fallible knowledge about a wide variety of things, and can help us to live peacefully and prosperously. On the other hand, they leave us exposed to errors and vulnerabilities that only philosophical reasoning can systematically diagnose. How, though, does the ambition to reason arise and get a hold?

One might hypothesize that, when people find their imaginative knowledge insufficient or misleading, their *conatus* prompts them to refine their universal notions and question the standards of truth on which they have been relying. This in turn, so the hypothesis might continue, leads them smoothly and seamlessly towards knowledge of the second kind. According to Spinoza, however, the answer is not so simple. At a psychological level, individuals and communities develop attachments to their imaginatively grounded beliefs and habits which in turn make them resistant to change. Even when they see that their beliefs are wanting, they are often unwilling to give up what they take themselves to know in favour of a more adequate but faintly grasped alternative (E IVp6; II/214). Moreover, at a social level, bodies of knowledge are reflected in distributions of power, and established experts are generally unwilling to put their dominance at risk. 'Hence it happens', for example, 'that one who seeks the true cause of miracles and is eager, like an educated man, to understand natural things...is generally considered and denounced as an impious heretic by those whom the people honour as interpreters of nature and the Gods' (E I App.; II/81). Within communities organized around imagining, attempts to reason are sometimes deeply challenging and profoundly unwelcome. So if reasoning is to become the basis of an established way of life, as opposed to a sequestered minority interest, communities must first find ways of using their imaginative resources to create conditions in which resistance to knowledge of the second kind is not so strong as to be crushing, and in which there is space to develop a philosophical form of existence aimed at truth.

Since hostility to reasoning may originate in many quarters and take many forms, attempts to use imagination against it will themselves be culturally specific, and Spinoza's own writings offer a case in point. In the Dutch Republic, as he represents it in the *Theological Political Treatise*, the most strident enemies of philosophical reasoning were the members of a powerful group of Calvinist theologians, who took themselves to know what doctrinal truths any faithful person must believe. Armed with this set of certitudes, they opposed the style of philosophizing practised by Spinoza and his circle, and intermittently attempted to suppress its methods and conclusions.[6] In this context, then, the general problem of creating a society hospitable to philosophizing mutated into the more specific problem of challenging a particular theological outlook, not only by confronting it head-on and pitting philosophy against an imaginatively based form of theology, but also by promoting an alternative form of religious life that allowed space for critical enquiry. If reasoning is to flourish, Spinoza contended, the theologians' conception of religion will have to give way, not in the first instance to a rational or adequate alternative, but to a more easy-going and inclusive religious practice that will not stunt philosophical inquiry. By appropriating the resources of imagination on which the theologians relied, and using them to defend a different account of religion's demands, *cognitio* of the first kind could at least encourage reasoning by sustaining a way of life in which it was not subjected to harassment.

Writing from within a community where the Bible possessed unparalleled religious authority, Spinoza accepts the existing parameters of theological debate and defines the imaginatively grounded goal of religious life in biblical terms as a matter of loving one's neighbour (TTP XIII.8; III/168). Satisfying this demand, he claims, is all that true religion requires of us, and the function of religious beliefs and forms of worship is simply to help us achieve it by motivating us to live in a loving and steadily cooperative fashion. Since it matters very little how we bring this about, there is no need for us to agree with one another about religious doctrine. You may imagine God as a judge while I believe him to be immaterial, but as long as we both live cooperatively there is no religious reason to examine our differences. Nor is there any need to investigate the standards of truth and falsehood on which we base our beliefs. I may ground my conception of an immaterial God on my reading of the Bible, while your belief that God is a judge may be validated by your feeling that the Holy Spirit dwells in your heart. Our respective

---

[6] Verbeek 1992.

standards may both be deeply confused, having been picked up from incidental testimony or arbitrary associations; but if they enable us to live cooperatively there is no religious reason to challenge them (TTP XIV.16; III/175). A genuinely religious community therefore has a limited interest in the truth of people's beliefs and focuses instead on the way they behave. To sustain cooperation there is no need to inquire too closely into the epistemological processes by which individuals form their theological convictions, or the degree of confusion that their ideas exhibit. As long as they manage to live harmoniously or love their neighbours they should be allowed to follow their own beliefs and worship as they wish (TTP XIV; III/176).

At first glance this account of true religion seems set against the philosophical project of reasoning. Of all imaginative practices, religion seems particularly devoid of critical standards, particularly uninterested in developing them, and particularly tolerant of falsehood. To learn to live religiously is to learn to accept cooperative people as they are, however crazy, setting aside differences in religious belief and outlook and refusing to jeopardize the benefits of harmony by probing their convictions. While the social and political advantages of such a stance may be clear enough, particularly in a society where theology has traditionally been a source of contention, it is not easy to see how abandoning the collective quest for truth can create circumstances in which the possibility of reasoning is enhanced.

Spinoza's response to this objection is straightforward. To be sure, true religion does not require people to examine their religious beliefs critically, and is indeed tolerant of a great deal of falsehood. However, by enabling individuals and groups to arrive at their own convictions and live in the light of them, it creates conditions in which they have the opportunity to cultivate the habit of examining their ideas and practices, and are free to alter them in the light of their investigations. Moreover, as testing the truth or falsehood of one's beliefs by subjecting them to increasingly rigorous standards of confirmation becomes an option, true religion makes space for people of a philosophical bent who want to press this process of clarification as far as they can, and go all out for truth. As long as philosophers continue to live cooperatively, they are not only individually free to think in the privacy of their own studies, but also collectively free to cooperate publicly with one another in developing their adequate understanding. True religion therefore creates and validates a way of life in which philosophers have latitude to transcend the limits of imaginative thinking and learn to reason.

To make the transition from the first to the second kind of knowledge, a community must live in social and material circumstances where this possibility is not denied them, and true religion exemplifies such an ethos. This condition is far from trivial, but as it stands it is nevertheless comparatively weak. Although a religious way of life offers people the opportunity to reason, it does not encourage them to make use of it. On the contrary, it mainly tolerates the more or less relaxed epistemological standards around which their beliefs and practices are organized. However, if the religious way of life that Spinoza envisages is to challenge the dogmatic theologies of his contemporaries and foster the art of reasoning, it seems that it must achieve more than mere forbearance. As well as permitting religious ways of life to be grounded on philosophical reasoning, it must some-how positively encourage the growth of knowledge of the second kind.

Following out this line of thought, Spinoza elaborates his analysis of true reli-gion by drawing attention to the epistemological virtues it demands. To live cooperatively, he warns, one must in the first place avoid the hypocrisy of taking refuge in religious practices to which one is not committed, or placating oneself with what one recognizes to be religious fictions or fantasies (TTP XI.20; III/176). Such strategies are destructive because, although ideas that we acknowledge to be fictions can move us deeply and strengthen our resolve to live in a particular way, they lack the power of stable beliefs to generate steady patterns of action, and thus the habits of a cooperative way of life. In religion, where it is vital that one should be able to sustain the patterns of behaviour that constitute loving one's neighbour, one needs to operate on the basis of ideas that one regards as true, and is expected to give up religious outlooks that one no longer finds credible. One consequently cannot be indifferent to the question of what one does or does not believe, or to the criteria on which one's beliefs are grounded.

Alongside hypocrisy, Spinoza condemns the related vice of stubbornness (TTP XIV. 22; III/176–7). In the religious context he has in mind, stubborn people are those who insist on upholding discredited interpretations of Scripture, or reject ideas and outlooks on which cooperation evidently depends. Stubbornness impedes cooperation; but in excluding it, Spinoza imposes an expectation that religious people will be at least somewhat responsive to evidence and argument, rather than hanging on to their beliefs come what may. Easy-going as religion may be, it does not license one to believe absolutely anything, and to some extent requires individuals to be knowledge-seekers. It expects them to gravi-tate to whatever they sincerely regard as the best-supported religious outlook available, so that as a community modifies the morally certain basis of its com-mitment to true religion, beliefs and attitudes that were once acceptable may cease to be so. In Spinoza's view, for example, a person who continues to insist, in the face of extensive textual evidence, that all the recorded utterances of the biblical prophets are revealed truths, may be held to be guilty of stubbornness and thus of failing to live in a religious fashion. Cooperation has an intellectual dimension, and by obstinately refusing to take the opinions of one's opponents into account one violates the central religious tenet, 'Love your neighbour'. Since this demand does not apply to people who really do not understand a dispute, or otherwise fail to see its force, true religion will in practice remain pluralist. But because it embodies an openness to well-grounded argument, it imposes a critical pressure on a community's habits of thought and encourages people, where possible, to converge on religious convictions that satisfy the best available standards of moral certainty.

True religion is therefore not condemned to extreme levels of epistemological fragmentation, nor is it as indifferent to truth-seeking as at first appeared. The requirement of living cooperatively contains an epistemological dimension, and although one can lead an entirely satisfactory religious life on the basis of beliefs and practices that are deeply inadequate and confused, critically minded people are under something resembling a religious obligation to subject their theological convictions to epistemological critique. As Spinoza puts it, 'each person is bound to accommodate [the tenets of religion] to his own power of understanding' so that he can accept them 'without any hesitation' (TTP XIV.33; III/179). Admittedly, the debates in which this will involve them will be conducted in imaginative terms, using inadequate ideas acquired through signs and perceptions, and will thus fall short of the philosophical style of thinking from which knowledge of the second kind arises. But as Spinoza now goes on to illustrate, such debates can nevertheless instill attitudes and habits integral to reasoning, and can therefore help to cultivate the outlook and expectations on which it depends.

Practitioners of true religion may be motivated to live cooperatively by many diverse beliefs and practices, but if they are to avoid hypocrisy and stubbornness, each of them must be willing to examine their own beliefs when these are challenged. This process may, of course, be one of individual reflection, but Spinoza is more interested in the public debates, controversies, and struggles in which it can also be manifested. In his own case, the Dutch discussions that particularly concern him focus on disagreements about the nature and grounds of a truly religious life. Engaging with theologians who take it for granted that the Bible is the source of religious knowledge, he sets out to challenge the conceptions of moral certainty on which these opponents rely, focusing on their appeals to divine revelation. Treating theology like any other form of interpretative inquiry and viewing it as a matter of decoding signs, he assumes that we first of all need a hermeneutic theory that will allow us to determine, with moral certainty, what claims the text makes about God's revelations to the prophets. In some contexts, such as that of literary criticism, establishing the meaning of the text might be enough; but if we are to use conclusions about biblical revelation as the basis of a religious way of life, we also need some morally certain grounds for treating them as authoritative.

At this point, some of Spinoza's theological opponents appeal directly to divine revelation. But he remains unsatisfied. Rather than taking refuge in ignorance, he argues, we need to examine the biblical text to work out what sort of insight the prophets possessed, and on what topics they were authoritative. If we can provide convincing answers to these questions, we shall be able to conclude with moral certainty not just that the prophets happened to teach this or that, but that when they spoke about topics on which they were authoritative, what they said was true. We shall be morally certain not just that the prophets do as a matter of fact teach us to live cooperatively, but also that they were exceptionally well placed to know, on the basis of their imaginative experience, that God 'ordains' this way of life as particularly beneficial to us. Much as we trust physicists or gardeners in their own domains, so we shall have good reason to trust the prophets' testimony in their particular area of expertise. We shall then be able to justify our commitment to a biblically based interpretation of the character of a truly religious life, and will have coherent reasons for rejecting alternative accounts of what such a life involves.

The *Theological-Political Treatise* offers an argument to this effect: careful interpretation of the Bible shows that the prophets were human beings whose exceptional imaginative capacities gave them an extremely unusual degree of insight into moral questions about how to live. In this domain we therefore have reason to take their opinions seriously. Moreover, people who accept this argument put themselves in a position to live religiously on a morally certain basis, and are able to give a satisfactory discursive account of their reasons for living as they do. The epistemological norms around which their religious life is organized gain strength from the fact that they overlap with those underpinning less contentious imaginatively grounded practices such as narrative history or moral psychology; and as in these other cases, both the extent of theology's concern with truth and the particular truths on which it focuses are determined by its goal. Just as a historian needs to recognize and respect a certain range of facts if she is to tell the story of Rome, so there are various truths that a religious person needs to acknowledge and respect. She must, for example, live in a manner that is in fact cooperative (as judged by the prevailing morally certain standards), and accept any other truths that turn out to be necessary for realizing this end (TTP XIV.22; III/177).

As before, the religious authority of Spinoza's own analysis remains limited. Deeply as he may disdain the positions of his theological opponents, his argument is powerless in the face of individuals or groups whose cooperative lives are sincerely based on competing standards of moral certainty. However, among the qualities that true religion requires of them is an openness to his position, and by putting it into circulation, the *Treatise* places them under a religious obligation to consider it on its merits. Instead of sticking rigidly to their existing criteria of moral certainty, truly religious people will make intellectual engagement an aspect of their cooperative way of life and assess accounts of the basis of religion to the best of their ability. The question now is how far this exercise can help to create an imaginatively grounded social ethos hospitable to the development of the second kind of knowledge. Will a religious community whose members examine Spinoza's analysis of religion merely be made to reconsider the standards of moral certainty by which they vindicate their beliefs, or will they also be brought closer to the more stringent demands of philosophical reasoning? One of the aims of the *Theological-Political Treatise* is to narrow the gap between knowledge of the first and second kinds by developing an imaginatively based way of life oriented towards reasoning. Against theologians who give priority to revealed truths, understood as supernatural pronouncements of the deity, Spinoza's defence of the authority of religion rests on an examination of the natural events with which philosophical reasoning is also concerned, and urges us to explain religious phenomena in ordinary causal terms (TTP II.1–2; III/29). Furthermore, rather than allowing us to accept divine revelation as an inexplicable *fait accompli*, it encourages us to apply the Principle of Sufficient Reason that lies at the heart of the *Ethics*, and to refuse to acknowledge the so-called mysteries of religion.[7] People who accept his justification of true religion will also accept the validity of a particular intellectual stance—a stance that can operate in the imaginative domain, but is at the same time definitive of reasoning. They will become acquainted, as it were, with the attitude that underlies reasoning, and will begin to live by it.

True religion therefore gives a community the freedom to explore ideas and ways of life that are compatible with cooperation, while fostering the epistemic virtues of sincerity and openness and allowing for the development of standards of moral certainty that validate the explanatory demands of reasoning. In these three ways, an imaginatively based form of knowledge generates social conditions that are not only conducive to the development of rational understanding, but also inculcate some of its habits and norms. The activity of imagining, as Spinoza conceives it, can at its most sophisticated handle evidence derived from perceptions and signs with critical acumen, and arrive at compelling conclusions—so much so that it is natural to wonder what else reasoning should require. But Spinoza's reply is clear. Whereas the ideas with which we imagine are confused, those with which we reason are clear and distinct or adequate. To cultivate a philosophical way of life we therefore need a stock of adequate ideas, and in order to see how the transition from the first to the second form of knowledge can be made we need to consider how our adequate ideas are acquired.

In a number of his works, Spinoza's argues that some adequate ideas—the so-called common notions—are made available by sensory experiences common to all human beings, and are in principle accessible to anyone. For example, according to the *Ethics*, our experience of our own bodies and their interaction with bodies external to us gives each of us access to the adequate idea that a body is capable of motion and rest (E IIp13 lemma 2; II/98). However, the mere availability of this idea is not enough to guarantee that a given individual will be able to articulate or reason with it. The idea will only become active in people who are free from prejudice in the sense that their imaginative ideas do not stand in the way of their capacity to recognize what bodies are actually like. Deriving adequate ideas from one's experience is thus a matter of setting aside one's inadequate

---

[7] On Spinoza's use of the Principle of Sufficient Reason, see Della Rocca 2003a and 2008.

assumptions by some means or other, whether by reflection, travel, experiment, or discussion; and these processes in turn depend on collective forms of inquiry and education that will be more developed in some situations than others. As we have seen, Spinoza holds that they will tend to be more widely available in truly religious communities, where a commitment to avoid stubbornness and hypocrisy puts people under pressure to consider challenges to even their most refined standards of moral certainty, and where the goal of cooperation permits the freedom to philosophize. A truly religious way of life provides propitious conditions in which adequate ideas can become available and be used to generate knowledge of the second kind.

In the *Ethics*, this process is presented in a particular light. Since Spinoza is anxious to show how reasoning can ultimately generate knowledge of the third kind, he is especially keen to explain how we acquire the adequate ideas of the attributes of God from which intuition proceeds, and correspondingly less interested in other adequate ideas that follow from these and lie further down his philosophical food chain (E IIp37, p38; II/118). However, we should not conclude that adequate ideas of God's attributes are the only basis on which reasoning can get started, and indeed, Spinoza's argument suggests that we can derive many other adequate ideas from experience, or from experience mediated by other aspects of imagining. For instance, as his geometrical examples indicate, we must be able to acquire adequate ideas of numbers and geometrical figures. Equally, the various axioms on which the *Ethics* relies must be adequately known if the rational standard of its argument is to be preserved. In addition, some of its postulates about the human body contain, as Spinoza explains, 'hardly anything that is not established by experience' (E IIp17s; II/105). Turning to the *Theological-Political Treatise*, we find further examples of adequate ideas about ourselves that also seem to be derivable from experience and reflection. 'It is far from true that everyone can always be easily led solely by the guidance of reason' (TTP XVI.22; III/193); 'No one neglects to pursue what he judges to be good, unless he hopes for a greater good or fears a greater harm' (TTP XVI.15; III/191–2); 'A contract can have no force except by reason of its utility' (TTP XVI.20; III/192); and so on.[8] Thus, while knowledge of the second kind can be spun out of the fundamental ideas of body and mind that occupy a privileged place in the *Ethics*, it can also begin from other adequate ideas that are less philosophically basic. In the circumstances that a truly religious way of life secures, groups of philosophically minded people will therefore be free to acquire different sets of adequate ideas, and use whatever set they possess to articulate an adequate standard of truth. With this norm in hand, they will then be able to follow out their own particular interests and develop different areas of rationally grounded knowledge.

---

[8] See Garrett 2012.

The goal of reasoning, Spinoza tells us, is 'nothing but the truth' (TTP XIV.38; III/179). While imaginative practices such as true religion subordinate their concern with truth to their own particular ends and let these ends determine whether or not a given truth is salient, philosophy takes an interest in everything that can be rationally understood, and ranges over all adequate ideas, whatever their subject matter. There are no truths that it does not enable one to think about, and this is part of its power (E Vp9). But since there are also no particular truths from which it must begin, it can start from any adequate ideas that an individual or community can come by. This does not mean, however, that its progress is completely indiscriminate. Like the imaginative practices we have been examining, the end of philosophy gives it a shape and invests some truths with particular significance; and by examining this affinity between imagining and reasoning, we can get a fuller grasp of the ways in which a truly religious way of life supports the project of philosophizing.

Among the adequate ideas that philosophers need to recognize in order to extend their rational knowledge are a number of claims about the value of a cooperative way of life. Taking a piecemeal approach to the second kind of knowledge, philosophically minded people bent on increasing their adequate ideas may, for example, devote themselves to reasoning about politics or physics; but if these activities lead them to neglect the demands of cooperation, they are liable to defeat their own enterprise by damaging the social environment on which it depends. As we have seen, this risk can be offset by true religion, which holds a cooperative way of life in place. For instance, a cooperative community may find ways of neutralizing the less than cooperative habits of a group of natural philosophers; or the natural philosophers themselves may combine a commitment to reasoning about physics with an imaginatively grounded, religious determination to live cooperatively. In these ways, imagination or knowledge of the first kind can sustain reasoning, and thus the growth of knowledge of the second kind. Spinoza is keenly aware of the need to exploit this relationship, but he is also convinced that reasoning can be self-sustaining. Rather than leaning on the morally certain standards of truth that knowledge of the first kind embodies, philosophers can bring their own more demanding epistemological norms to bear on their own activity, and develop an adequate understanding of the conditions on which its continuity depends. Moreover, their overall end of pursuing the truth makes this area of rational knowledge salient, and gives them a particular interest in it. Whether they are concerned with physics or politics, metaphysics or psychology, they need to know how to safeguard the business of philosophizing.

Turning to this issue, philosophers might, of course, conclude that the cooperative ethos of true religion is less effective as a means of promoting rationally grounded knowledge than a way of life in which false beliefs are firmly suppressed. The goals of true religion and philosophy would then conflict, and each would oppose the other. But Spinoza utterly rejects such a possibility. It is, he argues, not an accident that our religious commitment to living cooperatively is borne out by our philosophical understanding of the best way to promote the pursuit of truth, and that our imaginative grasp of how to live most freely anticipates the conclusions reached by reasoning (E IVp36s; II/235). The standards of moral certainty on which imaginative practices rely are, after all, standards of truth. They partially, and in some cases largely, capture insights that adequate ideas subsequently confirm. We therefore have a general epistemological reason for expecting that our imaginatively based grasp of a way of life that promotes philosophical inquiry will not be cancelled by reasoning. Rather, an adequate understanding of the conditions in which philosophy flourishes should echo our best-considered interpretation of the demands of true religion.

How, then, will philosophers devoted to the pursuit of truth set out to live? According to Spinoza, they will unite to extend their collective understanding, will be careful not to jeopardize their goal by antagonizing people who are not committed to it, will avoid trying to impose their way of life on others who do not share their ends, and will not undermine truly religious ways of life, even if they are grounded on falsehoods (E IVp26, p27, p67–p70). In short, they will live, like any truly religious community, in a cooperative fashion. In the *Ethics*, these conclusions are integrated into a body of *scientia intuitiva* or knowledge of the third kind, and are derived by rational steps from an adequate idea of the attributes of God. However, if philosophers are to avoid derailing their own project, they cannot wait until they have reached this level of insight. An adequate understanding of the reasons for living cooperatively needs to be available to them, whether or not they have yet grasped the metaphysical premises on which intuitive knowledge depends.

As piecemeal reasoners striving for knowledge of the second kind, philosophers therefore have an instrumental interest in acquiring an adequate conception of a cooperative way of life. Truths about the grounds for living in this fashion and the demands that it imposes are of special relevance to them, and stand out from other adequate truths with which they are also concerned. Moreover, this creates a further continuity between true religion and philosophy. The end of true religion, namely cooperation, is a means to the end of philosophy, namely truth, and simultaneously a component of that end.

Learning to live cooperatively is vital to both ways of life, but occupies a role in reasoning that is at once instrumental and constitutive. To make the transition to knowledge of the second kind, a community of religious people therefore does not have to alter its social orientation. Rather, it has to strengthen and unify its grasp of the reasons for living as it does by making its understanding of them more adequate. In place of the diverse outlooks on the basis of which religious people organize their collective life, philosophy holds out the prospect of a unified and compelling understanding of the grounds for living cooperatively, together with a way of life in which a shared commitment to these grounds further enhances the capacity to cooperate.

Equipped with this practical knowledge, a philosophical community puts itself in a secure position to pursue its goal by concentrating on whatever areas of inquiry turn out to be most fecund for generating adequate ideas; and according to the *Ethics*, truths about how to live are ultimately less fecund than truths about God, from whom infinitely many things follow in infinitely many ways. Because understanding God best serves the purpose of pursuing truth, this is where philosophers should focus their attention. But doing so is a collective and social undertaking that cannot proceed without the skills and insights that true religion initially fosters. As Spinoza acknowledges, the continuity between a truly religious and a philosophical existence means that it may in practice be difficult to determine where one gives way to the other. Formally speaking, the transition occurs when inadequate ideas are replaced by adequate ones, but this is a gradual process. It is possible, for example, to have an adequate idea of some properties of a triangle but an inadequate idea of others and as we have seen, an inadequate idea can be more or less deeply confused and thus more or less close to adequacy (Letter 56). Since an adequate conception of a cooperative way of life represents the end-point or limit of a long process of clarification, there is no moment of rupture between a sound imaginative grasp of the demands of true religion and a rational understanding of its character and benefits. Both belong to a continuous process of learning to live cooperatively, which forms, as it were, the ethical bedrock of philosophizing.

2

When does Truth Matter?

The Relation between Theology and Philosophy

I

One of the central aims of Spinoza's *Theological-Political Treatise* is to vindicate the view that philosophy and theology are separate forms of enquiry, each with its own domain of knowledge.[1] The two domains do not conflict, and neither has any authority over the other. Spinoza has pressing political reasons for defending this conclusion; it plays a central part in his attempt to establish that theologians can safely leave philosophers alone to get on with their studies, and vice versa. But many commentators have objected that his argument is unsatisfactory. Despite his protestations, they have claimed, he does not succeed in showing that philosophy and theology are mutually independent, but instead gives epistemological precedence to philosophy. I shall argue that this objection fails to understand the nature of Spinoza's position and wrongly charges him with inconsistency. However, in order to appreciate the coherence of his view, and see what Spinoza is doing when he develops it as he does, we need to take account of an aspect of the historical context of his work that has not been much explored. By looking beyond the immediate disputes to which the *Treatise* responds and getting a richer sense of the classical debates and traditions on which Spinoza draws, we can not only gain a better understanding of how, in his view, theology and philosophy are related; we can also appreciate the broader lineaments of his position and question the commonly held opinion that he pioneers a naturalistic conception of philosophy. Far from separating philosophy and religion, as contemporary naturalists do, Spinoza regards philosophizing as a form of religious activity and an exercise in piety.

[1] Originally published in *The European Journal of Philosophy*, vol. 20:1 (2012), 91–108. Reprinted with permission of the European Journal and Oxford University Press. I am grateful to Alexander Douglas, Harry Frankfurt, Moira Gatens, Jane Heal, Nick Jones, Melissa Lane, Warren Montag, Michael Moriarty, Serena Olsaretti, Quentin Skinner, and Theo Verbeek for their helpful comments on earlier presentations of this essay.

II

Nowadays, the relationship between theology and philosophy is not on the whole a pressing issue; but in seventeenth-century Holland it was deeply contested. Throughout a long-running dispute, a broadly Aristotelian division of labour between the two forms of enquiry was challenged by Cartesian philosophers, whose investigations trenched on areas over which theologians had habitually exercised authority. By crossing the traditional boundaries around their own discipline, the Cartesians posed an intellectual problem: what topics was their own approach capable, and incapable, of dealing with? But they also precipitated a practical and highly politicized struggle over the proper extent of the freedom to philosophize. On one side, the more orthodox theologians of the Calvinist Reformed Church held that philosophical enquiry should be guided by the conception of God and nature revealed to the prophets and recorded in the Bible. On the other side, Cartesians argued for a self-legitimating philosophy grounded on reason. Roughly speaking, the philosophers claimed that they should be allowed to pursue their enquiries independently of the theologians, while the orthodox theologians viewed the philosophers as a threat to true religion and the institutions of the Church.[2]

A tempestuous debate between these two groups was initially carried on in the universities, where Cartesians fought for permission to teach Descartes' philosophy alongside the established Aristotelian curriculum. But the conflict gradually became more widespread and intense, until, in 1656, the States of Holland felt the need to promulgate a decree directing professors to refrain from all invectives and abstain from all odious and insidious suggestions. They were 'to present the truth simply, and avoid drawing hateful consequences that could be expected to give offence to others'.[3] The States' attempt to broker a compromise was, however, only a partial success. At regular intervals, one or other side would overstep the boundaries imposed by the decree, provoking their opponents and destabilizing a fragile liberty to express a range of philosophical opinions.

It was at one of these uneasy moments, when the freedom to philosophize seemed to be under threat from the Reformed Church, that Spinoza composed the *Theological-Political Treatise*.[4] Written in the second half of the 1660s and published in 1670, the work is among other things a political intervention on behalf of a form of philosophizing unrestricted by theological prescriptions, and is directed against the convictions and political aspirations of orthodox Dutch Calvinism. By the time Spinoza sat down to write, a number of other authors had

---

[2] Verbeek 1992, Douglas 2015.   [3] Rowen 1978: 407.
[4] The *TTP* was written between 1665 and 1670 when the Dutch Reformed Church's consistories successfully opposed the publication of several theologically challenging works. See van Bunge 2001; Nadler 1999, 263–70; Israel 2001, 185–205.

already attempted to pour oil on troubled waters by arguing that theology and philosophy are distinct forms of enquiry and can peacefully co-exist.[5] Following the same strategy, Spinoza accordingly explains that the main purpose of the *Treatise* is to separate faith from philosophy (TTP XIV.5; III/174). If there is one thing he is trying to do, he insists, it is to show that philosophical investigation is distinct from the theological enquiries on which faith is grounded, and that the two domains are not in competition with each other. Theologians do not need to fear that the work done by philosophers threatens their knowledge or status, any more than philosophers need to worry that theologians are in a position to impose limits on the conclusions they can legitimately defend.

Spinoza clearly has political and personal reasons for defending this position; but given that it is one of the main claims he seeks to establish in the *Treatise*, it is vital to the overall success of his project that his argument for it should also be philosophically compelling. Summing up his achievement, he certainly seems to think it is. 'I have shown how philosophy is to be separated from theology, what each of these principally consists in, that neither should be the handmaid of the other, but that each remains in charge of its own domain, without coming into conflict with the other' (TTP XV.43; III/188). Or again, 'We conclude unconditionally that Scripture is not to be accommodated to reason, nor reason to Scripture' (TTP XV.25; III/185). From the moment the work was published however, commentators have criticized or puzzled over an apparent tension between these conclusions and the case that Spinoza makes for them. Despite his confident tone, there are moments at which he seems to undermine his avowed position by giving philosophy the upper hand, awarding it an asymmetrical authority to stand in judgment over the conclusions reached by theologians.

Since this tension lies on the surface of Spinoza's text, he could hardly have failed to be aware of it; and since his book is addressed to philosophical readers who could presumably recognize an inconsistency when they saw one, he would surely have expected them to be sensitive to it (TTP Pref. 33; III/12). What, then, are we to make of it? Responding to this problem, some commentators have been tempted by the thought that Spinoza is masking his true convictions. He himself believes that philosophy is stronger than theology and is capable of assessing at least some of theology's claims, while the reverse is not the case; but because he is trying to engineer a truce between philosophers and theologians, he represents their endeavours as mutually independent. By making his argument equivocal he allows his philosophically minded readers to appreciate the true scope of philosophical enquiry, but he also hopes to buy off potentially troublesome theologians with the reassurance that theology operates in a distinct domain.[6]

---

[5] On earlier exponents of this approach see van Bunge 1989, 52–4, Verbeek 1992; 1993; 1999; 2003, 95–7.

[6] Strauss 1965: 1-31; Strauss 1988: 142–201.

Other commentators, standing back from so pragmatic an interpretation, have acquitted Spinoza of political cynicism, but have nevertheless dwelt on the insufficiency of his argument. Whatever his intentions, they observe, he does not in fact put theology and philosophy on an equal footing, and in this respect his project is a failure.[7]

While each of these readings can garner some textual support, neither is persuasive. The first is hard to credit because it obviously and radically underestimates the theologians of the Reformed Church, who were hardly likely to fall for such a transparent ruse. They wanted a fully convincing assurance that their authority was not subject to the judgments of self-styled philosophers, and on this account Spinoza had not provided one. The second, more cautious interpretation escapes this criticism; but it nevertheless fails to do justice to the fierce drive towards philosophical coherence that is such a pronounced feature of Spinoza's works. Given his overarching commitment to consistency, it would be extremely surprising if he were to have settled for an evidently unstable position. So before concluding that his account of the relation between theology and philosophy is slack or hypocritical, it is worth asking whether the apparent tension to which it gives rise can be resolved in Spinoza's own terms, and indeed, whether he himself resolves it. I shall argue that he does. While his critics are right to point out that theology, as Spinoza represents it, is not entirely on an equal footing with philosophy, this does not undermine his claim to have established that the two forms of enquiry are in a relevant sense distinct. They are to be seen as both separate and overlapping, and as simultaneously independent and dependent.

III

The defining difference between theology and philosophy is not, according to the *Treatise*, one of content. There is no specific subject matter that is essentially the preserve of one form of enquiry rather than the other, although each may in practice focus on certain distinctive topics. Instead, the two are distinguished by their methods and goals. The method that theology uses is rooted in a kind of thinking that Spinoza calls imagining, which starts from the experience of particular things that we gain through words and images. Our perceptions, memories, passions, and fantasies all belong in this domain. So do the everyday forms of inductive and means-end reasoning that we bring to bear on them, and the bodies of historical or inductively grounded knowledge that we construct from these materials. Knowledge deriving from imagination in turn possesses an

---

[7] This objection is implicit in Lambert Van Velthuysen's critique of the *TTP* in the letter he wrote to Jacob Ostens in 1671. See Spinoza 1966: Letter 42 from Velthuysen in Spinoza 2016. For a broader discussion of the objection see Verbeek 2003, 28–37.

epistemological status that Spinoza characterizes as moral certainty, and which he contrasts with the philosophical certainty attaching to clear and distinct ideas: 'unlike a clear and distinct idea, the simple imagination [of a thing] does not, of its nature, involve certainty' (TTP II.2–4; III/30–1). Moral certainty guides most of our activities and is quite sufficient for many human purposes; but it is not indubitable and—at least in principle, though not always in practice—leaves space for disagreement and revision.

Working with these resources, theology brings historical or inductively grounded forms of reasoning to bear on Scripture in order to identify the commands of the divine law revealed to the prophets. It then encourages communities to live as the law dictates by exploiting the persuasive force of biblical narratives and exemplars. Its overall aim is the practical one of cultivating obedience to the divine law, which amounts, in Spinoza's minimalist interpretation, to the injunction to love your neighbour (TTP XIV.6; III/174). Although this fundamental tenet is morally rather than philosophically certain, its truth is so firmly guaranteed by the history and style of the Bible that it is not in practice open to question. As Spinoza assures his readers, 'we can easily grasp the intention of Scripture concerning moral teachings. In that area we can be certain of its true meaning. For the teachings of true piety are expressed in the most familiar words, since they are very ordinary, and no less simple and easy to understand' (TTP XV.68; III/111). Theology's task is thus to teach the divine law, and to help people live together in the harmonious manner that it dictates. As the etymology of the term 'religion' suggests, its defining aim is to bind people together.

Philosophy, by contrast, is an exercise in a more abstract species of reasoning. It relies on a demonstrative method to uncover the relations between types of things—particularly the most universal features of nature—and its goal is truth (TTP XIV.37; III/179). Moreover, the truths at which it arrives constitute a type of knowledge that is indubitable and, in Spinoza's view, exceptionally empowering. In principle, this kind of knowledge is open to anyone, since all human beings have some of the adequate or absolutely certain ideas from which philosophizing begins. In practice, however, few people possess the skills and level of application needed to demonstrate the consequences of these accessible premises. Whereas the obedience at which theology aims is grounded on imaginative ways of thinking that are part and parcel of everyday life and lie within the reach of ordinary folk, the quest for the philosophical goals of truth and wisdom is a more rarefied business (TTP XV. 36; III/187). Philosophy therefore does not have such a widespread or immediate impact as theology, and one should not expect its conclusions to be generally understood.

Straightforward as it may seem, Spinoza's account of the division between philosophy and theology radically diverges from the conception of theology upheld by orthodox theologians within the Reformed Church, and in doing so challenges their conception of the basis and scope of their own authority. Perhaps the most central point of contention lies in a topic that Spinoza discusses at length, namely the epistemological status of the tenets of faith around which Calvinist religious practice was organized. According to the Reformed Church, the central commitments of a religious life are revealed in Scripture and set out in the Church's *Belgic Confession*.[8] The fact that these tenets of faith have been revealed by God is a guarantee of their incontrovertible truth, and truly religious people will unhesitatingly subscribe to them. Faith, in short, requires one to hold certain specific and certain beliefs about God and the duties he imposes, and at least part of the task of theologians is to show that these beliefs are confirmed by the highest available epistemological standards.

Filling out the implications of his contrasting conception of theology, Spinoza is quite prepared to allow that tenets of faith play a vital role in enabling people to live in an obedient or pious fashion. He is also happy to admit that the tenets of faith contain a number of claims about the deity—for example that God exists, and that God is just. But as we have seen, he does not agree that theology is capable of providing an indubitable defence of their veracity, or even that it should attempt to do so. Its task is not to arrive at certain truths, but to encourage conformity to the divine law, 'Love your neighbour'. Theology 'determines the tenets of faith only insofar as is sufficient for obedience; but precisely how they are to be understood, with respect to their truth, it leaves to be determined by reason, which is really the light of the mind' (TTP XV.21;III/184). Rather than setting out a sequence of claims that satisfy the philosophical standard of truth, tenets of faith identify beliefs that serve the purpose of encouraging people to cooperate with one another, and thus support the goal of theology. Their function is to identify ideas and outlooks that are likely, as a matter of logical or psychological fact, to motivate individuals to live in accordance with biblical doctrine (TTP XIV.30; III/178).

Putting this view into practice, Spinoza rejects the Calvinist account of the role played by tenets of faith. According to his view, a claim such as 'God is just' has the status of a tenet because, humanity being what it is, people can only steadily obey laws that they regard as equitable. In order to conform to what theology represents as the divine command to love your neighbour, individuals need to conceive of God as a just deity who will apply the law fairly and consistently, and will not cheat or betray them. What should be of concern to theology, then, is not the philosophical truth or falsehood of a tenet, but its motivating power; and in order to achieve their proper goal, theologians should focus on the question of how belief in a tenet can be used to encourage a community to live obediently in accordance with the divine law. To achieve this end, a community must of course have a sufficient belief in the given tenet for it to guide their behaviour, and part

---

[8] Schaff 2007, Articles II, III, VII.

of the theologian's task is to make tenets of faith highly credible, judged by appropriate standards of moral certainty. But neither they nor their audiences need to be able to vindicate their beliefs by the mathematically certain standards of philosophical reasoning. So long as theologians achieve their goal of encouraging a cooperative way of life, their divergences from philosophically vindicated truths are of no theological significance and do not detract from the integrity of their enterprise.

By differentiating philosophy and theology and setting the two practices to attain distinct ends, Spinoza claims to establish that each is independent of the other, and yields a valuable form of knowledge that the other cannot provide (TTP XV.2; III/180). However, despite these efforts at even-handedness, there remains an epistemological sense in which theology occupies second place. Suppose, for example, that a morally certain tenet of faith were to be disproved by means of a philosophical demonstration. Given the superior level of certainty that philosophy provides, theologians would surely be required to bow to philosophical authority. To be sure, the knowledge that the tenet was false need not immediately undermine its theological function of promoting cooperation, or prevent religious people from appealing to it. But a philosophically minded theologian who cared about the highest standards of truth would be constrained by the force of the relevant demonstration to revise his views, and to subordinate the authority of Scripture to that of philosophy.

Spinoza does not confront this possibility directly, but he nevertheless gives philosophy the upper hand. As he explains in the *Treatise*, philosophy teaches us that our greatest good consists in a kind of intellectual knowledge that ultimately depends on, and consists in, knowledge of God or nature. The more we learn about types of natural things, and above all about ourselves, the better we come to understand the causal processes that constitute God's essence. Furthermore, because this kind of knowledge is profoundly empowering, the most effective way to empower ourselves is to concentrate on knowing God or, as Spinoza also puts it, loving God. Showing how this goal can best be achieved is part of the task of a complete ethics (TTP IV.13; III/60); and as Spinoza's own *Ethics* reveals, it turns out to depend on cooperation. In the first place, rationality requires us to live in the state rather than in solitude, and thus to cultivate shared ways of life (E IV P73; II/264–5: EIV P40; II/241). In addition, if one is to make any significant progress in extending one's philosophical understanding, one must cooperate with people who are already bent on the same end, while simultaneously doing one's best to persuade those who are not yet committed to the project of understanding to join in. 'It is especially useful to men to form associations, to bind themselves by those bonds most apt to make one people of them, and absolutely, to do those things that strengthen friendships' (E IV App. xii; II/269). The injunction to live cooperatively therefore falls within the purview of philosophy as well as theology, and the central doctrine that theology teaches 'agrees with reason' (TTP 15.24;

III/185). But because, as the *Treatise* confirms, it does not matter how the injunction to live cooperatively is reached, 'as long as it obtains the supreme right, and is
the supreme law for men' (TTP XIX.4; III/229), philosophers can derive and
legitimate it for themselves. At least to this extent, they have no need to rely on
theological instruction, but possess their own route to moral knowledge; and here
again, the epistemological superiority of philosophy threatens to undercut the
independence of theology. When philosophers and theologians disagree, it is the
philosophers who will have the final say.

This *sotto voce* asymmetry presents a challenge to orthodox Calvinism, and
indeed to any theological outlook that regards its own epistemological standards
as the best available. Although Spinoza reassuringly contends that theology and
philosophy will proceed on roughly parallel tracks, never diverging over theology's most fundamental commitments, a theologian's claim to know that these
commitments are true nevertheless remains ultimately subordinate to the judgment of philosophy. By itself this may not seem very worrying—after all, Spinoza
is adamant that moral certainty is more than adequate in most areas of life. But as
well as undercutting the purportedly 'equal but distinct' status of the two practices, the asymmetry implicit in Spinoza's account questions a further aspect of
Calvinism by casting doubt on its assessment of theology's moral significance.
According to the Dutch Reformed Church, the moral core of theology revolves
around the notion of eternal salvation, conceived as the final end of human existence. In order to be saved, one must conform to the doctrines taught in the Bible
as these are interpreted by the Church; and as the Church's *Confession* asserts,
salvation depends on faith rather than on works. To count among the faithful,
and thus to be a candidate for salvation, it is not enough to live in an obedient or
cooperative fashion; one must also sincerely assent to the relevant tenets of faith.[9]

Among the things that Spinoza is trying to achieve by defining theology as he
does is to subvert this Calvinist outlook. Contrary to the Church's position, he
argues, theology's goal is not to prescribe a given set of beliefs, but to help people
live in a certain way. As we have seen, its aim is to encourage obedience or cooperation, and tenets of faith are merely functional props in this process, to be assessed
in terms of their effectiveness rather than their truth. So in order to tell whether
someone is living religiously in the manner that theology recommends, we do not
need to probe their convictions. All we need to consider is their works, that is to
say, their way of life. 'If the works are good, they are faithful, however much they
may disagree with other faithful people in their doctrines' (TTP XIV. 16; III/175).

Spinoza is here attacking the Church's picture of the role of salvation within a
religious life. At one level he does not disagree with the Calvinist position. As
he freely acknowledges, the promise of salvation plays a vital practical role in

---

[9] Schaff 2007, Article XVI.

promoting cooperation. If people did not believe that those who live cooperatively will be saved, they would be less strongly motivated to obey the divine law (TTP XIV.27; III/178). At another level, however, there is a deep disparity between Church doctrine and the view articulated in the *Treatise*. According to the latter, as we have by now come to expect, theological tenets relating to salvation derive their status from their motivating power rather than their philosophical truth. It therefore does not matter, from a theological point of view, whether the Church gives a philosophically correct explication of the nature and force of salvation as long as it succeeds in encouraging people to practise obedience. Thus, where Calvinism presents a religious life as a means to, or a sign of, salvation, Spinoza reverses the causal order. A belief in salvation is for him a means to a religious life, insofar as it sustains the desire to live in a cooperative fashion. Furthermore, this view has a radical impact on the way salvation is conceived. Since it is the final goal of religious existence, and the goal of religious existence is simply obedience or cooperation, salvation of the kind that religion extols no longer figures as an exalted end, lying beyond our earthly life.

For a Calvinist, then, one of the most discomfiting features of Spinoza's account of theology is that it transforms an ambitious theological conception of salvation as eternal life into a comparatively mundane goal that does not even presuppose a knowledge of doctrine, let alone the intervention of divine grace. The saving faith offered by religion consists simply in the advantages of a cooperative or obedient existence (TTP XIV.13; III/175). To make matters worse, it is clear to a careful reader of the *Treatise*, and even clearer to a reader of the *Ethics*, that the benefits of a life lived in accordance with the religious requirement to love your neighbour fall far short of those that flow from a life devoted to philosophical understanding. The kind of imaginatively based cooperation that theology helps to sustain is undoubtedly valuable, and constitutes a form of salvation for which everyone has reason to strive. But it cannot compete with the empowerment generated by a philosophically grounded love of God, which, as Spinoza observes at the end of the *Ethics*, constitutes our true salvation (E V P36c; II/303). Where Calvinism gives pre-eminence to religious salvation and condemns the benefits of philosophy as morally negligible, Spinoza turns this order on its head. It is philosophy that holds the key to moral liberation and reveals the ultimate standards of the good against which those of theology can be measured. In moral as well as epistemological matters, it has the upper hand.

As his critics have pointed out, these interconnected asymmetries seem to vitiate Spinoza's project. Rather than presenting theology and philosophy as independent practices, each with its own method and telos, he appears to represent them as overlapping and unequal. Philosophy, the stronger party, is capable of assessing claims made by theology, the weaker party, which has no reciprocal authority to judge the results of philosophical enquiry. So despite Spinoza's protestations to the contrary, philosophy and theology are neither independent nor equal, and his argument fails. While I shall claim that this conclusion does not fully capture the position defended in the *Treatise*, there is evidently something right about it. Spinoza clearly does think that philosophy is ultimately more powerful than theology, and can in some respects encompass and surpass it. But the remaining problem is to see how he can hold this view while also maintaining that theology and philosophy are distinct, so that neither is the handmaid of the other.

IV

To resolve this difficulty, it is helpful to shift one's attention from the dispute about the relation between theology and philosophy to another of the historical debates in which Spinoza intervenes, this time concerning the ancestry of the Calvinist interpretation of salvation that the *Treatise* opposes. Like many other features of his outlook, Calvin's conception of salvation as an other-worldly condition is deeply indebted to Saint Augustine who, in his *City of God*, pits himself against a group of pagan philosophers. These thinkers, of whom Cicero is among the most prominent, have in Augustine's view failed to confront the depths of human depravity, and have consequently misunderstood the nature of the good. 'With wondrous vanity, [they] have wished to be happy here and now, and to achieve blessedness by their own efforts.'[10] But because human virtue can never be free from the struggle against vice, the supreme good cannot be attained in this world and lies only in eternal life.[11]

In Spinoza's lifetime, this debate about what human beings can hope for remained very much alive. On the one hand, an Augustinian outlook continued to inform the theology of Calvinism, and was propagated by the Reformed Church. On the other hand, the philosophical orientation that Augustine repudiates had been revived by the Erasmian humanists of the northern Renaissance and was firmly entrenched in the humanist educational curriculum that had become standard across northern Europe.[12] This pattern of instruction culminated in the study of moral philosophy; and perhaps the most ubiquitous of the texts used to teach the subject was Cicero's *De Officiis*.[13] Since one of the aims of Cicero's work is to defend the very position that Augustine had attacked (namely that perfect virtue lies within human reach), educated Dutchmen who had not forgotten what they learned at school would have been familiar with two competing outlooks: the other-worldly notion of the good life upheld by the Reformed Church, and its more optimistic Ciceronian counterpart.

---

[10]   Augustine 1998, xix.4.919. On Augustine's conception of wisdom see Menn 1998, 130–144.
[11]   Augustine 1998, xix.4.918, 924.   [12]   Grafton and Jardine 1986; Black 2001; Charlton 1965.
[13]   Cicero 1913.

Spinoza himself had received a humanist training at the school in Amsterdam run by Franciscus Van den Enden,[14] and there is consequently every reason to think that he would have been familiar with the Ciceronian analysis of virtue. Like his contemporaries, he would have rehearsed its features, recognizing it both as a philosophical alternative to Calvinism, and as a means of contesting the Church's notion of salvation. Revived and rewritten, it could form the basis of an anti-Calvinist position, and this, I shall argue, is part of the strategy employed in the *Treatise*. The account of the relationship between theology and philosophy that Spinoza articulates is modelled on a Ciceronian analysis of virtue; and by viewing it in this light we shall be able to see how it is that Spinoza can conceive of the two practices as independent, while also giving philosophy the upper hand. His solution to the problem we have identified is historically informed, insofar as it exploits an influential Ciceronian view that would have been well known to many of his readers. But by recasting the latter in his own terms, he arrives at a position that coheres with his own philosophical commitments.

In *De Officiis* Cicero distinguishes two levels of virtue. People who are perfectly virtuous blend and reconcile duties arising from the individual virtues, and in doing so manifest the overarching quality of *honestum*.[15] From their point of view, being wise, just, temperate, and courageous are not distinct skills directed at distinct ends, but are aspects of a comprehensive capacity to respond virtuously to all situations, however complex and multi-faceted they may be. At the same time, perfect *honestum* brings with it a way of life. Virtuous people are drawn to one another, and the bonds of friendship uniting them are so strong that each loves the other as himself and they become as one.[16] Contrasted with perfect *honestum*, however, is what Cicero, following the Stoics, describes as second-level or second-grade *honestum*, which provides what he calls a likeness or *similitudo* of its perfect counterpart,[17] and constitutes a moral standard to which ordinary people can aspire.[18] Those who possess it are familiar with the duties that each virtue imposes, and are in general able to fulfil them;[19] but while they largely behave as they would if their *honestum* were perfect, there is nevertheless something they lack. Their grasp of how to live a virtuous life does not obliterate trade-offs between one virtue and another, so that they are sometimes forced to choose between, say, courage and prudence. Nor are they always capable of seeing how virtue resolves apparent conflicts between right action and utility (*utilitas*).[20] Working at the level of second-level *honestum* their conception of what it would be virtuous to do will sometimes conflict with their conception of what would be most advantageous.

---

[14] On Spinoza's use of classical sources see Proietti 1985. On what Spinoza may have read at Van Enden's school, see Frijhoff and Spies 2004, ch. 4; Klever 1991; Nadler 1999, 109.

[15] *DO* I.v.15.   [16] *DO* I.xvii.55–6.   [17] *DO* III.iii.13–15; III.iv.16.

[18] *DO* III.iv.18. On Dutch discussions of the use of *simulacra*, see Blom 1995: 171.

[19] *DO* III. Iii–iv.   [20] *DO* I.iv.12–13; I.xlii.52.

It is possible, in Cicero's view, to progress from second-level *honestum* towards its perfect counterpart by extending one's philosophical understanding of what true virtue consists in. But while sages who reach these heights are rare, second-level *honestum* is much easier to achieve. This level of virtue is suited to ordinary people living in ordinary political circumstances, and Cicero's analysis of it is accordingly developed in the course of a discussion of life in the state.[21] 'The men we live with,' he remarks, 'are not perfect and ideally wise, but do very well if they possess semblances of virtue (*simulacra virtutis*).'[22] Among such people, the key virtue to be cultivated is justice. To sustain the benefits of a civil order, the members of a community must be able to live together under the law; and this condition in turn rests on the ability of a ruler to encourage individuals who only possess second-level *honestum* to act justly. Citizens must learn to identify their individual utility with that of the community as a whole, even when doing so is onerous or compromising.[23]

How, though, should rulers set about such a difficult project? One of the means that political authorities can use to teach ordinary people what political life requires is to exploit a range of narratives and anecdotes, illustrating the advantages of living equitably and the troubles that are liable to arise when justice is flouted. The many historical incidents recounted in Cicero's own works are an instance of this technique, and serve to indicate in concrete terms what a just way of life involves. At the same time, they are designed to arouse the desire to live justly, and to motivate both rulers and citizens to do their best to sustain an equitable way of life.[24] The fact that Cicero employs this technique makes it clear that he is addressing individuals who have only attained second-level *honestum*. (If their *honestum* were already perfect they would know how to act virtuously in all situations and would not need to be taught.) So there is a link within his theory between second-level *honestum* and a set of tools for inculcating virtue which appeal to histories and fictions.

In the *Treatise*, Spinoza replicates both these central features of Cicero's architecture, while partially reconstructing them with his own materials. Like Cicero, he distinguishes two levels of virtue, and associates the higher with the kind of rational understanding that philosophy yields. Only philosophically grounded knowledge can enable one to steer an unswervingly virtuous course through the exigencies of life, and show one how to reconcile its many demands. However, again like Cicero, Spinoza identifies less exalted ways of life that are grounded on the workings of imagination and answer to the requirements of second-level *honestum*. The resources of imaginative thinking can be used to make the demands of a virtuous life accessible, and to motivate people to act much as they would if their *honestum* were more perfect. This, moreover, is where

<hr>

[21] *DO* I.vii.20.   [22] *DO* I.xv.46.   [23] *DO* III.vi.26.   [24] *DO* II.xi.42.

theology comes into play. Its aim is to cultivate a form of second-level *honestum* that falls short of a way of life grounded on understanding, but nevertheless emulates it as far as possible.

In spelling out the nature and role of theology, Spinoza draws on Cicero's discussion of political life as the principal arena in which second-level *honestum* is cultivated. As we have seen, theology's goal is to encourage people to achieve piety by obeying the divine law, 'Love your neighbour'. But as Spinoza now adds, obeying the divine law 'consists in the exercise of loving kindness (*charitas*) and justice', and is fundamentally a matter of living equitably with others (TTP III/226). Here, then, is a first continuity: according to the *Treatise*, the theological virtue of obedience coincides with justice, the virtue that is for both Cicero and Spinoza the key to a successful political order, so that theology helps to sustain the goals of the state. Next, and still following Cicero's lead, Spinoza takes up the view that narratives and exemplars can be used to sustain political authority. Since rulers cannot expect their subjects to exhibit philosophical rationality, they need to work on the passions that dominate the imaginative thinking of ordinary people. They must persuade their subjects to obey the law by representing political cooperation as beneficial and desirable; and they need to rely on a repertoire of imaginative devices such as narratives and exemplars in order to do so. For Spinoza, however, these tools are also the mainstay of theology. Much as a ruler may, for example, appeal to a national history to generate enthusiasm for the law, so theologians appeal to the Bible to illustrate what obedience or justice requires, and to inspire people to emulate the models it provides.

By merging the methods and goals of politics with those of theology, Spinoza creates, as the title of the *Treatise* indicates, a theologico-politics, in which our duty to God coincides with our duty to the state. Both require us to live justly, and the imaginative means by which religious authorities instil this message blend with those that states employ to achieve the same end. To put the point another way, theology becomes an aspect of the Ciceronian political project of maintaining just cooperation under the law, and to this extent the goals and methods of politics and theology largely coincide. Where people possess only second-level *honestum*, their grasp of individual virtues can be shaped by a repertoire of theological exemplars and narratives that show them how to behave in certain types of situation, and inspire them to live up to a theologico-political ideal in which justice, obedience, and piety are combined.

Although exemplars can play a part in cultivating a social ethos, and can be applied to particular circumstances, the guidance they offer is bound to be less than comprehensive. For one thing, narratives deal with some types of situation rather than others, and may not throw any light on a given predicament. For another, no particular exemplar can be expected to weigh with everyone; to be effective, it must resonate with an individual's experience, character, and situation (TTP II.13; III/32; XIII.25; III/171–2). To overcome these limitations, an imaginatively based practice such as theology will need to be pluralist. As Spinoza explains, its exemplars must be sufficiently diverse to appeal to people of many different kinds and must as far as possible allow individuals to hold and express beliefs that sustain their ability to cooperate, whatever these may be (TTP XIV.21–2; III/176–7). Nevertheless, given the imperfect virtue of the people it is dealing with, and the incompleteness of the guidance it offers, theology cannot be expected to produce a form of cooperation immune from conflict. Strong as its motivating power may be, the kind of harmony at which it aims can only be consistently sustained when it is backed up by the political power of the state. This implies, in Spinoza's view, that ultimate authority to interpret the religious duty of obedience must lie not with the officials of the Church, but with the political ruler or sovereign. Conflict can only be kept in check if 'every exercise of religious duty [is] accommodated to the peace and preservation of the state', and the supreme duty imposed by religion consists in piety or obedience to one's country. So, for example, if a man demands my shirt, piety may require me to give him my coat; but when this action would damage or threaten the republic, piety requires me to hand him over to the law, even if this may result in his death (TTP XIX.23; III/232).[25]

Theology and politics thus operate together to generate second-level *honestum*. But the cooperative existence that they promote is still only a simulacrum of the perfect virtue that flows from philosophical understanding. According to the *Ethics*, people who have acquired a certain amount of philosophical insight will recognize that understanding is the most empowering goal they can pursue, and will appreciate that, in order to acquire it, they must create a common way of life directed to this end. As their understanding grows, they will become increasingly capable of creating and sustaining a community whose members are comprehensively committed to cooperating with one another for the sake of further understanding, and will want understanding for others as much as for themselves (E IVP37; II/235). The foremost aim of this type of community of the wise is undoubtedly understanding itself: 'For understanding is the first and only foundation of virtue, nor do we strive to understand things for the sake of some end' (E IVP26; II/227). But its members will also recognize that, in order to enlarge their understanding as effectively as possible, they must cooperate by practising the full range of virtues (E IVP37s1; II/236). The individual virtues that second-level *honestum* upholds therefore do not disappear; rather, each emerges as a necessary component of the philosophical quest for understanding, and plays a unique and irreplaceable role in this process. Furthermore, once a wise person sees how the individual virtues contribute to the overall goal of understanding, they will, in Spinoza's view, be able to overcome the limitations of second-level *honestum* that Cicero describes. They will see how to reconcile the demands of individual virtues and achieve the unified moral outlook that Cicero identifies

---

[25] For further discussion of this claim see Essay 10.

with perfect *honestum*. In addition, they will appreciate that sacrificing a virtuous course of action to the demands of utility or self-interest amounts to sacrificing the pursuit of understanding, and consequently has no place in a life devoted to philosophical knowledge (E IVp72; II/264).

Spinoza thus incorporates the central aspects of perfect *honestum* into his conception of understanding; but he does not take over Cicero's account in its entirety. Instead, he adapts it to his own already complex system, and in doing so introduces a number of modifications. Two of these are especially striking. In the first place, Spinoza's alignment of imagination with passivity and understanding with activity, together with his account of the adequate and inadequate ideas in which activity and passivity consist, yields a distinctive interpretation of the Ciceronian claim that second-level *honestum* is a *similitudo* of its perfect counterpart. When theologico-politics inculcates second-level *honestum* into the members of a community, instilling in them the habits of justice and obedience, their actions will largely mirror those of a community of wise persons whose cooperation is grounded on understanding. However, the members of the first group will remain passive, and will lack the active control over their actions that understanding provides (E IIIP1; II/140). What theologico-politics can achieve, then, is a passive enactment of active understanding, and Spinoza provides a systematic analysis of what the relevant kinds of passivity and activity involve.

A still more telling shift concerns the proper description of a perfectly virtuous way of life. As we have seen, Cicero describes the capacity to live in a maximally virtuous fashion as perfect *honestum*, whereas Spinoza identifies the fulcrum of a virtuous life with understanding or *intelligentia*. Following out the implications of his claim that one is active only insofar as one understands, Spinoza goes on to assert that anything we do on the basis of understanding relates to *fortitudo* or strength of character. This in turn encompasses *honestum*—the desire by which a man who lives according to the guidance of reason is bound to join himself to others in friendship (E IVP37s1; II/236). Here, *honestum* figures as one rational virtue among others, but as the one most immediately manifested in cooperation among the wise, and most closely linked to harmony and justice. 'The things that beget harmony are those related to justice (*iustitia*), fairness (*aequitas*) and *honestum*' (E IV App. XV; III/270). *Honestum* is thus the capacity to promote and sustain the form of rational friendship integral to a fully virtuous way of life, and is an aspect of perfect virtue. It corresponds, at the rational level, to the theological virtues of obedience and piety, together with the civil virtue of justice, which contribute to the imaginatively based form of cooperation that is a mark of second-level *honestum*. So while Cicero uses the notion of perfect *honestum* to designate a capacity for perfect virtue,[26] Spinoza's use of the term is more specific, and more

---

[26] *DO* I.xx.66; I.xliv.157.

closely associated with social cooperation. In his conception of a perfectly virtuous life, the social virtue of *honestum* is integrated into the determination to live as reason or understanding recommends.

These features of Spinoza's argument reorganize and revise the position that Cicero lays out; but they do not undermine the structural isomorphism with which we have been concerned. Both writers rely on a two-tier conception of virtue, and both conceive its levels along basically similar lines. With this conclusion in hand, we can now return to our original question and ask how Spinoza's adoption of a two-tier model provides him with the means to resolve the tensions that have been held to mar his analysis of the relation between theology and philosophy. How might such a model enable him to reconcile his claim that each of these enquiries has a separate end, with philosophy's evident capacity to encompass and outdo theology?

V

When, in the *Treatise*, Spinoza describes the goal of theology as distinct from that of philosophy, he speaks in the imaginative terms that belong to everyday life and are the currency of second-level *honestum*. Taking up Cicero's reminder that, when he separates the virtues, he is not speaking with philosophical precision, but talking in popular or everyday terms.[27] Spinoza presents the theological goal of obedience as distinct from the philosophical goal of understanding or wisdom. In doing so, he adopts the outlook of people whose grasp of themselves and the world is mainly informed by their imaginative experience, and whose understanding of virtue remains at the second level. The practice of theology, he confirms, is separate from that of philosophy in the sense that it does not depend on philosophical skills or knowledge, so that one does not need to be a philosopher in order to live in an obedient or cooperative fashion. As everyone agrees, 'Scripture was written and published not only for the learned, but for all people of every age and kind', so that anyone can use it for theological ends (TTP XIV.10; III/174). At this level, one can be obedient without being wise (TTP XIV.28; III/172), and there is a clear sense in which these two virtues, along with the practices in which they are embedded, are distinct. The imaginative domain of second-level *honestum* does not show how these virtues can be integrated, but for ordinary purposes this does not matter. People can live without philosophizing, and as long as they are collectively able to make use of the resources of theologico-politics, they can sustain a cooperative existence and enjoy the benefits it brings.

---

[27] *DO* II.x.35.

Once a community begins to philosophize, however, this second-level view ceases to constitute its entire outlook, and gradually gives way to a form of life in which the virtues no longer appear to be distinct, but are seen to be inextricably united. Moreover, it is only from this perspective that wise men can fully grasp what virtue is, and become capable of leading a truly virtuous life. Looking back on the second-level *honestum* they formerly possessed, they can appreciate the incompleteness of the understanding on which it was based, and the weakness of the bonds that sustained their obedience or cooperation. Although they can still see why they used to regard the virtues as distinct and liable to conflict, they now appreciate what their earlier view lacked, and can correct its practical limitations. The goal of theology has become absorbed into that of philosophy, and the pursuit of cooperation has become integral to the pursuit of wisdom. More generally, the viewpoint of second-level *honestum* has been replaced by one in which it is impossible to be fully cooperative without being wise, or fully wise without being cooperative. In one sense, then, philosophy has replaced religion; but in another sense it has itself become a form of religion. It shares religion's capacity to bind and, as the *Ethics* makes abundantly clear, brings with it a form of rational piety. 'The desire to do good generated in us by our living according to the guidance of reason, I call piety', Spinoza tells us (E IVp37s1; II/236). And again, 'especially necessary to bring people together in love are the things which concern religion and piety' (E IV App. XV; II/270).

It is true that, in the *Treatise*, the nature of the relationship between the two levels of *honestum* is not entirely clear. This is partly because Spinoza tends to shift from one perspective to the other, creating an impression of inconsistency or even sleight of hand. Although he is for the most part content to inhabit the viewpoint of imagination and to present theology as distinct from philosophy, he also wants to remind his readers that there is more to life than an imaginative outlook, and allows the terms of philosophical understanding to enter his discussion. In addition, confusion is created by the fact that, in this text, Spinoza says relatively little about the content of philosophical understanding and its relation to theology. Only in other works does he offer a sketch of the rational way of life that is consonant with perfect virtue, and show how this both mirrors and contrasts with the cooperation that theologico-politics sustains.

However, once we recognize that the *Treatise* implicitly adopts a two-tier Ciceronian conception of virtue, we can begin to see how Spinoza's argument possesses an overall consistency. And when we read it in the light of the more comprehensive analysis of philosophical virtue set out in the *Ethics*, the character of his position becomes clear. There is no inconsistency in Spinoza's claim that the ends of theology and philosophy are distinct. Instead, each practice represents a different stage in a process of moral empowerment, and as communities or their members progress from one stage to the next, their outlooks change. Virtues that once seemed separate come to be seen as necessarily connected. Claims that used to qualify as tenets of faith cease to serve their previous function.

Recognizing Spinoza's debt to a Ciceronian conception of *honestum*, and thus to the legacy of classical humanism, attunes us to a model of moral knowledge that allows him to reconcile the separateness with the convergence of obedience and understanding. At the same time, it helps us to appreciate what he is trying to achieve. Despite initial appearances, his aim is not to isolate philosophy from theological intrusion, in a manner that one might be tempted to see as an antici-pation of Enlightenment secularism.[28] Nor is it to defend a philosophical approach that is naturalist in the contemporary sense of the term.[29] Rather, he is employing a classical model in order to present a religious or theological way of life as an anticipation or likeness of the higher form of virtue and piety that philosophy engenders. By adopting a recognizably pagan stance to which Calvinism is his-torically opposed, Spinoza challenges the intellectual antecedents as well as the doctrines of orthodox Calvinism. Theology, he contends, is not the means to true salvation. Rather, it is a serviceable but transcendable aspect of everyday life.

---

[28] For a notable example of this stance, see Israel 2001.

[29] Among many recent commentators who have interpreted Spinoza as a naturalist in one or more modern senses of the term see Della Rocca 2008; Hampshire 2005; Morrison Ravven 2003, 70–4; Garrett 2008, 4–25.

3

Spinoza on Superstition

Coming to Terms with Fear

Fear has recently become one of the ruling preoccupations of politics, and also of political philosophy.[1,2] The fears of private citizens and governments, together with the ways in which anxiety is managed or exploited, are widely discussed in both popular and philosophical contexts, and the attempts of governments to play on fear for their own ends are an everyday topic of conversation. But while we are familiar enough with the existence of fear as a powerful force within political life, it is not obvious how we should position it within our theoretical discourse. How, if at all, does it fit into accounts of the normative goals of politics, whether these are taken to be security, peace, or justice? How does it bear on notions such as citizenship or identity? What place, if any, does it have in our understanding of rights or capabilities? Although questions such as these unleash a host of possibilities, one fruitful means of thinking about the place of fear in contemporary debate is to return to an old topic, supposedly sloughed off during the Enlightenment: the issue of superstition.

Superstition was regularly characterized by classical writers as a response to fear, and their view was reiterated throughout the Renaissance and the early modern period. Within this tradition, however, one of the most penetrating and questing interpretations of superstitious practices was offered by Spinoza, who makes his analysis the basis of a wide-ranging form of critique. Like his predecessors, he is deeply hostile to superstition, which can induce people, so he claims, 'to fight for slavery as they would for their survival' (TTP Pref. 10: III/7). However, by implicitly acknowledging an affinity between practices that are superstitious and practices that serve to strengthen commitment to a cooperative way of life, he qualifies his own disapproval. If the project of containing the fears on which superstition feeds depends on institutions and conventions that are themselves not far from being superstitious, it may not be enough to condemn the phenomenon

[1] Originally published in 'Spinoza on Superstition. Coming to Terms with Fear', *Mededelingen Vanwege het Spinozahuis* 88, 2006. Republished with permission of the Spinozahuis.
    I am grateful to Raymond Geuss for his response to a presentation of material contained in this essay, and to Nancy Bremmer, Annabel Brett, Miranda Fricker, Kinch Hoekstra, Lena Haldenius, Axel Honneth, Rachel Paine, Robert Pipppin, Anthony Price, Amon Raz Krakotkin, Theo Verbeek, and Anne Whittle for helpful comments.
[2] For a particularly influential example of this trend see Sklar (1989).

Spinoza on Learning to Live Together. Susan James, Oxford University Press (2020). © Susan James.
DOI: 10.1093/oso/9780198713074.001.0001

outright. Instead, we shall need to examine an issue that is often marginalized in seventeenth-century thought, and ask whether superstition can play a productive part in dealing with anxiety.

More, perhaps, than any of his contemporaries, Spinoza appreciates the role of the passions in social and political life, and conceives politics itself as a process of passionate negotiation. In our everyday lives, he proposes, objects or states of affairs affect us as broadly harmful or beneficial, and we respond to them accordingly. In some cases we make judgments about them; but incorporated in all our responses are evaluative assessments, manifested in our affects. When I gaze out over the lake, I do not just perceive it, but feel exhilarated by its beauty or dispirited by its bleakness. Passions such as these are an aspect of our ordinary relationship with the world, and although they are shaped and modified by our individual temperaments, and by our individual and collective histories, they are grounded in a common set of bodily dispositions which help to determine the character of human life. On the one hand, we are prone to broadly positive affects such as love, pride, or self-esteem, which we experience as empowering and satisfying. On the other hand, we are susceptible to passions such as grief or shame, which we find disempowering or debilitating. Moreover, one of the most fundamental principles of Spinoza's philosophy is the idea that each of us tries to avoid these debilitating affects by striving to achieve a position where our affects are as empowering as possible, and our connections with others are as satisfying as we can make them (E IIIp9, p11; II/147).

This project of avoiding or circumventing negative passions is particularly delicate when empowering and disempowering affects are closely intertwined, as is the case with hope and fear. Our hopes are fixed on future states of affairs, and even before we have attained our goals the very act of hoping for them is satisfying and invigorating. However, because future outcomes are to some extent uncertain, hope is always accompanied by a degree of anxiety about the possibility of failure, and because this experience is unpleasant, no one can overcome the desire to be free from it (TTP XVII.2: III/201). There is, according to Spinoza, no hope without fear, and the strengthening quality of the one is inevitably balanced by the disempowering tendency of the other (E III p18s2; II/155).

Fear is a crucial ingredient of superstition because, according to Spinoza, it makes people credulous (TTP Pref. 2; III/5). Suppose I am afraid and come upon a source of hope. In this mood it is unlikely that I shall pause to examine the epistemological credentials of the hope in question, and more likely that I shall just embrace it and feel comforted. If, for example, I am worried about a friend who is having a dangerous operation, and you tell me that a swan flying over the lake is a good omen, I may not pause to note that there is no causal connection between the swan and a successful outcome, and then sort out my feelings accordingly. Instead, I am likely to clutch at the hope and enjoy feeling better. One can imagine a situation where your words give me hope, even though I know perfectly well that the swan is not a good omen. Spinoza, however, is primarily concerned with a different epistemological and emotional scenario, in which I am sufficiently vague about the causal structure of the world to be capable of believing that the swan and the outcome of the operation are causally connected. At the heart of his analysis lies the claim that people suffering from anxiety are in general more strongly motivated to find a source of hope than to ensure that their beliefs are well grounded, and that those who are hopeful are disinclined to put their hopes at risk by questioning the grounds on which they are based. Thus, fear may produce a kind of psychological rigidity;[3] but it may also manifest itself in what looks like intellectual laziness or lack of curiosity, when this is driven by an unwillingness or inability to challenge the passionate judgments that sustain one's optimism.

The disposition to deal with anxiety by resorting to hope plays an important role in superstition, but is not enough to generate a superstitious practice of the sort that primarily interests Spinoza. Such practices also incorporate a second device for blocking fear, this time by the creation of self-esteem. Someone who is surrounded by admirers or buoyed up by pride may experience a level of self-satisfaction great enough to override their worries, so that a further way to defeat anxiety is to seek out circumstances where admiration or adulation increase one's confidence and sense of invulnerability. (As Spinoza wryly observes, 'no one who has lived among men has failed to see that, when they are prospering, even if they are quite inexperienced, they are generally so full of their own wisdom that they think themselves wronged if anyone wants to give them advice' (TTP Pref. 2; III/5).) Superstition flourishes in conditions where these two psychological dispositions come together. Consider the predicament of two parties who can manage to alleviate their fears if the first is able to offer hope to the second, while the second is able to increase the self-esteem of the first by accepting the hope it holds out. Suppose, to take Spinoza's own principal example, that the first party is a Calvinist preacher, while the second is the Amsterdam populace, and imagine further that because the populace is fearful it is disposed to latch on to any source of comfort that it finds credible. By giving it the means to hope (for instance by representing himself as capable of interpreting the will of God) the preacher both validates and at the same time allays the people's anxiety.[4] And in the process he wins their admiration, thereby increasing his own confidence and displacing his own fear. There is thus a sense in which the populace is a perpetrator as well as a victim of superstition, and the same is true of the preacher.[5]

---

[3] Bacon links this to superstition when he describes the latter as erecting 'an absolute monarchy in the minds of men.' Bacon 1996, 373.

[4] See Deleuze, 1997, 27.

[5] For an illuminating discussion of superstition and the masses, see Balibar, 1994, 3–37.

As Spinoza presents superstitious practices here, they are constituted by groups who possess different kinds and levels of power, and depend on one another to combat their fears.[6] To illustrate their interdependence, he takes the standard example of organized religion, and in the *Theological-Political Treatise* focuses his readers' attention on the superstitious relationship between priests and peoples, whether pagan, Jewish, or Christian. However, considered in itself, his account does not assume that superstition consists in holding any particular type of belief, or in admiring any particular kind of authority. The passionate judgments around which superstition revolves have to be about something, and in the cultures Spinoza is concerned with it is religious authorities who uphold superstitious practices in order to bolster their own pride and status, and who offer superstitious cures for the fears of ordinary people. But in a different set of circumstances it could be otherwise. Superstition could in principle be promoted by political ideologies, natural science, philosophy, or medicine, and could be maintained by politicians, doctors, and scientists among others. So the implications of Spinoza's analysis extend far beyond the critique of organized religion, and arguably beyond his own political concerns.[7] One can get a sense of their scope by comparing the claim, 'If you go to church regularly you will be saved' with 'If you support the Stadtholder you will be safe from the Spanish' (and by comparing both of these with their modern equivalents). We can think of contexts in which the functionaries who make these claims are offering to alleviate the anxiety of their supporters by holding out a hope, and are sustaining their own confidence by doing so, and in such circumstances they would answer to Spinoza's analysis. In fact, if all humans are prone to superstition, as he believes, we should not be surprised that practices of various kinds are put to superstitious use (TTP Pref. 4; III/5–6).

Given that anxiety is unpleasant, superstitions that diminish it seem to serve a useful social function. Yet Spinoza is relentlessly critical of them. Although he acknowledges the affective relief they provide, he nevertheless insists that superstition is an exceptionally dangerous and destructive phenomenon, and offers three arguments for his view. One is that superstitions create unstable and alternating hopes and fears. Rather than simply providing a means of getting rid of an anxiety, the hope that superstition holds out keeps it in play in the very act of offsetting it. ('If you pray regularly, you won't go to Hell after death.') Furthermore, people who are in the habit of placing their faith in superstitious hopes are liable to be repeatedly disappointed, and to find themselves continually re-exposed to debilitating fears. Because the process of being let down and

---

[6] It is possible for an individual to occupy the position of a group, as in the case of Moses.

[7] Despite Althusser's account of Spinoza as a theorist of ideology, many commentators continue to consider superstition solely in the context of religion. A recent exception is Warren Montag, who presents superstition as a model for the formation of all the inadequate ideas that Spinoza regards as characteristic of the human imagination. See Montag 1999.

looking for yet another source of hope is itself an anxious one, there is a sense in which superstition creates the passion it is designed to allay, and is therefore self-defeating (TTP Pref. 5; III/6). Worse still, the process of persistently attempting to overcome fear by moving from one superstitious practice to another makes individuals and communities habitually unfaithful, and their inconstancy, combined with the credulousness we have examined, is liable to generate social unrest (TTP, Pref. 6; III/6).

Spinoza's second argument notes that individuals or groups who are trying to sustain their own confidence by winning the admiration of others are forever on the look-out for supporters, and are willing to compete in order to attract them. (One sees this, he complains, in the Dutch Calvinist Church, which has become a forum for orators who seek to attract admiration, to outdo their adversaries, and above all to gain the applause of the populace (TTP, Pref. 15–16; III/8).) This competitive climate gives rise to factions, which are liable to try to settle their differences by violent means. One of the most lethal consequences of superstition is therefore that it undermines security by making it difficult or impossible for governments to maintain order.

The view that superstition generates political conflict is widely held among seventeenth-century writers, and Spinoza frequently reiterates it, for example in his discussion of the Pharisees. 'When men begin to argue with the fierce heat of superstition, and the magistrate aids one or the other side', he comments, 'they can never be calmed, but must be divided into sects' (TTP XVIII. 12; III/223). In the *Theological-Political Treatise* this pessimistic stance is linked to the broader, Tacitean claim that the gravest threat to the security of the state lies in internal differences rather than in external powers (TTP XVII. 18–19; III/204). Rulers who correctly fear their own subjects are liable to resort to superstition in an attempt to control their anxieties, but the superstitious practices on which they rely are liable to give rise to quarrelling factions, thus further challenging their authority. Spinoza's Roman examples are designed to demonstrate that states can indeed get caught in this downward spiral (TTP Pref. 8; III/6). However, they also draw attention to a suggestion that is harder for him to accommodate, namely that the destructive effects of superstition depend more on the power of the parties involved than on the nature of superstition itself, so that some superstitious practices may be politically harmless. Spinoza does not allow for this, and seems to exaggerate the connection between superstition and conflict; but one can nevertheless see why he does so. For while superstitious practices need not lead to fighting in the streets, they relieve our anxiety in a way that makes us vulnerable to cooption by the politically powerful, and thereby sow the seeds of struggle.

This sombre conclusion is taken up in a third argument, which criticizes superstition on the grounds that it is pacifying. The habit of clinging to ill-considered sources of hope is bad for us, individually and collectively, because it inhibits our ability to develop more secure strategies for fending off the debilitating affect of fear, and catches us in a cycle of hope and anxiety from which it is difficult to escape. The trouble with superstition is that it prevents us from staring our fears in the face by examining their causes, and thus inhibits the growth of a kind of psychic independence and strength of character that enables us to combat anxiety more effectively. Our investment in the hopes that lie at the centre of superstitious practices stands in the way of open-minded enquiry, encouraging us to 'scorn reason' (TTP VII.4; III/97), and avoid the patient task of forming and revising hypotheses that Spinoza recommends in his *Treatise on the Emendation of the Intellect*.[8] So while superstition is a natural response to anxiety, to which we are all prone, and while 'it's as impossible to save the common people from superstition as from fear' (TTP Pref. 33; III/12), it is nevertheless shortsighted, and increases our susceptibility to the conflicts so far outlined.

How, then, can superstition be avoided? Although Spinoza acknowledges that one can sometimes discredit a superstitious practice by showing that the beliefs on which it is based are false, he cannot regard this approach as providing the whole answer. If superstition is a means of alleviating an endemic form of anxiety, anyone who wants to diminish its influence will have to address the fear on which it feeds, taking account of the possibility that the mere information that a certain hope is false may not enable those who depend on it to abandon their superstitious habits (E IVp1s; II/211). In fact, even a general understanding of the nature and shortcomings of superstition may not stop one from making use of it. In the grip of anxiety, and encouraged by others, we may continue to form hopes that we would be able to avoid in cooler circumstances, and may find ourselves unable to bring our knowledge of causes and effects to bear on our immediate situation. Rooting out superstition is therefore not simply a matter of dissipating falsehood, and unless the anxieties that fuel it are addressed, inconstancy, conflict, and pacification will continue to stand in the way of empowerment.

Spinoza offers two connected responses to this problem. The best and most reliable way to relieve anxiety about the future is to do our best to understand the world by learning about its causal structure. Collective understanding of this sort empowers us by enabling us to see what we are capable of achieving, and how we can best realize our goals. Furthermore, it modifies our fears, because the more it empowers us, the greater is the satisfaction we derive from it, and the greater our determination to use it to counteract the suffering caused by negative affects. This aspect of *fortitudo*, as Spinoza calls it (E IIIp59s; II/188), therefore acts as a counterweight to our tendency to short-circuit investigation by forming superstitious hopes, and enables us, to a greater or lesser extent, to resist credulousness and pacification. At first glance, this rational strategy seems vulnerable to the obvious worry that coming to understand the uncertain threats by which

---

[8] Spinoza 1985.

we are surrounded (whether wars and global epidemics, family break-ups or incurable illnesses) may increase rather than reduce anxiety, and strengthen the disposition to resort to superstition. Spinoza does not deny that this can happen, or that knowledge can sometimes lead individuals to despair, but he nevertheless argues along Stoic lines that the process of coming to understand the causes of our fears can provide a kind of insight that modifies our experience of them. Understanding is itself invigorating, and produces a form of delight that lies outside, and counteracts, the unstable nexus of the passions. Moreover, once the collective habit of self-examination gets firmly embedded in a society and becomes a recognized source of emotional satisfaction, commitment to self-understanding may counteract the tendency to take refuge in superstition by enabling individuals to *feel* its limitations. Self-respect and contentment may become bound up with the fortitude that prevents us from latching on to poorly grounded hopes, and may come to be invested in a desire to manage uncertainty by confronting the fear it creates.

At the same time, understanding is meant to provide a solution to the problematic relationship between superstition and conflict. One of the insights that a proper appreciation of the causal order reveals to us, according to Spinoza, is that the most effective way for humans to empower themselves is to live cooperatively under the civil law. As we gain a better understanding of the world, we acquire reasons for avoiding the forms of competition and aggression to which superstitious practices give rise, and these reasons in turn shape our passions. People who appreciate the limitations of competitive strategies are no longer so strongly drawn to them, and because they can imagine more effective ways of dealing with their fears than resorting to superstition, they no longer derive as much satisfaction from it as before.

In the *Ethics* Spinoza invests the notion of understanding with an almost religious aura, and portrays the philosopher who attains it as participating in the divine. But he also emphasizes that, while understanding exists and can be cultivated, it never exists alone, and can always be put under pressure by the disposition to deal passionately with anxiety by resorting to superstition. To differing degrees, individuals are moved by understanding and the fortitude in which it is manifested, and also by the normal range of affects, and in many of us the former is relatively weak. As a result, we remain subject to fluctuating passions, and are often torn between hope and fear in the manner of the unfortunate multitude described in the Preface of the *Theological-Political Treatise* (TTP Pref. 8; III/6). So although the pursuit of understanding is the surest means of countering superstition, this technique will often not be sufficient, if only because the moderation, sobriety, and presence of mind that are constituents of fortitude will sometimes move us less than the judgments embedded in our passions. To avoid the instability and pacification that are integral to superstition, we therefore need to look for other ways to divert the hopes and fears on which it feeds.

Spinoza's response to this point takes a political turn that is both problematic and suggestive. It is obvious, he assumes, that people are better off when they are able to live peacefully together than when superstitions generate the threat of conflict between them. Moreover, the citizens of an orderly polity have less reason than anyone else to fear social unrest, and thus less reason to resort to superstition. Nevertheless, in order for individuals to live harmoniously together, their passionate investment in doing so must be stronger than their commitment to superstitious practices that are powerful enough to threaten the fabric of society. As we have seen, understanding encourages the avoidance of conflict by offering people a way to cope with fear; but Spinoza now goes on to suggest that, when understanding is in relatively short supply, as it usually is, societies and their members can use the affects themselves to counteract the consequences of superstition.

One thoroughly conventional aspect of Spinoza's analysis is his assumption that superstitious practices trade on the images, rituals and narratives that he classifies as fruits of the imagination. Productive of passion as they are, these devices are a fertile means of arousing superstitious hope and admiration; but, as Spinoza goes on to suggest, they can also be employed on behalf of a harmonious way of life to strengthen a passionate commitment to cooperation and peace. By borrowing the tools of superstition, its opponents can create what one might call devotional practices that avert rather than promote conflict, and provide an antidote to disempowering affects such as fear. Developing this line of thought, he reminds his readers that passionate people are different from one another, and are moved by appeals to the imagination in different ways. Some, for example, may find patriotic narratives a sustaining source of pride and loyalty, while others may be inspired to live more charitably by images of universal humanity. Some are comforted by sectarian religions, while others draw strength from the ceremonies of an established church. To cater for this variety, the state will have to make room for diverse devotional practices, each adapted to fostering reverence for, or identification with, the values or way of life on which it depends (TTP XIV. 32–3; III/78–9).

A striking feature of this approach is that it does not matter whether the narratives around which a devotional practice revolves are true. People may hold beliefs that contain not a shadow of truth, 'provided the person who accepts them does not know they are false' (TTP XIV.20; III/176). For example, it is immaterial whether the religious believe that God is a fire or a spirit, that he is just or merciful, or whether he acts from free will or from the necessity of his nature (TTP XIV.32; III/178–9).[9] What is vital is that some belief or other should be incorporated into practices that strengthen our ability to live cooperatively by generating the

---

[9] The epistemological implications of this view are spelled out in Verbeek, 2003, 30.

positive affects on which this effort rests.[10] So, for example, Spinoza defends the importance of allowing a number of religious confessions to coexist within the state on the grounds that this can encourage citizens to live according to the law, and can strengthen their aversion to extra-legal conflict.

Since devotional practices are part of the institutional structure that prevents people from behaving in ways that are individually and collectively disempowering, this view plays a crucial role in Spinoza's account of the means by which a community promotes a peaceful way of life. However, it is a strange position for him to take, since devotional practices look remarkably like the superstitious ones of which he is so critical. How can the former support cooperation when the latter do nothing but threaten it, and how can false devotional beliefs be empowering, while false superstitions bring vacillation and inconstancy? The difference between the two types of practice purportedly lies in the passions they arouse and the functions they are able to serve. Unlike superstitions, devotional practices arouse *devotio*, a form of love combined with wonder, which easily changes into love as its objects become familiar (E IIIp52s; Dftns of the Affects X).[11] The satisfaction and empowerment that individuals derive from devotional practices can therefore give them a sense of confidence in their values and a steady commitment to their goals. As Spinoza's examples illustrate, devotion to the figure of Christ, fortified by Christian narratives and ceremonies, can generate love for the cooperative way of life outlined in the New Testament.[12] So too a love of one's country can work in a similar way to promote political harmony (TTP XIX.22: III/232).

This difference in the constitutive passions of devotional and superstitious practices should presumably play a part in explaining how the first supports a steady commitment to cooperation while the second induces inconstancy. While the hope that contributes to superstition is always destabilized by its relation to fear, the wonder that contributes to devotion, and the simple love to which it gives rise, are represented as possessing a fixity that brings the heart to rest. This characterization is of course idealized, since *devotio* remains an element in a network of shifting affects, and can be displaced by other passions. Nevertheless, it contrasts significantly with the hope generated by superstition, which, as Spinoza defines it, is intrinsically connected to uncertainty, and always offset by anxiety and doubt. While these negative affects inevitably press on it, presaging disempowering patterns of behaviour such as competition and conflict, this is not the

---

[10] There is a long tradition of argument to the effect that narratives about the fatherland can serve as examples of virtue, and can shape the civic passions. On the way it was adapted by Protestant writers, see von Friedeburg 2005, 81–98.

[11] In some Roman sources, *superstitio* carries a connotation of excessive devotion. Readers attuned to this overtone might have interpreted Spinoza as contrasting an excessive response (*superstitio*) with an appropriate one (*devotio*). Beard, North and Price, 1998, 217.

[12] On the use of ceremonies to create reverence, see TTP V.32; III/76.

case with devotion, which instead engenders confidence. For example, it would be impossible to feel devotion to a thoroughly unreliable deity, because its very unreliability would block the formation of the affect, only leaving room for hope; but it *is* possible to feel devotion to a God, a country or an ideal that is unthreatening and has served one well. Moreover, this passion brings with it patterns of action that Spinoza regards as empowering, such as constancy and a willingness to defend whatever one loves. Because one feels devotion for an object only when one is reasonably confident of it, and because this passion is empowering, it is not prey to the infidelity that accompanies hope and fear, and thereby avoids one of the main political disadvantages of superstition.[13]

As Spinoza sees the matter, superstitious people are unable to make much progress towards understanding because their fears, and the conflicts in which they become embroiled, stand in the way. Each time their hopes are disappointed they are given the opportunity to identify a past mistake (to realize, for example, that a would-be prophet who claimed to have divine powers is a fraud) but the anxiety that such discoveries provoke will often prevent them from appreciating the limitations of superstition as a means of dealing with fear. What is needed is a different way of calming anxiety, a strategy capable of creating conditions in which individuals and groups can engage in empowering forms of reflection and practical experiment. Devotional practices can help to sustain the political security that is a minimum condition of counteracting fear, by exciting love in individuals of a certain temperament. They therefore foster a cooperative way of life, and at the same time make way for understanding by empowering those who take part in them. To be sure, they cannot be expected to do all the work; Spinoza concedes that in some circumstances the use of threats is the only way to guarantee obedience to the law, and thus to create conditions in which peace can be maintained and the conditions of understanding kept alive (E IVp 54s; II/250). But since this approach to the problem runs the risk of exacerbating superstition, a wise ruler will rely on devotional practices as far as possible.

The general point of appealing to devotion is therefore clear enough; but it is more difficult to disjoin it from superstition than the argument so far suggests. An investigation of the continuities between the two practices reveals an ambivalence in Spinoza's account that sits uneasily with his unqualified hostility to superstition and encourages us to reconsider its relation to the pursuit of understanding. A first problem springs from the claim that, while superstition leads to civil conflict, devotion contributes to harmony. As we have seen, this is an exaggeration. A superstitious practice that successfully reduces my anxieties, and a practice that strengthens my resolve to live cooperatively, may both play a role in encouraging me to live peacefully with others, so that, as far as their immediate

---

[13] See Verbeek 2003, 26–8.

consequences are concerned, there may be nothing to choose between them. Furthermore, because the content of a practice does not guarantee that it will produce a specific passion, practices may excite devotion in one group and super-stitious hope in another, or may arouse hope and devotion by turns. 'Words have a definite meaning only from their use. If they should be so organized that, according to their usage, they move the people reading them to devotion, then those words will be sacred. So will a book with the words organized that way. But if the same words should be organized in another way, or a usage should prevail according to which they are to be taken in an opposite meaning, then . . . they will be unclean and profane' (TTP XII.11; III/160).

A second problem relates to Spinoza's claim that devotion is more stable than hope, and raises once again the question of why this should be so. Given that the beliefs on which it rests need not be true, why is devotion to a God or a country any less liable than a superstitious hope to fail us and lead to disappointment? One aspect of the difficulty is that devotion is likely to give rise to hopes of one sort and another, and thus to fear. For instance, patriotism may induce me to hope that my country will be successful and glorious, and to worry that my wishes are going to be thwarted. Furthermore, when devotion springs out of inadequate judgments, it can easily be unsettled by changes of belief. If the object of my devo-tion is a kind and loving God, for example, my feeling for the deity will surely be damaged when I come to believe that he is vengeful, and here too I may suffer the anxiety that predisposes me to superstition. By way of reply, Spinoza can point out that devotional practices are plural, so that when one of them ceases to work I can always embrace another. In fact, he occasionally speaks as though we each have a duty to find a practice that suits our individual temperament and stirs the heart to obey (TTP XIV.32; III/178–9). One might wonder why this is any better than telling someone who has been let down by a superstitious practice to go and find another. But the main issue to which it draws attention is Spinoza's assump-tion that, whereas superstitious practices are locked in competition and therefore produce conflict, devotional ones can peacefully coexist. What explains this fun-damental difference, on which so much of his analysis depends?

It is tempting to suggest that, whereas superstitious practices revolve around claims that are fervently believed and therefore conflict with one another, devo-tional ones are ironically entertained. (For example, people who discover that their fellow feeling is strengthened by singing hymns may decide to go to church, but they need not believe the words they sing.) In fact, however, Spinoza firmly resists this possibility (TTP XIV. 20; III/176). The affects that arise in such cir-cumstances are, he claims, fleeting and superficial, so that only devotional prac-tices to which we are epistemologically as well as emotionally committed can generate sufficiently strong and enduring passions to bind us to a harmonious way of life. Perhaps this is so. But it is then hard to see why devotional practices are not, like superstitious ones, a source of conflict. For although the love they generate is by definition empowering, individuals who experience this affect pre-sumably remain subject to the principle enunciated in the *Ethics* that, insofar as human beings are passionate, they strive to make others agree with them. People who advocate one devotional practice are therefore liable to compete with those who advocate another, and their devotion may give way to mutual hostility.

I have been presenting the task of distinguishing devotional from superstitious practices as an obstacle for Spinoza, and in a way it is. However, it is more pro-ductive to see it as contributing to an internally subversive yet fruitful strand of thought within his philosophy. This begins with his explicit recognition that political possibility is partly shaped by our affects, so that a satisfactory political theory needs to take account not merely of our rational capacities but also of our passionate ones. Furthermore, we need to recognize that these latter capacities are shaped by several forces. One is understanding, which in Spinoza's view has the greatest potential to release us from the destructive consequences of our own psy-chological dispositions. But it does not exist in isolation. Our ability to acquire and benefit from an understanding of ourselves and the world we inhabit partly depends on the passions themselves—on the desires, hopes, and fears that arise out of everyday experience and serve to organize our aspirations and ambitions (EIII. Dftn. of the Affects, XXVIII; II/197–8). If our affects enable us to feel that it is better to try to live cooperatively than to use our energies in conflict, we then face the problem of how to keep them trained on this goal. How can we dissipate the fears that are liable to drive us apart? How can we dramatize to ourselves both the benefits of a cooperative life and the dangers of hostility, and in doing so reinforce our desire for a peaceful form of existence?

Having identified this set of problems as central to political philosophy, Spinoza addresses them by examining not so much the content of our passionate judgments as the functions they serve and the strategies in which they can be incorporated. Equipped with this approach, he tries to separate good strategies from bad. However, as I have tried to show, his attempt to keep them apart also serves to bring out their continuities. The encouragement of devotion cannot be neatly separated from the production of superstition, nor is it clear that the first is invariably fruitful and the second destructive. Sometimes, in spite of what Spinoza says, a good way to cope with fear may be to resort to superstition and place one's faith in hopes that are potentially divisive. And sometimes, as he allows, an effective way to cope with anger or hatred is to rely on devotion, and make use of ultimately misleading narratives or practices to strengthen solidarity. Like the power of devotion to maintain harmony, the ability of superstition to calm our fears can be productive. And like superstition, devotion can generate conflict. Neither strategy is foolproof, and both can be destabilized by competi-tion rooted in fear.[14]

---

[14] As Spinoza will go on to suggest in the *Political Treatise*, this is partly why democratic societies turn into monarchies. TP VII.5; X. 1–10.

This merging of superstition and devotion shifts the former from its usual position on the map of oppositions underlying much early-modern philosophy. In the first place, since superstition is no longer intrinsically connected to religion and can manifest itself in politics or philosophy, identifying it is part of a general form of critique. Furthermore, if superstitious practices, as much as devotional ones, can contribute to a harmonious civic life, it is no longer automatically a moral lapse to espouse them. They belong to the set of institutional and psychological mechanisms through which both rulers and ruled tame their anxieties, and thereby help to maintain their ability to live peacefully together. Although Spinoza firmly holds on to a distinction between superstition and understanding, his analysis makes it difficult to sustain the view that superstition is always destructive and can play no part in creating the conditions on which the growth of understanding depends. Putting this point the other way round, devotion is in some ways closer to superstition than his account suggests. While the love in which it consists provides an inbuilt urge to cooperation, it is not secure. So although devotional practices are more promising than superstitious ones as a means of fostering understanding, both are unstable. It is true that Spinoza sometimes marginalizes this similarity by characterizing the narratives around which devotional practices are organized as shadows or anticipations of the universal moral law revealed by understanding. When devotion enables us to behave cooperatively, he claims, we live as we would if we understood this law, and to that extent participate in a rational way of life. However, it remains the case that the passionate judgments constituting our devotion are inadequate, so that our commitment to a harmonious form of existence is liable to change with our individual or social circumstances. The effectiveness of the practices we can use to counteract fear and its consequences varies greatly from one situation to another, so that superstition, as well as devotion, may play a fruitful role in political life.

In the final book of the *Ethics* Spinoza outlines a form of understanding that floats free of the affects, and of the fluctuations of power and feeling that are integral to them. It is arguable that this aspiration, itself the ultimate goal and reward of the practice of philosophy, contains elements of superstition, insofar as it holds out the hope of a life beyond fear and quells the anxieties of philosophers by validating their status. (Needless to say, Spinoza would dismiss any such suggestion; but since his ability to do so depends on his insistence that understanding relieves us of anxiety, anyone who is sceptical about this claim may also doubt his conclusion.) Nevertheless, we may perhaps accommodate his ideal image of philosophical understanding by viewing it as the resolution of a less ambitious conception of reasoning that runs throughout his work. According to this interpretation, reasoning is the process of using the limited understanding we possess to extend our knowledge of causes and effects, modifying both our ideas and the affects with which they are intertwined as we go along. To understand the causes of our superstitious fears, for example, we first have to gain enough self-confidence to confront them; but understanding their causes and consequences will in turn strengthen this confidence, and give us the means to grasp, in both thought and action, the limitations of fears to which we were (and may to some extent remain) subject.[15] This technique can be used by both rulers and ruled to combat disempowerment; and since an individual has very little power, the practice of reasoning, like the other practices we have considered, is bound to be a collective one.

Many contemporary political philosophers remain strongly inclined to suppose that what they have to deal with is a realm of rational individuals who are susceptible to arguments, and whose passions generally fall into line with their rationally grounded conclusions. What we have to provide, it is often assumed, is a reasoned account of the principles on which a free, or just, or equal society should be based. If the reasons are good, people will accept and internalize them, and in this way our efforts will have an effect on political life. As we have seen, Spinoza does not reject this view. He agrees that we ought to try to understand our situation as best we can, and adds that understanding modifies our emotional responses. But he also shows that there is something crucial that such a model leaves out, namely that our ability to appreciate and act on the fruits of understanding is shaped by passionate judgments, which are in turn moulded by the practices that political societies contain. To revert to his key example, our capacity to live cooperatively can be destroyed by anxiety or strengthened by devotion, and these passions, together with the judgments in which they are embedded, are themselves fostered or dissipated to different degrees by circumstances. Applying this point to the practice of political philosophy, we need to see political theories as embodying a set of implicit assumptions about the emotional capacities that citizens must possess if the theory in question is to be realizable; and we need to recognize these dispositions as an important aspect of the theory itself. Nevertheless, philosophers often fail to take the step of making these capacities part of their subject-matter, and this in turn cuts them off from the further project of considering the conditions on which such abilities depend. Rather than seeing our capacity for political reasoning as embedded in passionate dispositions such as the ones we express in superstition and devotion, they are inclined to treat it as an independent variable with a force of its own. In taking this stance they neglect a set of problems that Spinoza illuminates, and marginalize an aspect of politics that is no less vital than the normative principles to which so much attention is rightly paid.

We therefore need to try to advance the insights Spinoza has given us by pursuing the questions his philosophy raises. As I have argued, his work encourages us to dwell not only on the relations between hope and fear, but also on the interconnections between superstition, devotion and understanding. Like him, we find ourselves in circumstances where political narratives play on our fears and

---

[15] See Gatens and Lloyd 1999, 40–57.

loyalties; and like him, we face the task of dealing with the powerful passions these arouse in us. If, as the *Theological-Political Treatise* suggests, the practices that alleviate fear with hope cannot be neatly separated from those that arouse devotion, so that our commitment to a cooperative way of life is habitually touched by, and mingled with, superstition, we need to think again about the place of superstition in contemporary political life.

4

Narrative as the Means to Freedom

Spinoza on the Uses of Imagination

Throughout his philosophical career, Spinoza was concerned with the problem of how the members of societies can be motivated to sustain harmonious and empowering forms of communal life.[1] Given that we need to live together in order to survive, and yet have divergent desires and interests, there is a seemingly ineradicable tension between the urge to cooperate with one another and our wish to go our own way, both sides of which must be accommodated in any stable political system. If we are to avoid the frustrations and miseries engendered by conflict, we need to be able to reconcile our more individual aspirations with the demands of a shared way of life. But what forms of self-understanding are most effective in helping us to move towards this goal, and in what conditions can they be successfully cultivated?

In developing his response, Spinoza never loses sight of the fact that creating and maintaining a harmonious way of life is a fundamentally practical project, simultaneously made possible and constrained by circumstances. But he nevertheless takes account of the fact that the manner in which the members of a particular society handle the conditions in which they find themselves will partly be determined by their conception of the kind of understanding most relevant to resolving their differences. Hence the question he faces: what sort of knowledge is most efficacious in enabling people to reconcile their individual desires with the requirements of their collective life?

Within the history of ethics we can broadly distinguish two lines of response. According to a universalist approach, we are best served by a systematic and compelling grasp of universal moral principles that we can then apply to our own situations. By contrast, advocates of a particularist view argue that we need something more specific: an interpretation of ourselves and our circumstances that generates resources for dealing with them.

[1] Originally published in Yitzhak Y. Melamed and Michael A. Rosenthal eds, *Spinoza's 'Theological-Political Treatise'* (Cambridge University Press, 2010), pp. 250–76. Reprinted with permission of Cambridge University Press.

I am particularly grateful to Akeel Bilgrami, Aaron Garrett, Moira Gatens, Charles Griswold, Joel Kupperman, Melissa Lane, Amelie Rorty, Michael Rosenthal, Daniel Star, and John Troyer for their comments on earlier presentations of the material included in this essay.

Spinoza on Learning to Live Together. Susan James, Oxford University Press (2020). © Susan James.
DOI: 10.1093/oso/9780198713074.001.0001

The opposition between these two stances is venerable and deeply entrenched; but universalism has recently been subjected to a renewed wave of particularist criticism from philosophers who contend that moral reasons are never completely general. One version of this position appeals to the holistic nature of reasons in order to argue that the answer to the question 'What do I have best reason to do?' is always determined by features of the specific situation under consideration, and thus varies from one case to the next.[2] A further version contends that we give meaning and value to situations and actions by fitting them into narratives about our place in the world that, while they may express shared values, are less than universal. Only through narratives can we generate the thick descriptions in which moral meaning is conveyed, and provide accounts of what is going on that are sufficiently detailed and focused to explain and justify our actions. So much so that, without this resource, we could not hope to assess possible courses of action as conducive to, or destructive of, a cooperative way of life.[3]

The disagreement between defenders of this latter version of the particularist position and their universalist opponents underlies a range of current debates in ethics, political philosophy, and the philosophy of action. While aspects of the history of their disagreement are often invoked to illuminate one or other position, it is perhaps surprising that Spinoza's distinctive contribution to the argument has not been much explored. Resisting the temptation to opt for one side at the expense of the other, he argues that our capacity to live cooperatively grows out of a situationist capacity for constructing narratives, which in turn explain and justify our actions. At the same time, we realize our highest good when we become capable of acting on the kind of principles that the universalist extols.

This inclusive stance both allows and constrains Spinoza to address the problem of how to reconcile universalism with particularism. How do the narratives that give moral meaning to our collective lives mesh with our commitment to general principles? What contribution can each approach make to our attempts to create the cooperative ways of life on which our ability to live as we wish depends? Rather than trying to keep the two views apart, Spinoza explores their mutual dependence, carefully mapping the borders at which they meet and tracing the paths that lead from one to the other. Travelling in one direction, we rely on narratives to become capable of being motivated to act on general principles; moving in the other, our principles are made liveable through the narratives that make our individual and collective lives intelligible. There is much to be said about each of these journeys, and about the points at which they intersect as we track from the situational to the universal and back again. Here, however, I shall focus on Spinoza's account of the ways in which we depend on narrative to become more

---

[2] Dancy 2004.   [3] MacIntyre 1981, Hutto 2007.

capable of living by universal principles. As I shall try to show, the breadth and subtlety of his analysis opens up a set of possibilities and problems that are not only philosophically rich in themselves, but also add a fresh dimension to contemporary discussion of the kinds of understanding that promote social and political cooperation.

Spinoza aligns the approaches I have described as universalist and particularist with two distinguishable ways of thinking. We take the universalist approach when we engage in the abstract form of thought that Spinoza calls reasoning or understanding, and aim to grasp the unchanging and exceptionless laws governing types of things such as human minds (E IIp44c2; II/126). As we use our reason to extend our knowledge of the laws of human nature, we come to recognize general features of the type of collective existence that is, as Spinoza puts it, most empowering for humankind. For example, so the *Ethics* tells us, everyone has good reason to promote their ability to reason (E IVp36, E IVp37; II/234–5); equally, 'a man who is guided by reasoning... desires to maintain the principles of common life and common advantage. Consequently, he desires to live according to the common decision of the state' (E IVp73; II/265). Furthermore, when reasoning operates as it should, it motivates us to act on our understanding, both by yielding incontrovertible grounds for doing some things rather than others, and by strengthening our desire to put our rationally grounded knowledge into practice (E IVp59; II/254).

The true understanding of the world that reasoning provides is in Spinoza's view extremely powerful, but it is not easy to come by. Almost everyone has the capacity to cultivate the practice of reasoning, but few have the opportunity to do so, and still fewer appreciate its benefits (E IVp37s2; II/238). This latter insensitivity is mainly due to the fact that most of us are absorbed in the distinct and wide-ranging kind of thinking that Spinoza calls imagining. Imagining, in this technical sense of the term, encompasses the thinking and behaviour that we base on our experience of particular things, situations, and processes. It includes our perceptions and expectations, our memories and fantasies, together with the passions that run through them. It also includes the kinds of informal reasoning we employ to string these experiences together, such as the means–ends inference that makes me decide to go out for half an hour because the saxophonist next door rarely practises for longer than that, or the inductively based suspicion with which I delete an email offering me a million dollars. In short, imagining is our everyday and favoured way of imposing meaning on our experience. 'Because deducing a thing solely from intellectual notions often requires a long chain of perceptions, plus extreme caution, mental perceptiveness and restraint—all of which are rarely found in men—men would rather be taught by experience...' (TTP V.36; III/77).

When an individual imagines, the meaning they ascribe to an event, and thus the way they fit it into their broader interpretation of the world, is determined by their own history (E III, Postulates 1 and 2; II/139–40). The pattern of our past experiences shapes the way we see and feel about new events and states of affairs, so that the story of what has happened to us in the past remains present, informing our grasp of what is going on and constituting an interpretative standpoint. Spinoza does not describe this process as the creation of a narrative (*narratio*)—a term he mainly reserves for a particular manifestation of imaginative thinking, namely the narratives contained in the Bible and in histories—but I think it is appropriate to see the entire activity of imagining in these terms.

As with any narrative, imaginative thinking expresses the point of view of a narrator and puts together a more or less coherent story about what is going on. And, as with any narrative, later stages of the story may prompt its narrators or audiences to reinterpret what went before, so that the past to which we relate our current imaginings is never fixed. When individuals or groups imagine, they do not construct narratives from scratch, because they are always already absorbed in existing meanings and points of view. To be sure, they may or may not be able to articulate them—for example, one might well be unable to recount the narrative underlying the sudden antipathy one feels for a woman one passes in the street. Nevertheless, when we make use of imagination to describe, explain, or justify, its narrative structure comes to the surface as we recount the past experience on which our current judgments are based, or explain how a situation strike us. Furthermore—and here we come to the point at issue—such narratives, together with the affects they contain, ground our grasp of the things that matter to us, of the means to achieve them, and of the forms of cooperation that will help us to realize them. Among many other things, they give us our conceptions of cooperative ways of life, and shape our willingness (or lack of willingness) to live by them.

We therefore have two potential sources of insight into the project of creating ways of life that will accommodate both our desire to pursue individual goals and our dependence on other people. One of them—philosophical reasoning—is universalist. It focuses on unchanging properties of types of things and the atemporal laws that govern them. The other—imagining—is particularist, and charts our individual and collective interpretations of specific things and events. But what contribution does each of these kinds of thinking and acting make to our ability to live together in a harmonious fashion? Spinoza's answer is rooted in his doctrine of the *conatus*—his view that each of us strives to maintain ourselves as the individuals we are, and where possible to increase our power to maintain ourselves (E IIIp6; II/146). This striving is manifested in every aspect of our existence, including physical processes such as the homeostatic mechanisms governing the temperature of our bodies, and the entirety of our thinking. Both through imagining and reasoning, then, we try to get the kind of grip on ourselves and our circumstances that will empower us, by enabling us as far as possible to create a way of life in which we experience high and secure levels of physical and psychological satisfaction.

In outline, the role of philosophical reasoning in this process is relatively straightforward. By giving us a true understanding of ourselves and the world, reasoning shows us what we can and cannot achieve, disabuses us of various pervasive errors about the nature of our capacities (E I App.; II/77–83), and reveals what types of action will and will not be empowering. If we were completely rational, we would follow the dictates of reason and agree on an optimal way of life (E IVp35c1; II/233). As things are, however, we are only somewhat rational. Alongside our efforts to empower ourselves through reasoning, we also strive to maintain ourselves by imagining, and this way of thinking exposes us to various systematic forms of misunderstanding that limit our ability to cooperate effectively.

It is important not to exaggerate the dysfunctional character of imagining, as Spinoza conceives it. Despite its deficiencies, it provides us with a largely efficacious grasp of the world and ourselves, and underpins many sensible habits and decisions about what to do and how to live. Indeed, unless this were the case we would not survive. Nevertheless, Spinoza is impressed by the extent to which imagining fails to track the truth as it is revealed by reason, and tends to blur the line between accurate perception and fantasy. We see this above all in the general human disposition to put an empowering interpretation on our experience, thereby making it satisfying and encouraging. As the *Ethics* explains, 'the Mind strives to imagine only what affirms or posits its power of acting' (E IIIp54; II/182) and 'avoids imagining things that diminish its own power or that of the body' (E IIIp13c; II/151). In our efforts to persevere in our being, we blend realism and fantasy in varying degrees, sometimes taking refuge in projection or denial, and sometimes facing up to disempowering truths with courage or fascination. Contrary to an imaginatively fuelled assumption that we make about ourselves, straightforward observation is extremely difficult to achieve. 'Indeed, when men see or hear something new, unless they take great precautions against their preconceived opinions, they will for the most part be so prejudiced by them that they will perceive something completely different from what they see or hear has happened, particularly if the thing that has been done surpasses the grasp of the narrator or the audience, and especially if it makes a difference to his affairs that a thing should happen in a certain way.' Hence the commonplace observation that two historians or chroniclers may describe an event in such divergent terms that it is hard to believe that they are talking about the same thing (TTP VI.53; III/92).

The central claim here is that, rather than simply recording our experiences, we are disposed to make them affirmative and to resist interpreting them in ways that are physically or psychologically debilitating. In this sense, there is an element of fantasy built into our everyday thinking. The mind strives to imagine what affirms its own power of acting. As interpreters, our narratives are selectively organized to achieve a certain effect, in which truth tracking is subsidiary to empowerment.

In order to appreciate the appositeness of Spinoza's view, it is helpful to remember that the trait he is describing operates at a familiar level. In Joseph O'Neill's 2008 novel, *Netherland,* the protagonist, Hans, is a Dutch banker working in New York. On a flight back from London he is given a chocolate bar, and although the bar is frozen he starts to eat it.

When I took my first bite I felt a painless crunch and the presence of something foreign in my mouth. I spat into my napkin. In my hand, protruding from brown gunk, was a tooth—an incisor, or three quarters of one, dull and filthy.

Dazed, I called over an attendant.

I found a tooth in my chocolate bar, I said.

She looked at my napkin with open fascination. Wow...

Then she said carefully, Are you sure it's not yours.

My tongue lodged itself in an unfamiliar space. Shit, I said.

Hans's striving to conceive of himself as someone with a full set of teeth is not an isolated event. In interpreting what is happening to him, he implicitly draws on a pre-existing sense of himself as a competent man who would be ashamed if he thought he was falling apart. This self-evaluation is in turn embedded in a narrative that sustains his conception of the kind of person he is: he is physically attractive, extremely good at his job, a sportsman, and so forth. Here we can begin to see how the narrative that gives Hans a certain orientation to the world also manifests the striving of his *conatus.* It shapes his effort to persevere in his being and, in this particular incident, does so to the point where a wish becomes father to the thought that the tooth in the chocolate bar belongs to someone else. Like Spinoza's historians, Hans and the flight attendant start out by describing their situation in radically different ways, and it is only through their exchange that they arrive at a common account of what has occurred. As it happens, their common account is true: unfortunately, it is Hans's tooth that is lodged in the chocolate bar. But our shared narratives do not always converge on truths. Many of our ordinary beliefs are in Spinoza's opinion profoundly mistaken, so that the scraps and stretches of narrative on which we agree are often only half-truths and are sometimes simply false. The urge to empower ourselves that drives us to interpret our experience in ways that are more or less fantastical will not necessarily be checked by other people; on the contrary, as we shall see, they may equally well corroborate or elaborate our fantasies. Moreover, as Spinoza sees the matter, there is nothing exceptional about this mixing of fantasy with fact. It is what imagining is like.

The fantastical element in imagining can therefore cut both ways. It may bind people together and, as we shall see, can be a potent unifying force. But it is also liable to undermine the effectiveness of the very efforts to cooperate that it engenders. A first and significant difficulty stems from the porous boundary between fact and fantasy that we have just examined. If, for example, a community bases its efforts to cooperate on a narrative that significantly overestimates its capacities, it will run the risk of failure. In addition, however, Spinoza is convinced that imaginative thinking embodies an inherent tendency to generate division and conflict between agents, whether individual or collective (E IVp32; II/230–1). This problem stems from the fact that each of us has our own passions and desires, grounded on our own histories, and strives to persevere in our being in our own way (E IIIp57; II/186). The narratives we create will consequently embody diverse conceptions of the ends that are worth pursuing and the ways of life that are tolerable, and as we strive to realize them, our aspirations are bound to clash. To make matters worse, some of the psychological laws that are integral to imagining set us at odds with one another. We are naturally disposed, for instance, to want other people to share our desires, and are liable to hate them for failing to do so (E IIIp31; II/164). But when they do love what we love, and we find ourselves competing with them for scarce goods, we are prone to envy them (E IIIp35; II/167). Once again, our viewpoints are bound to diverge; and given that we have to live together, they are bound sometimes to give rise to personal and political conflict.

Because the laws governing our affects form an ineliminable dimension of imaginative thinking and are not easy to offset, the implications of Spinoza's analysis look dark. If imagining is inherently fantastical, it will be unable to correct its own tendency to produce narratives that are erroneous and potentially divisive. If it is inherently antagonistic, it is not obvious how it can make a constructive contribution to the project of creating a stable and cooperative way of life. If it is always prone to generate narratives that collide, surely it is bound to impede rather than promote cooperation. It seems, then, that the version of the particularist approach on which we have been focusing cannot yield the kind of insights that we need in order to build reliable, cooperative forms of existence, so that we would do better to turn to the universalist approach exemplified by philosophical reasoning.

Spinoza agrees that, if human beings were thoroughly rational, this would be the right conclusion to draw (TTP V.20; III 73–4). As it is, however, the option is not available. Since the imaginative dimension of our thinking is inescapable, we simply have to reckon with it. However, this state of affairs is not as bad as one might fear because, despite the limitations we have discussed, there are ways in which imagining can enhance our ability to create harmonious and satisfying ways of life. Taking up first the fantastical impetus of imaginative thinking, and then its sheer diversity, Spinoza argues that each of these features possesses a productive aspect.

Judging by the historical record, communities have from time to time been strikingly successful in uniting around a narrative that has enabled them to live cooperatively. Moses, for example, generated a remarkably cohesive community by persuading a group of newly released slaves with no experience of the benefits of citizenship to live in accordance with a comprehensive set of laws. He achieved this feat by representing the Jews as the subjects of a divine legislator who could be trusted to reward their obedience. By providing them with a narrative that answered to their beliefs and yearnings, he gave them a largely compelling reason to obey the law. The effectiveness of Moses' narrative was, however, completely independent of its truth since, according to Spinoza, there is no anthropomorphic God who imposes laws on individual nations or holds out the prospect of reward and punishment. Moses 'imagined God as a ruler, a lawgiver, a king, as compassionate, just, etc., when all these things are attributes only of human nature' (TTP IV.30; II/64). In this case, at least, the fantastical element of imaginative thinking was not destructive. On the contrary, it empowered the Jews by enabling them to create a secure state.

If a narrative is to shape the behaviour of a particular group of people, they must be motivated to act as it recommends, and this willingness in turn depends on a number of conditions. First, whether or not the narrative is true, the people concerned must believe it to be so. (In the *Theological-Political Treatise*, this claim is grounded on the relatively uncontentious assumption that we are generally more strongly motivated to act on claims that we take to be true than on claims we hold to be fictional (TTP XIV.20; III/176).) Secondly, Spinoza finds in the Old Testament a number of strategies for creating and sustaining a desire to live in accordance with the values that a narrative extols. One of the less successful ways in which Moses tries to persuade the Jews to conform to the law is to threaten anyone who disobeys with punishment. However, as the Bible indicates (and Spinoza agrees), harmony born out of fear is without trust (E IV, App. XVI; II/270–1), so that individuals who only cooperate on this basis will 'act very unwillingly... All they care about is saving their necks and avoiding punishment.' (TTP V.22; III/74). Since we experience fear as disempowering, our *conatus* ensures that we strive to resist situations that make us afraid, and in the case of the Jewish law this sometimes encouraged people to turn away from God, or to imagine that they were sufficiently powerful to avoid divine punishment. Moreover, when they acted on these convictions they partly undermined the scheme of cooperation on which everyone's mutual benefits depended.

It is therefore more constructive to provide empowering grounds for obedience, and 'that's why Moses... introduced religion into the Republic, so that the people would do their duty not so much from fear as from devotion' (TTP V.29; III/75). According to the *Ethics*, devotion is a kind of love we feel for people whose capacities far outstrip our own, and who therefore excite our wonder or veneration (E IIIp52s; II/181). To feel this affect for God is, in part, to love him; and because we experience love as empowering, a person who gains satisfaction from loving an infinitely powerful deity will normally seek to maintain this relationship by obeying the divine law. However, as Spinoza's analysis of the passions also allows us to infer, even this strategy is not completely stable, and is liable to be derailed by the element of veneration that devotion contains. In venerating God for capacities that far outstripped their own, the Jews were made aware of their comparative impotence, and were reminded of the extent to which they were dependent on a being who held them in the power of his hand. The sense of vulnerability that they experienced in turn made them anxious. (Can we really trust him? Are we not enslaved to his inexorable power?) As the Pentateuch testifies, a desire to escape this form of subordination intermittently eclipsed their veneration for the divine law, making way for narratives that embodied competing interpretations of their collective experience and recommended other courses of action.

Spinoza's attention to the obstacles that Moses encountered brings us to the second set of problems endemic to any form of cooperation grounded on narrative. Because the narratives to which a community appeals will invariably be diverse, the binding power of any single narrative will be inherently limited. Furthermore, since the balance of power between narratives shifts with the passions that motivate individuals to act on them, a successful narrative must continually adapt to changing times. We see Moses grappling with these only partly superable difficulties as he cajoles, threatens, and bargains, attempting to encourage and amaze the Jews into an enduring condition of steadfast obedience to the law. (It was because he aimed to break their stubborn heart, Spinoza remarks, 'that he addressed them with the sound of trumpets, with thunder and with lightning, not with arguments' (TTP XIV.36: III/179).) The story of his attempt to inculcate a level of single-minded devotion that would guide the actions of virtually all his people suggests that, at least in some circumstances, such a strategy can work remarkably well. But as we have also seen, it is bound to come up against the labile nature of human affect. Unless an approach to the creation of harmonious ways of life that is grounded on the narrative resources of imagination can accommodate the variety and changeability of our grounds for action, its success is bound to be limited.

Turning to this problem, Spinoza points out that imaginative diversity is not invariably an obstacle to cooperation. For example, communities commonly offer their members a number of disparate interpretations of the benefits of obeying the law, and accept that some individuals conform to it because they fear punishment, others because they hope for gain, still others because they love their country, and so on (TTP XVII.6; III/202). As long as most people have a motivating reason for obedience, the goal of cooperation is achieved, and there is no immediate need for greater homogeneity. So although the narratives that constitute imaginative thinking provide an imperfect means of combating political conflict, they are sometimes strong enough to achieve this goal. The Spinozist version of particularism we have been considering therefore yields an answer to our problem that can in practice be sufficient.

It is clear from Spinoza's outspoken defence of religious pluralism that he appreciates the force of this conclusion. Given that humans interpret their circumstances through many distinct religious narratives, a useful way to generate empowering forms of life is to exploit this very diversity in the name of social unity. Permit people to hold any religious beliefs that strengthen their ability to obey the law. Encourage individuals to interpret the core beliefs on which obedience depends in whatever way makes them easiest to accept. Refrain from inquiring too closely into the particular convictions on which obedience is grounded (TTP XIV.34; III/179). Don't worry about the fact that many of these convictions will be false, but judge them solely on the basis of their practical consequences (TTP XIV.32; III/178). In short, allow people to generate their own reasons for conforming to the divine law by constructing their own narratives.

This approach to the creation of religious harmony also informs Spinoza's analysis of its political counterpart. Because individuals and sects have different conceptions of what the divine law demands, a community needs an authority to pronounce on the matter. In principle, the Scriptures can fulfil this role, since any careful reader can identify their core doctrine (TTPXII.33; III/165); but in practice we know that the biblical account of the law can be interpreted in many conflicting ways. If peace is to be maintained, someone must adjudicate between the claims of competing sects, and the only agent with the power to do so is the sovereign of the state. The interpretation and enforcement of divine law thus becomes a part of the civil law over which the sovereign exercises control. 'The supreme power...which has the sole responsibility of preserving and protecting the rights of the state, has the supreme right to maintain whatever it judges concerning religion' (TTP XIV; 63; III/199). A sensible sovereign who takes to heart Spinoza's argument for the benefits of religious pluralism will therefore permit a profusion of religious narratives. However, there seems no reason why this strategy should be confined to religion. If it succeeds in generating obedience to the tenets of the divine law that the civil law incorporates, why should it not generate obedience to other aspects of civil law as well? A sovereign should surely generalize from the religious case and look kindly on any interpretative narratives, whether historical, personal, political, or cultural, that motivate individuals or groups to cooperate.

While Spinoza recognizes that the promotion of ingenious versions of pluralism is often the most empowering strategy available to a community, he is still not convinced that this conclusion constitutes a satisfactory solution to our problem. His main reservation is the familiar one that, when states ground cooperation on a diversity of narratives, they remain vulnerable to the types of antagonism that the passions engender and will sometimes succumb to conflict or disintegration. Contemporary liberals are liable to regard this risk as a necessary cost of any tolerable political system; but Spinoza remains doubtful. Even where a relatively harmonious way of life exists, the divisiveness inherent in the passionate relationships underpinning it means that its destruction is always in the offing, and its multiple narratives are as likely to become a source of indecision and conflict as of unity. Observing this fact, one may simply resign oneself to living in a political community that falls significantly short of the ideal from which we began. Alternatively, one may decide to look again at the nature of imaginative thinking to see whether it contains further resources for building stronger forms of cooperative life.

Taking up the second of these options, Spinoza turns again to the Bible to re-examine the motivating force of different types of narrative. In general, people are more willing to act on a promise of empowerment than on a threat of disempowerment, and the Jews were consequently more stably motivated to obey a God worthy of devotion than one who traded on fear of retribution (TTP V.28; III/75). In both cases, however, they were expected to conform to the commands of an external legislator with whom it was impossible to negotiate, and although they had reason to believe that God would look after them, their subjection to him was nevertheless complete. Since he alone determined the law that bound them together, they were unable to fix the terms of their own common life, and a form of cooperation that was empowering in some respects was consequently disempowering in others. As well as binding the Jews to the law, the structure of the Mosaic narrative set an absolute limit to their striving to empower themselves, and in doing so created grounds for anxiety and resistance. The protection offered by God in the form of the law could also be experienced as a form of slavery, waiting to be overcome.

There is, in Spinoza's view, no way of escaping from this tension within the type of narrative that Moses bequeathed. Its constraints can only be overcome as changing circumstances create new possibilities, intertwined with revisionary narratives. The discussion of the constitutional history of the Jewish state contained in Chapter XV of the *TTP* charts a process by which control over the law shifts from one agent to another, thus creating a demand for narratives capable of legitimating and encouraging new forms of obedience. But it is in the New Testament that Spinoza locates what he presents as the most empowering outcome of this process. When the followers of Jesus Christ represent the law made by God as written on the fleshly tablets of the heart rather than on tablets of stone—that is to say, as a set of rules that anyone can understand and legislate for themselves—they draw on the resources of the Old Testament to construct a narrative that overcomes the limitations inherent in its predecessors. According to the outlook they offer, one need not submit to commands set by someone else in order to obey the law; rather, true obedience lies in obeying commands that one imposes on oneself. Instead of following the law because God requires it, one conforms to it because one appreciates that one has good reasons of one's own for doing so, and acts on this understanding. Needless to say, this conception of one's relationship to the law will only be compelling if one can be confident that one does in fact have good reason to obey it, and on Spinoza's reading, the narratives

contained in the Bible strive to make this view persuasive. Both testaments represent conformity to the divine law as the only means of achieving an unparalleled
level of power that benefits us as individuals and as members of communities.
According to the New Testament, moreover, the law is universal in the sense that
it applies to everyone and takes each person's interests into equal account. 'Before
the coming of Christ, the prophets were accustomed to preach religion as the law
of their own country;...but after the coming of Christ the Apostles preached
the same religion to everyone as a universal law...' (TTP XII.24: III/163). The
Apostles thus offer an image of a rule designed to uphold the common good that
imposes the same manageable demands on each of us, and which one can willingly obey in the confidence that one will receive one's fair share of benefits and
not carry more than one's fair share of burdens.

What makes the Scriptures attractive, then, is their resolution of the tension
between doing what we ourselves regard as best and doing what the law requires
of us. Their doctrine, one might say, presents in the compelling guise of a religious narrative the republican view that the only way to gain political freedom is
to legislate for oneself a law that upholds the common good. Spinoza represents
the emergence of this strong imaginative basis of cooperation as a significant conceptual transition in the history of humanity. But at a psychological and a historical level the story is of course more complicated. Psychologically, a grasp of the
universality of the law is not by itself enough to banish debilitating passions such
as fear. The prospect of punishment or the threat of corruption may still cause
citizens anxiety, and can be expected to qualify their confidence in any legal system under which they actually live. So the problems posed by conflicting passions
and narratives will not be completely resolved, although one might expect the
disempowering doubts associated with a narrative about a law that one obeys
willingly to be less boundless and enervating than those excited by a narrative
about a Mosaic God. The fear that comes with total submission to an unpredict-
able deity is not the same as the fear that a law upholding the common good may
be corrupted or go awry. Although anxiety will remain, its quality will be modified by the narrative of which it is a part, and it will play a different role in individual patterns of motivation.

Historically, the task of creating communities that are capable of living up to
the ideal held out by the Bible is, as Spinoza recognizes, immensely taxing. The
existence of a narrative in which the ideal is represented does not in itself make it
compelling, and in practice its effectiveness depends on a host of factors. For
example, some agent must be capable of making the narrative credible to a community, and that community must in turn be capable of using it to strengthen its
form of cooperative life. Spinoza seems to have thought that the Dutch state had
made a certain amount of progress in this direction. The idea that one has good
reason to obey the law when one legislates it for oneself on terms that apply
equally to everyone had been made concrete in the republican constitution of the

United Provinces and in the dogmas of some of its sects. However, despite their potential to empower, these institutionalized narratives remained fiercely contested. So much so that, when Spinoza was writing the *Theological-Political Treatise,* it even seemed possible that the Dutch republican regime would not survive.

In such circumstances, a more pragmatically minded theorist might well have taken refuge in the thought that an adequate degree of political unity can some-times be created out of imaginative diversity. But Spinoza is not yet ready to accept what he regards as a weak conclusion and, as before, the next phase of his argument grows almost dialectically out of the impasse he has reached. If the task of politics is to build ways of life in which cooperation is stably protected and upheld, the United Provinces, as Spinoza implicitly portrays it, has reached a significant point of transi-tion. Pulling in one direction, the narrative he locates in the Scriptures holds out an image of a strongly unifying form of cooperation, organized around an appreciation of the power that can be generated when the members of a community impose the law on themselves. However, like an oasis glimpsed from the desert, this ideal has so far only flickered into view. The circumstances in which it can be securely realized do not obtain, and recent attempts to establish it have met with limited success. Standing in its way, and pointing in other directions, are a number of competing narratives, offering different accounts of the nature and extent of the commitment to cooperation, and carrying with them the materials for religious and political conflicts that may do irreparable damage to the state.

From Spinoza's point of view, this situation is discouraging. But that very fact contributes to the danger the situation poses. Discouragement is potentially as damaging as the situation on which it feeds, because it is liable to reinforce a spirit of defeat in which the United Provinces may fall back on a less empowering way of life than the one it has already achieved, and resort to terror or devotion in order to enforce the law. Whatever the short-term benefits of such a strategy, it carries with it the likelihood of increased social and political conflict. During the 1660s and 1670s, Spinoza seems to have been convinced that the Dutch were at serious risk of curtailing their liberties by abandoning their republican constitu-tion. In his political and philosophical writings he is trying to resist this outcome by providing a narrative that will inspire his compatriots to continue to struggle for stronger forms of cooperation. The narrative he now goes on to offer is thus a political intervention designed to encourage the citizens of a polity to press for-ward towards a more stable way of life.

To move towards the ideal of a community in which the law is written on the fleshly tables of the heart, one must provide reasons for obedience that have a general appeal.[4] As Spinoza now goes on to claim, the kind of reasons that can best satisfy this demand are those derived from philosophical reasoning. Unlike imagining, which answers to particular and diverse experiences, reasoning yields

---

[4] See Gatens, 2009b, 455–68.

truths that are universal, eternal, and guarantee their own certainty (TTP IV.29–31; III/64). To rationally understand a law about what empowers human beings, for example, is to appreciate that it captures an incontrovertible feature of the human good, and that it applies to you as one human being among others. Like anyone else, you have a reason to recognize it and to give it weight when deciding what to do (TTP IV.16; III/61). Philosophical understanding therefore provides us with a universalist approach to the problem of cooperation. It uncovers general principles such as 'Be just,' or 'Strive to bind yourself to others by love' (E4p46), and shows us why we have reason to act on them.

This conception of reason is familiar enough; but what concerns us here is its role in Spinoza's argument. Spinoza does not claim that he or his contemporaries currently live in an environment where most people can in fact use philosophical reasoning to work out how they have good reason to live. Nor does he claim that even the most advanced philosophers of his time have enough understanding to give more than a fragmentary account of what these reasons are. And he certainly does not claim to know that his sketch of a rational community can be fully realized. He is not therefore appealing to philosophical reasoning as the basis for an immediate and accessible solution to the problem of creating stable and harmonious communities. Instead, he is offering an image of a way of life devoted to the pursuit of philosophical understanding, which, if we could achieve it, would enable us to contain the diversity of our imaginative outlooks and generate forms of cooperation far stronger than any we have so far managed to devise.

In the *Ethics*, Spinoza defends the need for an exemplar or model of human nature that we can set before ourselves and try to imitate (E4 Pref; II/208). Putting this approach to work, he offers us a model of a life organized around the pursuit of philosophical understanding, and invites us, his readers, to use it to give meaning and value to what we do. We are meant to internalize his ideal of systematic philosophical understanding and let it shape our lives. But in so far as we follow him, and live by a faith in the existence of reasons that we cannot actually grasp, we rely on our capacity for imagining. We are envisaging a way of life in which we have universalist reasons for cooperating from a particularist perspective in which our reasons for acting are for the most part shaped by the narratives through which we interpret our experience.

What will make the ideal of rationally grounded cooperation compelling to us? As we have seen, a first condition is that we should be able to hold it as true. But this is a stringent requirement, particularly if we acknowledge that the claim that reason can ground an empowering form of unity may be as much a fantasy as Moses' conception of a legislating God. Although Spinoza is confident that this is not the case, he is acutely aware that the philosophical arguments by means of which he demonstrates his conclusion are not within everyone's reach. How, then, is he to make his view persuasive? Presumably the most effective means of enabling people to appreciate the benefits that understanding brings is to teach them how to reason; but before he can take this route, Spinoza first faces the problem of convincing them that they should submit to being taught. Since they are not skilled in reasoning, there is no point in offering them a complex philosophical argument, and Spinoza therefore pursues the alternative course of appealing to their imagination. His first, comparatively basic appeal is to their experience, and thus to the narratives in which our grasp of our own capacities are embedded. We already understand ourselves as capable of reasoning and have some experience of the kinds of power to which it can give rise; so the suggestion that it might generate further effective conclusions should not strike us as outlandish. For this consideration to move us, however, we need to be convinced that the benefits of learning to reason will be worth the trouble, and here Spinoza makes a second and more interesting appeal.

As aspirant philosophers, he tells us, we are pursuing a kind of knowledge that will free us from the passionate conflicts of our everyday lives and increase our power. Among the rewards we shall gain from living in a community whose members recognize that they have good reasons to cooperate for their mutual benefit are the confidence and satisfaction that come from knowing that we shall be treated fairly, the ability to pursue our own ends within the limits of the law, and the support generated by enduring friendships. In addition, the project of understanding to which such a community is devoted will diminish our suscepti-bility to sadness and bring us joy. Here, as elsewhere in his work, we find Spinoza employing the resources of imagination in the service of reasoning, gilding his portrait of a life devoted to understanding with a familiar and empowering pas-sion. Part of what makes the image of a rational life desirable, and encourages us to struggle towards it, is its continuity with the familiar pleasures of forms of existence grounded on imaginative thinking. Our ability to identify with these pleasures can inspire us to promote the forms of cooperation from which we imagine them to spring. But what motivates us here is not so much a grasp of the rational basis of cooperation, which still lies ahead, as a narrative about what we might achieve and the satisfactions it would bring. Here, then, Spinoza gives the last word to the particularist approach.

The central conclusion of the argument I have traced is that the way of life endorsed by reason needs to be brought within imaginative reach if it is to mould our desires and actions. The general principles around which it is organized must be made liveable by being embedded in the narratives that shape our aspirations and give meaning to what we do. If we are unable to see how we could, or why we should, conform to the demands of what Spinoza describes as a rational life, an image of such a life will be no use to us. As he appreciates, it is only through more or less particular narratives that a commitment to cooperation can be brought alive. Universalism therefore cannot get along without the form of particularism that Spinoza defends.

5

Responding Emotionally to Fiction

A Spinozist Approach

I

Within contemporary analytical philosophy there continues to be a lively debate about the emotions we feel for fictional characters.[1] Our sadness at the death of Anna Karenina or fear of Dracula are thought to need explanation because they violate a supposedly normal state of affairs in which our feelings for an object are responsive to our beliefs about whether or not it exists. When, for example, you learn with relief that your friend was not after all involved in a road accident, you cease to feel anxious about her. Once you realize that there is nothing to be anxious about, the emotion fades. Why, then, does the knowledge that Anna Karenina is a fictional character not prevent us from feeling sad about her suicide? Why does the belief that the figure of Dracula on the screen is an actor in front of a camera not block the fear he arouses? As Colin Radford has argued in an influential article, there seems to be something anomalous and even incoherent about emotional responses such as these.[2]

The supposed incoherence that Radford identified is often expressed in the following paradox:

1. We experience (genuine, ordinary) emotions towards fictional characters, situations, and events.
2. We do not experience (genuine, ordinary) emotions when we do not believe in the existence of the objects of emotion.
3. We do not believe in the existence of fictional characters, situations, and events.[3]

[1] Originally published in in Anthony O'Hear ed., *Passions and the Emotions*, Royal Institute of Philosophy Supplement 85 (Cambridge University Press, 2019), pp. 195–210. Reprinted with permission of the Royal Institute of Philosophy.

I am particularly grateful to Sharon Achinstein, Jane Bennett, Anne Eakin Moss, Evelyne Ender, Moira Gatens, Joanna Hodge, Jonathan Lear, Yitzhak Melamed, Yi-Ping Ong and Christopher Thomas for their comments on aspects of this essay.
[2] Radford 1975, 67–80.   [3] I take this formulation of the paradox from Friend 2015, 217.

Since these three claims are jointly incompatible, discussion has tended to focus on which should be rejected, and from this approach a descriptive question has emerged: how can fictions elicit genuine emotions? Alongside the descriptive problem, however, discussion of the paradox has also given rise to a normative question: are the emotions we feel for objects we believe to be fictional in some way inappropriate or irrational? What normative standards do or should apply to them?[4]

The contemporary debates surrounding these questions are undoubtedly absorbing and challenging in their own terms; but it is arguable that they are also slightly perverse. How has a phenomenon as familiar and satisfying as our emotional response to fiction become so problematic? What presuppositions have successfully derailed the everyday assumption that our emotions move easily across the barrier between belief and fantasy without becoming descriptively or normatively dubious in the process? It is not easy to articulate this sense of uneasiness from within the current debate, where the outlook that gives rise to the paradox largely holds sway. To get a clearer view of it, we may therefore do better to approach it historically. Spinoza, I shall suggest, offers an account of our emotional investment in fiction that stands at a helpful distance from the ongoing discussion. He achieves this, in part, by rejecting a widespread assumption about the agents whose emotional responses to fictional objects are held to be problematic. In much of the literature it is taken for granted that these are agents of a certain kind, who habitually distinguish real from fictional objects and whose emotions are for the most part responsive to their beliefs about whether an object exists. It is against this background that their emotions for objects they believe to be fictional show up as aberrant. But in Spinoza's view this is the wrong place to start. The ability to keep our emotions in line with our beliefs is a complex skill, and rather than simply assuming it we need to consider how it is acquired. What abilities does it presuppose and how do we develop them? According to Spinoza, the capacity to conform one's emotions to one's beliefs is parasitic on the capacity to invest emotionally in one's ideas, regardless of whether they are fictions. Contrary to the assumptions underlying the descriptive question, our feelings for fiction are therefore not mysterious. They are part of our ordinary affective life, and it is by means of them that we cultivate the skill of focusing our emotions on the truth.

II

Spinoza's defence of this view grows out of his account of imagination, the everyday way of thinking through which we acquire ideas of ourselves and external things. Insofar as we imagine, he argues, our ideas of external things are ideas of

---

[4] For further discussion of the normative and descriptive aspects of current debate see Friend 2015.

the ways they have affected our bodies. 'When the mind regards external bodies through ideas of the affections of its own body, then we say that it imagines' (E IIp26; II/112). However, whereas many of his contemporaries tended to emphasize the perceptual content of such ideas, Spinoza gives priority to those 'affections of the body by which the body's power of acting is increased or diminished, aided or restrained, and at the same time, the ideas of these affections' (E IIId3; II/139). Our experiences of the way that external things affect us take the form of feelings of joy and sadness (E IIIp11; II/148–9). As well as perceiving a friend at the door, for example, the experience affects me with gladness, and as well as seeing her leave I am saddened. As this example indicates, imagining does not fail to acquaint us with the perceptible features of external things. Nor does Spinoza deny that some of our ideas are devoid of any affect; it is possible to perceive an object while remaining affectively indifferent to it. However, because we are attuned to the way that external things empower or disempower us, our stance to the world is not fundamentally one of affective indifference. We are oriented to experience external things as the objects of sadness or joy.

Spinoza also takes trouble to remind us that our ideas are not, as he puts it, mute images like pictures on a panel, and do not merely represent the way that things appear (EII p42s; II/132). Rather, 'an idea, insofar as it is an idea, involves an affirmation or negation', and affirms something as present (EII p49s[II]; II/131–2). To have a joyful idea of a friend at the door is to affirm that this is how things are—she is standing there waiting to be welcomed—and this affirmative outlook is a general feature of imagining. To quote Spinoza again, 'if the human body is affected by a mode that involves the nature of an external body, the human mind will regard the same body as actually existing or present to it...' (E IIp17; II/104). To have an idea of a thing or state of affairs is therefore to affirm that it exists; and when we imagine, we affirm that things are, perceptually and affectively, a certain way. Putting this point together with the last, the ideas that constitute the process of imagining are simultaneously perceptual, affective, and affirmative.[5]

Before we turn to the role of fantasy or fiction in the processes of imagination, two further aspects of Spinoza's philosophical position need to be highlighted. First, our ideas of the way things affect us do not occur in isolation. They are embedded in trains of thought and governed by psychological dispositions that prompt us to make particular kinds of connection between them. We organize them into increasingly finely differentiated types of joy and sadness, as when you distinguish the initial joy of seeing your friend from the joy of talking to her, or distinguish your love for her from your hope that her life will go well (E IIIp56; II/185). Equally, the occurrence of an idea sparks off associations with other ideas

---

[5] This view contrasts with the view that ideas are belief-like as it is interpreted in Bennett 2003, ch. 10; Lin 2006, 395–414; Della Rocca, 2003b, 200–31.

that have been connected with it in the past, so that a superficial resemblance between your friend and a stranger, for example, may prompt a surge of affection for the stranger (E IIIp15; II/151–2). Dispositions such as these move our ideas along, incorporating them into a complex process of thought.

Spinoza's second relevant claim is that our imaginative patterns of thought are manifestations of an overarching disposition to persevere in our being that he describes, as I have noted in earlier chapters, as an individual's *conatus* (E IIIp6; II/146). In all our thoughts and actions, we strive to maintain ourselves as the beings we are, and our failures and successes are manifested in our sad and joyful affects. Insofar as we empower ourselves we are joyful, and insofar as we become less powerful we are sad. To some extent, our efforts to live joyfully are rooted in reality—for instance, we try to spend time with our friends rather than with our enemies. But they are also shaped by elements of fantasy that gain a hold in two related ways. One stems from the fact that, even when our imaginative ideas of external things are haphazardly constructed from our experiences of being affected, we tend not only to treat them as reliable, but to build them into fantasies of empowerment. As far as the mind is able, Spinoza tells us, it 'strives to imagine those things that increase or aid the body's power of acting' (E IIIp12; II/150). This disposition can lead us to get ahead of ourselves by fantasizing about the properties of the individuals we encounter, as when you convince yourself that the stranger who resembles your friend is as intelligent and generous as she is. More dramatically, it can prompt us to fantasize about the existence of external things. In an effort to make sense of our experience and live joyfully in the light of it, Spinoza argues, we may for example imagine the existence of tree sprites, winged horses, or an anthropomorphic God.

Fantasies such as these are an integral part of imagining and share its characteristic features. Spinoza is confident that an idea of a tree sprite may be as affective and confidently affirmed as an idea of a friend, and may enter in the same way into a train of thought. 'With their eyes open', he observes, 'someone may imagine certain things so vividly that it's as though they had those things before them' (TTP I, fn. 44; III/28). By contrast with those contemporary theorists who approach the problem of our emotional response to fiction from the standpoint of agents who have a firm grasp of the distinction between the fictional and the real, Spinoza therefore begins from an imaginative form of thinking in which fact and fiction are not clearly separated. Since our basic imaginative stance is to affirm the existence of the objects of all our ideas, our imagining at least initially lacks the resources to distinguish fiction from reality and the conditions assumed by the contemporary problem of fictional emotions are not yet in place. Purely imaginative agents, as we have so far delineated them, do not distinguish existing things from fictions, or their affects for one from their affects for the other.

One may well feel that this analysis wilfully fails to mark a range of distinctions that must play a central role in any worthwhile discussion of our emotions for fictional objects. But this response arguably misses Spinoza's point. His conception of imagining is designed to draw our attention to a pre-philosophical and indeed primitive way of thinking, in which there are no clear distinctions between what are nowadays described as beliefs and fantasies. Moreover, he suggests, this is where we have to start. To understand how we learn to distinguish fictional from real objects, and our affective investments in the one from our affective investments in the other, we need to ask how, given the nature of imagining, we acquire these skills. Rather than presupposing distinctions that will make our emotions for fictional objects seem problematic, we need to consider how we come by them.

Spinoza's most illuminating discussion of this process revolves around an imagined example of a boy who believes that Pegasus exists, or to put it in the terms of the *Ethics*, affirms the existence of a winged horse. 'For what is perceiving a winged horse', Spinoza asks, 'other than affirming wings of the horse?' In order to stop affirming the existence of the horse, Spinoza goes on, the boy must acquire some other idea that excludes the existence of Pegasus. If he 'does not perceive anything that excludes the existence of the horse, he will necessarily regard the horse as present' (E IIp49s[III.B.(ii)]; II/134). Perhaps, for example, someone explains to him that winged horses are mythical; but whatever the process, it must arouse ideas that undercut his capacity to affirm the existence of the winged horse. As the *Ethics* sums it up, 'the mind does not err from the fact that it imagines, but only insofar as it is considered to lack an idea that excludes the existence of those things that it imagines to be present to it' (E IIp17c; II/105).[6]

By coming to affirm that winged horses are mythical, the boy becomes unable to affirm their existence. But although Spinoza describes this process in terms that make it sound as though our ideas can be divided into two groups, those that we do and do not affirm, he in fact acknowledges a complex middle ground. When the boy recognizes that the mythical character of winged horses is incompatible with their existence, there is a sense in which he ceases to affirm the existence of the horse. He may acknowledge, if directly asked, that Pegasus does not exist, and put this idea to work in some of his thinking. But to embrace this view consistently, thereby expressing a robust commitment to Pegasus's fictionality, he must also give up his affective investment in the horse's existence and redirect the affective satisfaction that the idea produces in him. This is a further step. The boy may, for example, continue to joyfully imagine himself riding across the skies on Pegasus's back, and as long as this idea enters into his striving to live joyfully, it will block his ability to fully exclude the existence of the horse.

Spinoza is confident that the process of excluding or ceasing to affirm an idea is as affective as it is cognitive (E IIIp19; II/155). Affects, he argues, can only be

---

[6] On the difference between affirmation and belief see Steinberg 2005, 147–58; Steinberg, 2017, 261–82.

countered by affects (E IVp14; II/219); so until the boy gets some affective benefit from accepting that there are no winged horses, he is liable to hang on to the idea that they exist. Only once some compensating satisfactions have been established will he be able to let go of the joy he derives from believing in the winged horse and take pleasure in ideas that are consonant with its fictionality. Even then, as Spinoza argues with the help of a different example, his original affects will not completely disappear. Our knowledge that the sun is far from the earth does not entirely prevent us from affirming that it is, as it appears to be, relatively close (E IIp35; II/117). Nor does our knowledge that it is far off entirely exclude the satisfactions we gain from the way it appears. We still take pleasure, for example, in the story of Icarus. In the same way, the boy's initial, unequivocal affirmation of the winged horse's existence will retain a place in his memories, patterns of association and fantasies, and will continue to play a role in his striving to live joyfully. He may continue to imagine himself riding through the skies, and the fantasy may remain a source of emotional comfort.

With this analysis, Spinoza delineates some of the workings of imagination that fall between wholehearted affirmation of an idea and a firm commitment to its fictionality. As we learn to exclude or marginalize ideas, we grasp the distinction between things that do and do not exist, and move beyond the primitive imaginative condition in which the difference between fiction and reality has no traction. But learning to apply this distinction consistently is a further skill. It is a matter of learning how to manipulate our conscious and unconscious disposition to affectively affirm ideas of objects whose existence, whether real or fantasized, makes us joyful, by modifying the emotional responses that are integral to imagining. We do this not only by excluding ideas, but by learning the social skill of confining them within specific practices such as storytelling or daydreaming.

Most people, Spinoza urges us to see, only have an imperfect grasp of this skill. To return to our example, the boy who is initially unable to control his idea of the winged horse—who sometimes affirms it, sometimes excludes it as his other ideas take him—may become more adept at compartmentalizing or quarantining his ideas, together with the satisfactions they embody. At school, in biology lessons, he may unhesitatingly affirm that winged horses do not exist, while continuing to glory in his adventures with Pegasus as he lies in bed at night. At school he may be able to give reasons for his claim and take pleasure in his knowledge; but at night these reasons may be easily supplanted by a world of fantasy. As Spinoza points out, learning how to apply one's grasp of the distinction between objects that do and do not exist within one's ordinary imaginative thinking, and shaping one's affects accordingly, takes application and skill (E IVApp. xiii). Because our imaginative dispositions are continually at work, our capacity to differentiate our affects for things we believe to exist from our feelings for those we believe to be fictional remains to some degree unsteady, so that our affects are not, as the contemporary paradox seems to demand, invariably responsive to our beliefs. We therefore should not be surprised that we respond emotionally to fictions, nor should we view this disposition as anomalous. Instead of wondering how such responses are possible, we should reverse the descriptive question and pose it the other way round. What does it take to make our affective responses follow our beliefs? Rather than being an exception to a general rule, our emotional responses to objects we believe to be fictional are for the most part a manifestation of the inescapable and wholeheartedly affective mode of thinking that early-modern philosophers call imagination.

III

Within the contemporary debate, the descriptive question on which we have so far been concentrating tends to be distinguished from the normative issue of whether our emotional responses to fiction fall short of rationality or are in some other way inappropriate. For Spinoza, however, the two questions cannot be separated, and some of the normative features of his argument have already come into play. We gain our initial grasp of normativity, he argues, from the operations of our *conatus*. When we strive for objects and ways of life that we think will make us joyful, we are simultaneously striving for things that we desire; and to desire or want something is to conceive it as good (E IIIp9s). The goodness under consideration here is wide-ranging and encompasses the many forms of satisfaction and joyfulness that we strive to cultivate. Nevertheless, it forms the basis of the more specific norms we subsequently develop, for example by distinguishing ethical from aesthetic joys and sadnesses. Since all our imagining, and indeed all our thinking, is a manifestation of our *conatus*, it is invariably oriented towards things we find good and to this extent is bound to be normative. Judged from this viewpoint, our emotional investments in fiction are an integral part of our efforts to cultivate ways of life that we find joyful or good.

To live well or joyfully, Spinoza contends, it is vital to learn to distinguish reality from fiction. A person whose grasp of the difference between the two is non-existent or weak will be dangerously vulnerable to sadness and liable to be classified as mad. However, learning to handle this distinction is not simply a matter of learning to exclude fictions and the affects they embody from one's thinking. Instead, we learn to live as joyfully and powerfully as possible by learning to integrate the satisfactions we gain from fantasy, and the pleasure of distinguishing truth from fiction, into our ways of life.[7] To illuminate this developmental aspect of Spinoza's position, it is useful to compare it for a moment with a psychoanalytic account of the uses of fantasy. Donald Winnicott's analysis of transitional objects is

---

[7] For powerful discussions of this view see Gatens and Lloyd, 1999; Gatens, 2012, 74–90.

chronologically remote from Spinozist philosophy, but he unselfconsciously echoes the view we have been tracing when he contends that very young children do not have the means to distinguish external objects from the internal objects they imagine.[8] So much so that a child may not recognize that its mother figure is a separate individual who comes and goes of her own accord, imagining instead that she is under its control.

As children mature, they have to come to terms with the difference between inner and outer objects and learn to live with their limited power to control them. One manifestation of this process is the emotional attachment of some children to what Winicott called transitional objects, such as an old piece of blanket or a teddy bear. Although an adult will view the blanket as an ordinary external object, it functions for the child as the repository of its idea of its mother figure, and is not clearly allocated to the inner or the outer realm. Moreover, by straddling the boundary between the two, the blanket enables the child to blur the division between the real and the fantasized until it becomes emotionally capable of living with it. Eventually, in the normal course of things, children abandon their blankets and affirm their separateness from their mother figures. But according to Winnicott, this process of emotional differentiation is never complete, and the feelings of loss that it involves remain in play. In our adult lives we continue to suffer from our inability to omnipotently control the world, and need outlets through which our sadness can be allayed. Practices such as art, religion, and daydreaming answer to this need. Within them, we can invest affectively in transitional objects, without having to confront the question of whether they are inner or outer, fictional or real.

Fictional objects, as Spinoza conceives of them, function like a child's blanket. As we make the transition from a primitive form of imaginative life in which the real and the fictional are not distinguished to ways of life in which this distinction plays a role, and as we gradually revise our ideas of what is and is not fictional, we—like Winnicott's child—must forego some forms of joy. At all stages, this loss arouses affective resistance and has to be affectively compensated for, so that practices of compensation are themselves integral to our imaginative way of life. When Spinoza implies that childhood is a less perfect condition than adulthood, one can see what he means (E IVp39s; II/240). From the point of view of a philosopher who is set upon attaining an active way of life informed by understanding, the powerlessness of a young child has nothing to recommend it. But as Winnicott helps us to appreciate, Spinoza also acknowledges a sense in which we never completely leave childhood behind. The delights of an imaginative outlook in which we do not have to come to terms with the otherness of external objects

---

[8] Winnicott, 1971.

continue to fuel our affective investment in the individual and collective fictions that are part of our imaginative lives.

These commitments emerge most clearly from Spinoza's treatment of religion. Some religious people, he argues, resemble the child who straightforwardly affirms the existence of a winged horse. Since none of their ideas exclude the existence of an anthropomorphic God, they affirm the existence of such a deity on the basis of the narratives contained in the Bible, and make him an object of their affects, without realizing that no such God exists (TTP II.52; III/42–3). But there are also people, including many seventeenth-century theologians and Spinoza himself, who believe that biblical narratives were written for ordinary as opposed to learned people and are adapted to their beliefs (TTP XIV.1). Rather than describing God as he truly is, they describe him in fictional, anthropomorphic terms as a lawmaker, ruler, and judge. For people who read the Bible literally, the question of whether their representation of God is fictional does not arise; but for the theologians it does. They believe that God has no anthropomorphic properties, yet many of them also derive religious strength from ceremonies in which God is represented in anthropomorphic terms.

Are such theologians to be condemned as irrational for failing to bring their affects in line with their beliefs? This is not Spinoza's considered view. As I argued in Chapter 2, the aim of religion as he sees it is not to teach the truth, but rather to foster a cooperative way of life organized around the commitment to loving one's neighbour. Learning how to use the biblical narratives to promote this goal in oneself as well as others is part of what a Jewish or Christian religious life involves. For those who wholeheartedly affirm the God of Scripture, this will be a matter of learning to love or fear him; but for the theologians and others like them the process will be more complicated. They must learn how to use ceremonial invocations of an anthropomorphic deity to strengthen their affective commitment to a religious way of life, whilst also using their greater understanding of God for the same end. To put the point another way, they must cultivate the skill of integrating an affective commitment to a critical biblical hermeneutics aimed at truth with an affective commitment to a transitional religious practice that does not press the question of whether or not an anthropomorphic God exists. Once again, this skill comes in degrees. Some theologians, like the boy who has very little control over his affirmation of the winged horse, may struggle to keep the two practices apart. They may, for example, be emotionally drawn to a theology imbued with anthropomorphism. Others, like the boy who has learned to confine his daydreams about Pegasus, may be adept at incorporating the pleasures of theological understanding and biblical narrative into joyful ways of life.

Spinoza encourages the readers of the *Theological-Political Treatise* to cultivate this skill for themselves, urging them to discover which biblical narratives speak to them and how they can most effectively use them to strengthen their commitment to religion (TTP XIV.32; III/178–9). They should ask themselves, he suggests, whether it is more inspiring to concentrate on Genesis or Joshua, whether it is more moving to listen to the text read aloud or read it to oneself, and develop forms of religious observance that answer to their affective characters. This is in effect a recommendation to create transitional objects and employ them within their own religious practices. But there is a point at which Spinoza seems to withdraw this advice. He also claims that people who fully understand that there is no anthropomorphic God, but nevertheless attempt affectively to affirm his existence, would be guilty of something like bad faith. 'I ask you, who can embrace something in his mind in spite of the protests of reason? What else is denying something in your mind but the fact that reason protests against it?' (TTP XV.10; III/182). Here, at last, he seems to voice a version of the normative worry so prominent in contemporary discussion. Cultivating the skill of moving between an idea of God that one believes to be true and an idea of the deity that one knows to be fictional is a self-indulgent refusal to live up to the demands of rationality.

In raising this objection, Spinoza is not, however, casting doubt on the value of the transitional practices we have so far discussed. Rather, he is drawing attention to the difference, as he construes it, between philosophy and other forms of knowledge, and reminding philosophers of one of the implications of their practice. Philosophical understanding puts the issue of existence centre stage. In its ideal form, it deals in true or adequate ideas and affirms the necessary relationships between them. To have a completely adequate idea of a triangle, for instance, would be to affirm all the ideas it necessarily presupposes, together with all the ideas that necessarily follow from it, and to wholeheartedly exclude all ideas that conflict with them (E I ax. 4; II/46). Equally, someone who has an adequate idea of a horse will wholeheartedly affirm the impossibility of a horse with wings, and wholeheartedly exclude its existence. In its ideal form, philosophical reasoning therefore leaves no room for probabilistic, partial, or compartmentalized affirmations of the kind that characterize imagining. It rules ideas in or out, and the more adequate one's ideas become, the more difficult it is to affirm anything they exclude. As Spinoza illustrates the point in the *Treatise on the Emendation of the Intellect*, the better one understands that bodies are finite, the harder it will be to affirm the existence of an infinite fly (TIE 58; II/22).

As well as depending on a range of cognitive capacities, the exercise of understanding presupposes certain affects. Adequately understanding an idea is not only a matter of appreciating that it is ruled in or out. It is also a matter of wanting to put the idea to work by employing it in one's attempts to increase one's adequate ideas and by refraining from affirming ideas that contradict it. Philosophical understanding must incorporate the desire to use and cultivate this form of knowledge. To pursue it wholeheartedly, a philosopher must take pleasure in increasing the adequacy of his ideas, and as this joy grows, Spinoza argues, the pleasures of fantasy will pale into insignificance (E Vp20v; II/293).

In its purest form, philosophical understanding therefore seems to remove our power to respond affectively to fictions by cancelling our ability to affirm them. The better we appreciate that an object doesn't exist, the less affective hold it will have over us. Moreover, as we approach this state of enlightenment, attempting to cultivate affects such as love or fear for a non-existent object such as an anthropomorphic deity will become increasingly difficult. The more adequately one understands that God does not have anthropomorphic properties, the less capable one will become of loving or fearing him for these traits. To attempt to do so would then be to try to fly in the face of ideas that one cannot but affirm. Epistemologically, it would be a failure to embrace one's philosophical knowledge and live in the light of it; ethically it would be a failure to embrace what Spinoza regards as the best way of life, informed as far as possible by understanding. As I shall argue at greater length in Chapter 13, these weaknesses would display a lack of *fortitudo*, the power to live as our understanding dictates.

It seems, then, that the perfect philosopher would meet the expectation assumed by the contemporary problem from which we began, and would possess the skill of keeping his emotional responses in line with his beliefs. His desires would reflect what he knows to be true, and he would no longer derive joy from fictions. However, while this power may be a feature of the form of knowledge that Spinoza introduces at the very end of the *Ethics*, the intellectual love of God, it is not clear how far he thinks we can achieve it. In the *Political Treatise*, for example, he explains that no one, however wise, can practise *fortitudo* all the time (TP VI.3; III/297–8). By implication, philosophers will for the most part retain desires that can only be satisfied within transitional practices, and will need to continue to cultivate the skill of using them. To this extent, they will continue to resemble the boy who quarantines or compartmentalizes his affects by moving back and forth between his knowledge of horses and his daydreams. But in their case, the relevant skills will consist in compartmentalizing the practice of philosophy from a range of imaginative practices in which fictions play a role, thus enabling themselves to experience a range of forms of joy. As we have seen, religion is one of these.[9] But as Spinoza indicates, the wise man also knows how to rejoice in transitional practices such as going to the theatre (E IVp45c2s; II/244–5) or imagining exemplary actions and characters (E Vp10s; II/288). Each of these practices is governed by its own social norms, and in each case these norms have to be learned, so that the wise man, like anyone else, must cultivate a range of skills. He must learn how to integrate his emotional responses to various kinds of fiction into an existence dominated by the pursuit of understanding, by employing transitional practices to maintain and advance the joyfulness of his life.

---

[9] On this aspect of religion see Rosenthal 2001, 535–57. On the relation between religion and artistic practices see Gatens 2015, 1–16.

In its middle reaches, philosophical understanding offers us ways to strengthen and direct these skills. Whereas Spinoza's boy has an imperfect control over his daydreams, Spinozist philosophers come to understand a good deal about themselves. They come to know, for example, how their affective responses are organized and how individuals and societies can manipulate them. Equipped with this knowledge, they are individually and collectively better placed to understand the imaginative mechanisms governing our emotional responses to fictions, and can to some extent train themselves and others to use them productively. They can self-consciously consider how to develop a particular skill, reflect on their progress, or critically assess the effects of an existing transitional practice. Under this kind of scrutiny, our emotional responses to fiction become an object of understanding and our transitional practices grow in sophistication. The counterparts of the blanket to which Winnicott's child unselfconsciously resorts include things like plays, religious narratives, and political ideologies, each of which assumes a complex set of individual and social skills and is subject to critical reflection. (The skills of actors and artists, for example, differ from those of even the most discerning spectators.) Such practices are transitional in the sense that they license us to stand back from the demands of exclusively pursuing understanding, implicitly acknowledging the strength of the joy we derive from our affective investments in fiction. For the most part we cannot do without them, and except at the very limit they therefore remain integral to philosophical forms of life. Part of the philosopher's task is to learn to reconcile the joy he derives from fictions with the project of pursuing understanding, by learning to move deftly between different practices, transitional or not. In doing so, however, he must also accept and learn to handle a certain degree of risk. However habitual the ability to compartmentalize becomes, the danger of losing control of it always remains, whether because the force of imagination temporarily increases under physical or psychological stress, or because the capacity to distinguish truth from fiction is permanently destroyed. We never lose the disposition to invest affectively in all our ideas, fictional or not, and our power to control it is always less than perfect.

PART II

THE POLITICS OF LIVING TOGETHER

6

Law and Sovereignty in Spinoza's Politics

Recently, several innovative writers have found in Spinoza's philosophy a conception of politics that speaks to many of the concerns of contemporary feminism.[1] By focusing on what Spinoza calls imagination, they have developed an interpretation of his work that offers a way to view sexual difference as a fundamental yet variable dimension of political life, a way to theorize the ineradicability of politically significant differences of feeling and opinion, a way to understand the central role of local narratives and symbols in the construction of identity, and a way to conceive the social dimensions of affect.[2] Taken together, these interpretations contribute to a view of politics as a process in which sovereigns and citizens can explore and criticize the self-understandings around which their common way of life is organized and can cooperate to enhance their freedom by devising effective forms of legislation. The overall aim of politics is thus taken to be that of preserving and increasing liberty; but each particular, embodied community needs to determine in its own case how freedom is to be lived (TTP XX 11–12; III/240–1). Despite the fact that Spinoza himself is unexpectedly dismissive about the political capacities of women, feminist theorists have shown how his approach can 'open up possibilities for the social critique of fictions which elude the resources of more conventional criticism'.[3] As male and female subjects come to appreciate how their imaginative grasp of their situation both empowers and constrains them, they strengthen their ability to assess and where necessary revise the laws and conventions by which they are governed.

This conception of politics draws support from the final chapter of the *Theological-Political Treatise,* in which Spinoza examines the limits of state power. Extending a line of thought already present in Hobbes's *Leviathan,*[4] he observes that, because sovereigns cannot control the minds of their subjects, they are

[1] Originally published in Moira Gatens ed., *Feminist Interpretations of Spinoza* (Pennsylvania State University Press, 2009), pp. 211–28. Reprinted with permission of Pennsylvania State University Press.

    I am particularly grateful to Maria Aristodemou, Alexander Douglas, Peter Fitzpatrick, Moira Gatens, Eric Schliesser and Theo Verbeek for their comments on earlier versions of this essay.

[2] These interpretations are indebted to the influential work of Gilles Deleuze (see Deleuze 1988 and 1990) and Louis Althusser (see Althusser 1976, ch. 4). Some of the most important examinations and elaborations of the themes identified above are to be found in Balibar 1994; Gatens and Lloyd 1999; Gatens 2000; Montag 1999; Howie 2002.

[3] Gatens and Lloyd 1999, 5.   [4] Hobbes 1994a, ch. 32.4.

Spinoza on Learning to Live Together. Susan James, Oxford University Press (2020). © Susan James.
DOI: 10.1093/oso/9780198713074.001.0001

unable to prevent individuals from thinking and judging as they please (TTP XX.6: III/240).[5] Coercive as the state apparatus may be, it will not be able to stop subjects from forming their own feelings and opinions; and since these vary as much as tastes, any polity is bound to contain an ineliminable groundswell of conflicting affects and judgments. Furthermore, because humans are in general no better at controlling their tongues than their thoughts (TTP XX. 8–9; III/240), any attempt to police the expression of ideas will run a high risk of failure. Sovereigns the world over therefore need to face up to the fact that they cannot rely on legislation to enforce or outlaw belief and must recognize that the law can at most impose a level of uniformity on what people do. Even here, however, a sovereign's power will be circumscribed by its subjects' power to resist, so that in order to survive, a sovereign must be sensitive to what its subjects will and will not tolerate.[6]

Spinoza's stress on the limits of state power plays an important part in his political philosophy; but although he encourages his readers to note that sovereigns must be prepared to negotiate with their subjects, his commitment to a consensual image of government is nevertheless ambivalent.[7] Sovereigns, as Spinoza portrays them, must be sufficiently powerful to make and enforce the law (TTP XI.28; III/194). In addition, they must be capable of determining what kinds of dissent amount to sedition, of punishing subjects whose opposition they regard as seditious, and of specifying the limits within which subjects may discuss and challenge their judgments. Finally, when a sovereign refuses to respond to criticism, its subjects remain bound to obey its laws, even when they believe those laws to be wrong (TTP XVI.27; III/194). So as well as sketching the lineaments of a politics of compromise, Spinoza is a steely defender of the view that certain elements of a sovereign's power, including the ability to determine the boundaries of negotiation, should be as absolute as possible.

What should we make of this tension between the presumption that certain elements of a sovereign's power must be fixed, and the more open approach to lawmaking emphasized by many recent commentators? Does Spinoza's delineation of the incontrovertible elements of sovereign power undermine the emphasis on negotiation that feminist scholars have found so productive, or can the two be reconciled? One influential response to this question, championed by Negri and Matheron, takes up a remark in the *Political Treatise* to the effect that the only absolute form of sovereignty is that held by a democratic assembly whose decisions, and hence laws, are themselves the outcome of negotiation and compromise.[8] In states where every subject plays a part in the process of making the law,

[5] For Hobbes's discussion of the same point, see *Leviathan,* 198–199.
[6] Gatens and Lloyd 1999, ch. 5; Balibar 1994, 110.
[7] See Balibar, 1994, 174f; Gatens and Lloyd 1999, 67–70.
[8] Negri 1997, 219–247; Matheron 1969, 330ff.

and thus possesses a share of sovereign power, no one has to be coerced into obeying laws they have not made for themselves. Laws about the non-negotiable aspects of sovereign power emerge from democratic forms of collective negotiation and decision making, and because this minimizes the threat of resistance, the sovereign's power is as absolute as possible.

This is an important and compelling line of interpretation, but I shall argue that it only partly resolves the tension with which we are concerned. To get a fuller grasp of the issue, we need to go back a bit and look again at what it takes for the sovereign of a state to achieve a near absolute level of power. Negri and Matheron's appeal to democracy presupposes that the power of a sovereign is measured in relation to the power of other human agents (principally the multitude of subjects), and their proposed solution is designed to dissipate conflict between the sovereign's ability to make the law and its subjects' ability to resist. But for Spinoza there is also a theologico-political aspect of the problem. To assess the extent of the sovereign's power to make law, one needs to consider whether this power is limited by nonhuman agents, and in particular by God. If the deity ordains laws that humans are obliged to obey, both the sovereign's authority and a consensual politics will be framed by the non-negotiable demands of divine legislation, and both will need to be re-examined in the light of this restriction. Concentrating on this second aspect of Spinoza's discussion, I shall argue that by taking it into account we can hope to cast new light on the apparent tension between the negotiable and non-negotiable aspects of sovereignty.

One of the most puzzling features of the sovereign's power, as Spinoza presents it, is the manner in which it depends on both imagination and reason. On the one hand, sovereigns must create and maintain their ability to control the law by using the interlocking resources of reason and imagination to negotiate with their subjects. On the other hand, Spinoza seems to treat the claim that a sovereign must possess certain specific powers as a finding of reason. The latter requirement not only conjures up a traditional image of a patriarchal sovereign whose word is law, but also comes as a shock in the work of a philosopher who is usually so sensitive to the interplay between imagination and reason. The abrupt transition from one to the other is uncomfortable, because the imaginative dimension of the sovereign's power, on which its effectiveness has hitherto been held to depend, seems suddenly to be laid aside.

For theorists who rejoice in the central place of imagination in Spinoza's politics, this may well be a troubling moment. However, as I shall show, tracing out the theological aspect of Spinoza's conception of sovereignty allows us to reconsider whether the claim that sovereigns must possess certain fixed powers is in fact grounded in reason rather than imagination. One of the central aims of the *Theological-Political Treatise* is to undercut the view that the sovereign's ability to make the law is limited by the law of God. By examining how Spinoza argues against this position, we can arrive at a better appreciation of the pressures that prompt him to endow the sovereign with non-negotiable powers, and also come to recognize that these powers are themselves indebted to imagination. At one level, the absoluteness of Spinoza's conception of sovereignty offers a challenge to a line of interpretation that revolves around imagination and has proved singularly productive for feminism. At another level, however, it can be shown to vindicate this line of interpretation by revealing that Spinoza's appeal to imagination runs even deeper than most commentators have appreciated.

The idea that the authority of the sovereign might be limited by the law of God is alien to many contemporary readers, but it played a crucial part in early modern debates about political power.[9] Spinoza's analysis of the problem therefore needs to be seen as a contribution to a complex set of controversies and as aiming to overturn a number of established views. A crucial point of reference for understanding what is going on in the *Theological-Political Treatise* is the political theory of Thomas Hobbes, to which it is deeply indebted.[10] So much so that Spinoza's discussion of this theme can be fruitfully interpreted, I shall suggest, as an attempt to consolidate and extend Hobbes's arguments. Broadly speaking, both Hobbes and Spinoza address themselves to readers who hold that God has made laws that human beings are obliged to obey, and which they can come to know in two ways.[11] The natural light of reason enables them to discover what the law of nature requires of them; and through scripture they can learn the content of the law revealed to the prophets. The obligatory force of divine law in both its forms gave rise to a difficulty that is lucidly stated in Hobbes's *Leviathan*. Without a knowledge of divine law, Hobbes explains, 'a man knows not, when he is commanded anything by the civil power, whether it is contrary to the law of God or not; and so, either by too much civil obedience, offends the divine majesty, or through fear of offending God transgresses the commands of the commonwealth'.[12] In two of his three political works, *De cive* and *Leviathan*, Hobbes offers a series of arguments designed to resolve this uncertainty by establishing that the law of God, whether natural or revealed, is only binding when promulgated by a human being, and that the power to promulgate the divine law lies solely with the sovereigns of states. The authority of sovereigns is thus not limited by any countervailing legal duty to God, and nothing can override their subjects' obligation to obey them. In the *Theological-Political Treatise* Spinoza develops this controversial

---

[9] See, for example, Richard Hooker: 'Being so prone as we are to fawn upon ourselves, and to be ignorant of as much as may be of our own deformities, without the feeling sense whereof we are most wretched...how should our festered sores be cured but that God hath delivered a law as sharp as the two-edged sword, piercing the very closest and most unsearchable corners of the heart unto which the law of nature can hardly, human laws by no means possible, reach unto?' Hooker 1989, Bk.1, ch. 12, 108–9.

[10] On the relation between Spinoza and Hobbes, see Curley 1991, 97–117; Verbeek, 2003.

[11] Hobbes argues that divine law does not bind atheists. Hobbes 1994a, ch. 31.2.

[12] Ibid., chap. 31.1.

claim and integrates the resulting view into his broader philosophical position. Drawing on a metaphysical conception of the deity that Hobbes explicitly rejects,[13] and an analysis of prophecy that goes beyond anything to be found in *De cive* or *Leviathan*, he arrives at a conception of law as a purely human phenomenon.

Because Hobbes and Spinoza are aiming to discredit the authority of two different types of divine law, their argument proceeds in stages, and both begin by criticizing the view that the law of nature poses a challenge to the sovereign. Their discussion is organized around Hobbes's etymological claim that a law in the strict sense of the term is a command. 'Law,' Hobbes asserts in *De Cive*, 'is not advice (*consilium*) but command (*mandatum*).' It derives 'from one who has power over those whom he instructs,' and it generates obligations, so that 'to do what one is instructed by law is a matter of duty.'[14] To discover whether the so-called laws of nature are really laws at all, one therefore has to consider whether they are commands. If we consider them as made by God, Hobbes concedes (introducing a possibility to which he will return later on) this may indeed be the case. However, if we consider them as 'proceeding from nature', we find that rational investigation of humans and their circumstances does not yield commands, but only what Hobbes describes as theorems or dictates of reason. 'What we call the laws of nature are nothing other than certain conclusions, understood by reason, on what is to be done and not to be done; and a law, properly and precisely speaking, is an utterance by one who by right commands others to do or not to do. Hence, properly speaking, the natural laws are not laws, insofar as they proceed from nature.'[15]

As Hobbes goes on to explain, the law of nature is constituted by theorems about our conservation and defence and deals both with the relations between individual human beings and with the honour or worship due to God.[16] Theorems on the first of these topics tell us to uphold various virtues such as 'justice and equity and all habits of the mind that conduce to peace and charity' and make up what is generally referred to as the moral law.[17] Thus, in accordance with what he takes to be a widely shared view, Hobbes holds that 'the natural law is the same as the moral law' and, by appealing to the status of the law of nature, he infers that what is usually described as the moral law is in fact not a law in the proper sense of the term.[18] While it tells us what it is good for us to do and possesses an

---

[13] 'Those Philosophers who sayd that the World, or the Soule of the World, was God, spake unworthily of Him; and denied his existence: For by God is understood the cause of the World; and to say the World is God, is to say there is no cause of it, that is, no God.' Ibid., ch. 31.15.

[14] Hobbes 1998, 153–4.

[15] Hobbes, 1998, 56. Compare 'These dictates of Reason, men used to call by the name of Lawes, but improperly: for they are but Conclusions or Theoremes concerning what conduceth to the conservation and defence of themselves; whereas Law, properly is the word of him that, by right hath command over others.' Hobbes 1994a, ch. 15.41.

[16] Ibid., ch. 31.8–13.   [17] Ibid., ch. 26.37.   [18] Hobbes 1998, 55.

authority 'legible to all men that have use of natural reason', it does not consist of commands and therefore does not oblige us.[19]

When Spinoza comes to discuss the same issue, he adopts Hobbes's definition. The word 'law', he reiterates, is commonly used to mean 'a command which men can either carry out or neglect' (TTP IV.5; III/58). However, because his conception of the law of nature differs from the Hobbesian one, his argument about its status proceeds along different lines. Putting aside Hobbes's conception of the laws of nature as normative precepts, he first points out that the term is also applied more widely to describe the behaviour of things that act in a fixed and determined way (TTP IV.2: III/57). For example, the fact that all bodies, on colliding with smaller bodies, lose as much of their own motion as they impart, is in this sense a law about bodies, and the fact that 'when a man recalls one thing, he immediately recalls another like it, or one he had perceived together with the first thing' is a law about human nature (TTP IV.2; III/57–8). On the assumption that laws are commands, it immediately becomes evident that these so-called laws of nature can only be laws in a metaphorical sense (TTP IV.5: III/58). Since we have rational grounds for believing that all laws of this sort are necessary and eternal, we have no choice but to be governed by them, and it makes no sense to think of them as edicts that can be obeyed or disobeyed.[20] The language of command simply cannot get a grip on a deterministic universe.

Spinoza consolidates this conclusion by drawing still more deeply on distinctive features of his metaphysics. One of the insights we can arrive at through rational philosophical enquiry, he claims, is that nature and God are one and the same and thus that the more we learn about nature the more we learn about God.[21] 'The whole of our knowledge, that is, our supreme good, not merely depends on our knowledge of God but consists entirely therein', so that 'we acquire a greater and more perfect knowledge of God as we gain more knowledge of natural phenomena' (TTP IV.11; III/60). Once we appreciate that this is the case, we can recognize that the immutable laws of nature are the workings of God's mind, and we can shake off an anthropomorphic conception of God as a ruler who issues commands. This set of claims both opens up a sense in which natural laws are divine and simultaneously reveals that a true idea of the deity is incompatible with a conception of him as a legislator. It therefore offers further support for the view that the law of nature is not a law in the sense of a set of commands.

For Hobbes, as we have seen, the natural law is simultaneously a moral law by virtue of its content. It consists of precepts specifying what we ought to do and forbear from doing. Furthermore, Hobbes goes on to claim, both the natural and moral laws are also divine because, in creating nature, the deity determined that

---

[19] Hobbes 1994a, ch. 33.22.   [20] See Curley 1979, 371.
[21] This general conception of God is explicitly rejected by Hobbes. Hobbes 1994a, ch. 31.15–17.

this particular set of eternal precepts articulates the good for human beings. Since Spinoza does not conceive of God as the creator of nature, this argument is not available to him, and he accordingly provides a different account of the relationships between natural, moral, and divine law. As we investigate nature, we acquire knowledge of a great variety of causal regularities, of which those concerning human good and harm are a subset. But while this process of coming to understand what is good for us yields knowledge of our own condition, it is not a matter of recognizing commands that oblige us to act in a certain way. By reasoning, we come to see that without an understanding of the natural world, including ourselves, we shall be incapable of working out either what ends are most beneficial or how to set about achieving them. This insight in turn enables us to infer that our supreme good, and the goal for which we should above all strive, is understanding. If we then consider the status of the precept 'The way for humans to achieve their supreme good is to pursue understanding', we find that, insofar as it is an immutable truth about nature, it is a natural law in the metaphorical sense; but insofar as it concerns human good, it is simultaneously a moral law. Furthermore, since nature and God are one and the same, this moral recommendation can equivalently be expressed as 'Love God'—that is to say, love God by devoting yourself to understanding him. Reformulating the recommendation in this fashion brings home to us that the object of the moral law is God, and that it is appropriate to describe the moral law as divine, since it is simultaneously about the good for human beings and about their relationship to the deity (TTP IV.13; III/60).[22] The recommendation 'Pursue understanding', which flows from both the natural and moral laws, is therefore equivalent to the key precept of the divine law, 'Love God.'

By merging the three types of legislation, Spinoza is able to apply his account of the status of the natural and moral laws to their divine counterpart and to conclude that the divine law is not strictly speaking a law at all. Since, as we have already seen, God is not the kind of being who issues commands, loving him cannot be a matter of obeying his decrees.[23] It offers us a set of recommendations that are in fact for our good, but it does not oblige us to follow them.

It remains to consider how knowledge of the recommendations we can derive from our understanding of God and nature can be turned into laws in the proper sense, that is to say, into commands. How can a recommendation that tells us how to achieve our own good become a law that we are obliged to obey? Hobbes's answer to the question hinges on three central claims. First, the law of nature is

---

[22] For a somewhat different account of Spinoza's view of the relation between natural and civil law, see Belaief 1971, 42.

[23] 'When one conceives God's freedom as that of a tyrant or legislator, one ties it to physical contingency or to logical possibility. One thus attributes inconstancy to God's power since he could have created something else—or worse still, powerlessness, since his power is limited by models of possibility.' Deleuze 1988, 69.

not transparent and therefore stands in need of interpretation. Before its precepts can be turned into commands, some authority has to determine what it recommends.[24] Second, a law in the sense of a command must be promulgated in such a way that those who are bound by it are aware of their duties. For example, 'the command of the commonwealth is law only to those who have means to take notice of it,' and so it must it must be written and publicized.[25] Finally, an utterance only has the force of a command when the agent who utters it has the power to ensure that it is obeyed. In the state of nature no one is capable of interpreting, promulgating, and imposing the recommendations that constitute the natural law, thus turning them into binding commands; in the state, the only figure possessing these powers is the sovereign. Hence, laws of nature can be transformed into commands only by a sovereign, and although they are 'naturally reasonable', it is only by virtue of sovereign power that they become laws.[26]

Hobbes's argument is based on the assumption, defended elsewhere in his political works, that it is possible for human beings to create circumstances in which a sovereign has the power to issue commands that its subjects are under an obligation to obey. But before Spinoza can adopt this starting point he needs to go more deeply into its presuppositions and engineer a compromise with his own conception of nature as a closed causal system. Philosophical inquiry tells us, he insists, that all natural events, including human actions, are determined by their causes and that what we regard as contingency is simply an effect of our ignorance. A strictly philosophical account of nature will consequently allow no room for the idea that human beings can choose whether or not to obey commands, and no room for laws conceived as commands that can be obeyed or disobeyed. Instead, antecedent causes will determine everything people do, including the way they understand and respond to laws. Spinoza unblinkingly embraces this inference. 'I grant, without reservation, that everything is determined by the universal laws of nature to exist and produce effects in a definite and determined way' (TIP IV.3; III/58). However, he immediately goes on to argue that we are usually unable to make much use of this conclusion in non-philosophical contexts. Because 'universal considerations concerning fate and the connection of causes cannot help us to form and order our thoughts concerning particular things' and because we have no knowledge of 'how things are really ordered and connected' (TTP IV.4; III/58), we are for practical purposes justified in viewing events as contingent and explaining some of them by an appeal to human agreement or decision.

This transition from a strictly rational conception of nature to the more familiar outlook on the world that Spinoza attributes to human imagination enables him to accommodate both the idea that people can choose whether or not to

---

[24] Hobbes 1994a, ch. 26. 22.   [25] Ibid., ch. 26.15.   [26] Hobbes 1994a, ch. 26. 22.

issue commands and the idea that they can choose whether or not to obey them.[27] It thus makes room for our ordinary notion of a law and simultaneously opens up space for a new definition. Legislation, Spinoza now explains, consists of laws that 'men prescribe for themselves and others, for the sake of living more safely and conveniently, or for some other cause' (TTP IV.2; III/57). To turn an understanding of what is metaphorically described as the moral or divine law into a law in this narrower sense of the term, some human agent must lay down the relevant claims as rules of conduct. If we add the background assumption that a law is a command, we can introduce the further stipulation that the agent in question must possess enough power to be capable of issuing orders that others will obey.

Although he does not particularly draw attention to it, Spinoza's explicit provision that laws are laid down by humans is highly significant. As we have seen, God is not in his view the kind of being who is capable of issuing commands (though we may still imagine him doing so). Only human agents, whether individual or collective, can impose rules of conduct on one another, and in fact they can make laws of two different kinds. They can create human laws, or rules of conduct designed to safeguard life and the state. They can also make divine laws concerned with the supreme good, namely, the knowledge and love of God (TTP, IV.9; III/59). So for the divine law to become law in the ordinary sense of the term, it has to be legislated by a human agent and imposed by human power. As Spinoza will go on to explain in more detail, the divine law may be realized by a wise sovereign who sees how to translate its recommendations into specific decrees that subjects are capable of obeying; and there is also, in his view, a derivative sense in which subjects may legislate the divine law for themselves by willingly obeying the sovereign's commands. In both cases, however, the law is a human creation and consists entirely of human decrees.[28]

While he defends this conclusion in his own way, Spinoza is basically in agreement with Hobbes's view that only human agents can transform either the law of nature or the moral law into commands. Nature itself does not impose legal obligations on human beings, and we must construct them for ourselves. This is a radical and provocative conclusion; but before either theorist can guarantee that there are no nonhuman sources of legal authority capable of challenging the sovereign's power, both theorists need to dispose of the further claim that, even if the law of nature does not consist of divine commands, the revealed law certainly does.[29]

In De cive and Leviathan Hobbes draws a sharp distinction between the laws of nature insofar as they proceed from nature and the same laws insofar as 'they

---

[27] 'All that one needs in order to moralise is to fail to understand. It is clear that we only have to misunderstand a law for it to appear to us in the form of a moral "You must." If we do not understand the rule of three, we will apply it, we will adhere to it, as a duty. Adam does not understand the rule of the relation of his body to the fruit, so he interprets God's word as a prohibition.' Deleuze 1988, p. 23.
[28] See Vatter 2004, 186–191.   [29] See Den Uyl, 1983, 10ff.

have been legislated by God in the Holy Scriptures'. In the latter case, he allows, 'they are very properly called by the name of laws; for Holy Scripture is the utterance of God, who issues commands in all things by the highest right'.[30] This concession seems to sit uncomfortably with the rest of his argument. If Scripture gives us access to divine laws that we are obliged to obey, these laws must surely derive from a source of authority independent of sovereigns and may at least in principle restrict or oppose their edicts. Moreover, in a society where biblical revelation is taken seriously, such a division of authority may become a source of faction and have destructive political consequences.[31]

Hobbes's response to this objection is intricate. Before God gave Moses the Ten Commandments, he argues, the only divine law was the law of nature. However, since we know from scripture that the Commandments were subsequently handed down by God himself, we need to ask, 'Who was it that gave to these written tables the obligatory force of laws?'[32] As we have seen, if we are to be bound by a command, we need to know that it was issued by a suitable authority and understand what it requires; but where prophecy is concerned, this raises an epistemological problem. A prophet such as Moses, who receives a direct revelation, knows that God has spoken and what he has demanded. By contrast, ordinary people to whom the prophet recounts his revelation cannot possess the same assurance, since both the Bible and everyday experience warn us that prophetic claims can be mistaken or insincere.[33] The mere fact that Moses told the Jewish people he had received the tables of the law from God consequently did not enable them to know that his testimony was accurate and could not oblige them to conform. Instead, what obliged them was the fact that, when Moses promulgated the law, he was already their sovereign and they had already agreed to obey him. Revealed laws therefore only become binding when imposed by a human sovereign, and 'all subjects are bound to obey that for divine law which is declared to be so by the laws of the commonwealth'.[34]

Once again Spinoza endorses this conclusion, but once again his argument for it constitutes an even deeper attack on Christian theology than anything Hobbes articulates. As we have seen, Hobbes's main reason for denying that subjects are bound by laws known through revelation is epistemological; unless one receives a revelation, one cannot be sure that God has issued a command. Whatever Hobbes may privately have believed, he does not explicitly challenge the view that God sometimes issues commands to prophets, but focuses instead on the problem of how we can know what these commands are. By contrast,

---

[30] Hobbes 1998, 66–7. Compare 'But yet if we consider the same Theoremes, as delivered in the word of God, that by right commandeth all things; then are they properly called Lawes.' Hobbes 1994a, ch. 15.41.
[31] See Strauss 1965, 101–4.   [32] Hobbes 1994a, ch. 42.37.
[33] Ibid., ch. 32.7.   [34] Ibid., ch. 26.41.

Spinoza's argument takes a yet more unorthodox step. What the Bible represents as laws, he explains, are not in fact commands made by a deity. Contrary to an established outlook, God cannot be the source of our legal obligations, and in fact there *are* no divine laws of a kind that can form a counterweight to the legal authority of sovereigns.[35]

This stretch of the *Theologico-Political Treatise* treads on dangerous theological ground, and Spinoza begins concessively by allowing that the Mosaic law 'can be termed the law of God, since we believe it to have been sanctioned by prophetic insight'. At first glance, this seems to imply that Moses did indeed articulate laws made by the deity and to echo Hobbes's position; but on closer inspection it becomes clear that this is not what Spinoza is saying. Prophets, he proposes, possess outstanding imaginative gifts and, through narratives, images, and metaphors are able to grasp the significance of situations in ways that elude ordinary people. However, since there is nothing exceptional about their intellects, we should not expect them to provide philosophical insights into the nature of the divine law or the supreme good. This conclusion is supported by the Old Testament, in which it is obvious that prophets, along with other key figures, often fail to understand the true nature of the deity. For example, we can see from the conversation between God and Adam, as it is narrated in Genesis, that even the first man did not appreciate that the law of nature is entirely determined. If he had realized this, he would have understood that it was not simply his own will that caused him to eat the apple offered to him by Eve and would not have described his action as a choice (TTP IV.26; III/63). However, we can also see that the narrative represents the situation as Adam imagined it, or to put the point differently, as it was revealed to him. He imagined God as a being who commanded him to act in a certain way and gave him the option of obeying or disobeying. In short, he conceived of God as a lawmaker; and the same applies to the prophets, including Moses, whose experience of God was of a deity who gave him a set of commandments and told him how to impose them on the citizens of the ancient state of Israel (TIP, II, 31–5; III/37–8). Such imaginative powers can be immensely productive as a means of persuading a people to cooperate for their mutual benefit; but insofar as they represent God as the source of commands, they rest on a misconception.

In taking a stand on the character and status of revealed law, Hobbes and Spinoza were entering into a sequence of fierce theological debates and challenging those biblical commentators and religious authorities who regarded the commandments contained in scriptures as obligations distinct from the civil law. Both authors approach this fraught discussion by arguing that a correct reading of the Old Testament shows that the Ten Commandments were part of an

---

[35] See Gatens and Lloyd 1999, 95–100.

elaborate legal code imposed by Moses when he became the ruler of the Jews (TTP, III.2; III/48), and both insist that the obligation to adhere to them derived from Moses's sovereign power, which enabled him to enforce the law through threats and punishments. The Ten Commandments were therefore part of Jewish civil law and are nowadays only laws in jurisdictions where the sovereign makes them so.

Turning to the laws supposedly taught by Jesus Christ, Spinoza again develops a line of argument already defended in *Leviathan*.[36] Unlike Moses, who saw how the divine law applied to the predicament of the Jews, and expressed his insight in a civil code that was exceptionally effective in maintaining a historically specific state, Christ was able to understand the tenets of the divine law in their universal or philosophical form. As we have seen, these tenets are not laws, but recommendations about how to achieve the supreme human good. So Christ was not a lawmaker, and if he occasionally presented his insights as commands, this was simply a concession to the intellectual limitations of his audience (TIP, IV.32–3; III/64–5). The New Testament therefore does not contain anything that purports to be a revealed law and presents no challenge to the rule of earthly sovereigns.

Looking back, we can see that the fulcrum of Hobbes's case for the absolute power of sovereigns is his sceptical attitude to revealed law. While he does not explicitly deny that God reveals himself to man, he insists that the workings of revelation are too mysterious and uncertain to ground laws that impose obligations on communities of ordinary human beings. Biblical evidence does indeed suggest that God sometimes reveals specific commandments through his prophets; but individuals who are not themselves the beneficiaries of revelation can never be sure that prophetic testimony is veracious and can therefore never have sufficient reason to regard it as binding. Unlike Hobbes, Spinoza takes a more anthropological approach and, rather than simply putting prophecy aside as epistemologically deficient, offers to explain it. When the prophets describe themselves as articulating laws decreed by God, they are interpreting a situation they only partly understand, and although they sincerely believe that they are communicating decrees made by a deity for human beings, there *is* no deity of the kind they imagine. Thus, they themselves are the true authors of the law. Just as individuals who possess great intellectual gifts can grasp the content of the divine law in its natural and moral guises by philosophical means, so prophets can come to appreciate it by imagination. But whereas a philosopher who understands it will recognize that it is not a law in the strict sense of the term, the prophets erroneously imagined it as a set of divine commands that humans are under an obligation to follow. In truth, however, what is known as the divine law merely identifies our supreme good and recommends us to pursue it. To become a law

---

[36] While Spinoza explicitly draws this conclusion in the *Theological-Political Treatise*, Hobbes is more circumspect. See Hobbes 1994, ch. 42.41–44.

that fits Spinoza's definition ('a rule of conduct laid down by men, for themselves or others, for some end') it must be interpreted and legislated by human beings.

Spinoza has now put in place two sets of arguments, each designed to undercut a particular conception of the laws made and enforced by God. The first, which appeals to our capacity for philosophical understanding, claims to show that, although reason gives us access to what are called laws of nature and to what is called the divine law, it also enables us to see that these are not commands. Instead, the natural and divine laws consist of truths and recommendations, which possess no legal status and do not impose any legal obligations. The second set of arguments then aims to discredit the view that a number of divine commands are recorded in scripture. This position is countered by claiming that the lawmaking God described in the Bible is a product of imagination. The prophets and their peoples may have conceived God as a legislator who would reward the obedient and punish sinners; but no such being in fact exists, and the laws attributed to him were ordained and enforced by human beings. Taken together, the two arguments comprehensively slough off the widespread early modern assumption that political life is shaped and limited by divine commands and banish even the shadowy figure of a divine lawmaker who continues to haunt the pages of Hobbes's philosophy.[37] Law, it emerges, is never something to be discovered, but always something that humans have to use their reason and imagination to construct.[38]

Can this reading of Spinoza's analysis of sovereignty help us to reconcile the consensual aspects of his politics with his insistence that sovereigns must possess the power to determine the boundaries of negotiation and criticism within the state? To put the point another way, does the argument we have been tracing help us to see why Spinoza might impose these limits on the imaginative process of negotiation through which diverse individuals are able to understand themselves as citizens who compose 'as it were one mind and one body'? To sustain his account of politics, Spinoza has to accord real force to civil legislation, since it is now the sole source of political order. Yet if law is to be effective, a number of conditions must be met, among them the basic requirements that sovereigns are able to understand themselves as issuing commands, and citizens to conceive of themselves as obeying freely. As we have seen, Spinoza has identified a sense in which these self-conceptions, on which the idea of law rests, are the fruit of imagination, since the conviction that humans are capable of commanding and obeying is a consequence of our inability to understand the multiple causes that determine our actions. For practical purposes, this imaginary perspective is the only one available to us, and insofar as it enables us to represent ourselves as loci of power, it is undoubtedly productive. However, while we cannot overcome the

[37] See Strauss 1995, 32; Schmitt 1996, 57.   [38] See Deleuze 1990, 259.

limitation inherent in this way of imagining ourselves, we are nevertheless capable of understanding the nature of its shortcomings. Like Spinoza himself, we
can appreciate that, from a philosophical point of view, law embodies a misconception about our own capacities. Thus construed, it appears as doubly human:
the self-understandings on which law rests are the fruit of an unavoidable yet
inadequate perspective deriving from human imagination; and the laws built on
this imaginary basis are entirely constructed by human beings. Without imagination there would therefore be no law, and no politics.

It is easy to see why this analysis might have shaken the confidence of Spinoza
and his contemporaries. The sovereign, previously subject to the law of God, now
appears as a fragile and isolated entity whose task is to create law in the face of a
series of challenges: from its subjects, from a lack of the quasi-prophetic imagination that will enable it to make its commands acceptable, and from the recognition that the legal framework on which its power rests ultimately derives from a
lack of understanding. Whereas the traditional picture had portrayed God as the
preeminent lawmaker, and had represented human sovereigns as small-scale
inheritors of his legislative power, Spinoza shatters this image. God does not issue
commands and, but for imagination, what humans inherit is his incapacity to do so.

Insofar as this dramatically more exposed conception of sovereignty is rooted
in imagination, the tension between consensual government and non-negotiable
sovereign power from which we began is not, after all, a tension between imagination and reason, but rather a tension between imagination's more and less malle-
able features. While the identities we construct for ourselves alter with individual
and collective experience, there is something peculiarly immovable about our
sense that some of our actions are voluntary and thus about those aspects of our
political practices that depend on it. As one of these, law is a resilient notion,
capable of functioning as the organizing category of political life. Nonetheless,
Spinoza questions the depth of its authority by making it the creation of a human
sovereign, who first employs the deeply rooted imaginative vocabulary of command and obedience, and then draws on imagination once again to devise a narrative capable of persuading its subject to accept the laws it makes. If we now
consider why the *Theological-Political Treatise* places such emphasis on the absoluteness of sovereignty, this fragility may be part of the answer. Political order
consists in the law made by an inherently precarious sovereign who is, as we have
found, challenged from many directions. The power to limit negotiation therefore
serves not so much as a vehicle for tyranny, but more as an attempt to counteract
the sovereign's vulnerability by giving it the means to protect its subjects and promote their freedom.

The analysis offered here of Spinoza's grounds for holding that a sovereign
must possess certain non-negotiable powers is not complete. Along with Hobbes,
Spinoza has additional psychological and political reasons for favouring such
an arrangement. Underlying them, however, is the challenging claim that the

sovereign's power to make law is the fruit of imagination and thus of a pervasive kind of misunderstanding. An appreciation of this conclusion allows us to reconsider and reject the view from which we began, that the absolute aspects of sovereignty run counter to the emphasis on imagination that plays such a vital part in feminist readings of Spinoza's political philosophy. This, we can now see, is at best a half-truth. To understand Spinoza's account of sovereignty, we need to appreciate the ways in which it depends on and emerges from imagination.

7

Natural Rights as Powers to Act

I

In both his political works Spinoza makes it clear that an understanding of the right of nature is fundamental to an account of political life. Before we can address the foundations of the state, the *Theological-Political Treatise* tells us, we need to elucidate 'the natural right of each person' (TTP XVI.1; III/189).[1] Returning to the topic at the beginning of the *Political Treatise*, Spinoza explicitly restates some of the arguments in his earlier works, and sets out his view of the right of nature once again (TP II.1; III/276). Many of the themes that run through these two texts have played an influential part in the history of political philosophy and continue to inspire contemporary debate. Spinoza's conceptions of free speech, democracy and the multitude are still being explored and contested, as are his ideas about the nature of religion and its place in the state. However, despite the central explanatory role that he accords to natural right, this feature of his political outlook has attracted less attention. Perhaps we should not be surprised since, at least at first glance, Spinoza's conception of right seems alien to the notions around which modern debates revolve. An individual's natural right or *ius*, he contends, is simply its right to do anything in its power, and 'each individual has a supreme right to do everything it can'. Fish, for example, 'are determined by nature to swimming, and the larger ones to eating the smaller. So it is by the supreme right of nature that fish are masters of the water and that the larger ones eat the smaller' (TTP XVI.2; III/189). Rather than treating natural rights in the manner of most modern discussions, as a distinctive feature of human beings and arguably other living things, Spinoza insists that all individuals, animate or otherwise, have the right to do anything in their power. In the human case, however, this view has startling implications. 'Just as the wise man has the supreme right to do everything which reason dictates, or to live according to the laws of reason, so also the ignorant and weak-minded have the

[1] I am especially indebted to Robin Celikates, Michelle Chun and Victoria McGeer for their thoughtful responses to earlier versions of this essay. I should also like to thank Aurelia Armstrong, Jane Bennett, Moira Gatens, Martin Lenz, Paola Marrati, Al Martinich, Yitzhak Melamed, Philip Pettit, Melissa Lane, Genevieve Lloyd, Alan Patten, and Hent de Vries for further comments and suggestions.

Spinoza on Learning to Live Together. Susan James, Oxford University Press (2020). © Susan James.
DOI: 10.1093/oso/9780198713074.001.0001

supreme right to do everything which appetite urges, or to live according to the laws of appetite' (TTP XVI.5; III/189–90).[2]

If natural right as Spinoza conceives of it has no moral boundaries—if, for example, it licenses rapists to rape as much as it licenses their victims to resist—it is not easy to see what his conception can contribute to contemporary discussion, or how it can figure as more than a historical curiosity within current philosophical and political analysis. This sense of its irrelevance may help to explain why it has attracted relatively little interest; but the silence surrounding it is nevertheless worth breaking. Spinoza's positioning of natural right as one of the principles on which the state is grounded suggests that, if we want to understand his political philosophy, we cannot ignore the role of natural right within it. To enter into his project, we need to consider what might have motivated him to define the right of nature as he does, and what kind of challenge he was issuing to more orthodox interpreters. What philosophical gains, if any, does he derive from his insistence that 'the right of each thing extends as far as its determinate power' (TTP XVI.4; III/189), and are these supposed benefits of any interest to us?

Early modern jurists inherited many overlapping conceptions of the law of nature and used them to legitimate a range of natural rights and duties. But when Spinoza turns to this topic he does not concern himself with specific cases such as a natural right to freedom or property. Instead he goes straight to the foundations of the natural law tradition and interrogates three of its most deeply entrenched premises: the assumption that the law of nature from which our natural rights flow is a set of divine commands; the view that natural law distinguishes morally licit from illicit actions and only gives us rights that are consonant with justice; and the presumption that we can come to know what natural rights we possess by reasoning.[3]

The foundational status of these doctrines is made clear by Hugo Grotius. Writing in his *Commentary on the Law of Prize and Booty*, Grotius builds a detailed analysis of the rights of war on a set of received assumptions. 'Just as the mathematicians customarily prefix to any concrete demonstration a preliminary statement of certain broad axioms on which all persons are easily agreed,...so shall we point out certain rules and laws of the most general nature, presenting them as preliminary assumptions which need to be recalled rather than learned for the first time, with the purpose of laying a foundation upon which our other conclusions may safely rest.'[4] Letting the Platonic resonances of this approach sound for themselves, and appealing to a series of classical authorities for support, Grotius gives 'first place and pre-eminent authority to the following rule: *What God has shown to be his Will, that is Law*'. The ancients, he explains,

---

[2] The startling implications have been noted, for example, in Matheron 1985, 176; Curley 1991, 318; Balibar 1998, 59–63; Barbone 1999, 91–2.

[3] For Leibniz's response to Spinoza's view see Laerke 2012, 127–33.

[4] Grotius, 2006, 19–20.

'designated as ... *iussa* [things commanded] those precepts which we designate as *iura* [laws]'; but the act of commanding is a function of power, 'and primary power over all things pertains to God'.[5] Grotius's first principle therefore states that all things are subject to divine laws, which take the form of commands. Next, he expects his readers to agree that these commands specify what is just and unjust. According to Plutarch, he points out, 'Jove himself is Right and Justice, and the most ancient and perfect of all laws'; and a similar view is held by Chrysippus, who tells us that 'no beginning, no origin, can be assigned to justice other than its derivation from God and from the universal aspect of nature'.[6] Finally, Grotius reminds his readers, the law is made accessible to us in two ways. 'The will of God is revealed, not only through oracles and supernatural portents, but above all in the very design of the creator; for it is from this last source that the law of nature is derived. Thus Cicero very wisely maintains that the study of celestial phenomena is beneficial in relation to justice, as well as in other ways, because the student 'becomes acquainted with the will, plan and purpose of the supreme ruler and Lord, to whose nature (so say the philosophers) the true rational and sovereign law conforms'.[7] Philosophical or rational enquiry yields an understanding of a natural law that reflects God's plan for his creation and governs all natural things including human beings.

When Spinoza challenges Grotius's three axioms, he is therefore attacking some of the deepest pieties of the natural law tradition.[8] Criticizing the first, he argues that the laws of nature are not divine commands. Rejecting the second, he defends the troubling view that justice has no intrinsic place in natural law. Subverting the third, he argues that a rational understanding of the law of nature is at odds with the teleological conception of divine command that Grotius expects his readers to take for granted. Together, these departures amount to a wholesale rejection of an established orthodoxy, and to appreciate the revolutionary character of Spinoza's argument we need to bear this in mind. Whilst he is not the only seventeenth-century philosopher to criticize the view of natural law that Grotius assumes, his repudiation of a cherished set of premises is in effect a demand for a radical change of outlook.

It is not, however, a demand to dispense entirely with the notion of the law of nature.[9] Spinoza's aim is rather to offer an alternative and more firmly grounded interpretation, both of the law and of the right it bestows. To succeed, he must ensure that his conception of natural right is recognizable to the readers he is trying to persuade. In order to avoid the accusation that he has simply changed the subject, the account he offers must share some of the features they regard as

---

[5] Ibid., 21.   [6] Ibid.   [7] Ibid.
[8] Matheron 1984; Steinberg, 2018, 46–50; Garrett 2003, 630–2; Bijlsma 2015, 267–83; James 2012, 84; Santos Campos 2012.
[9] Garrett, 2003, 635–7.

definitive of the right of nature, and sustain at least some of the arguments and conclusions to which they are committed. To meet these requirements, Spinoza adapts some established doctrines to his own philosophical ends, and recreates versions of the benefits that natural rights traditionally secure.

II

Spinoza's most direct criticism of Grotius's conception of the law of nature lies in his repudiation of the claim that it consists of a set of commands issued by God. Support for the orthodox view was often drawn from biblical representations of the deity as a ruler and judge who reveals his law to his prophets, requires communities to obey it, and punishes transgressors. But although some Dutch theorists embraced this image, many regarded it as fictional. Rather than offering a philosophically defensible portrait of God, they claimed, Scripture describes him in anthropomorphic terms, designed to encourage ordinary people to obey his commands.[10] Spinoza was firmly of this latter view. '[S]cripture does not teach things through their proximate causes, but only relates them in that order and with those phrases with which it can most effectively move people (especially ordinary people) to devotion. For this reason it speaks quite improperly concerning God and things, because its concern is not to convince people's reason but to affect and fill their fantasy and imagination' (TTP VI.49; III/91). To understand God, he argues, we must shake off a mistaken idea of an anthropomorphic deity whose laws resemble those of a civil sovereign and whose commands we may obey or disobey, and with it an anthropomorphic conception of the law of nature. Whatever the natural law is and whatever rights it licenses, it cannot be properly understood as a set of divine commands.

This view was not unprecedented. As we have seen in Chapter 6, it had, for example, been influentially propounded by Thomas Hobbes, whose political works Spinoza knew.[11] But Spinoza's defence of it rests on two lines of argument that go beyond Hobbes, one a philosophical account of a God who has no anthropomorphic features, the other a diagnosis of the psychological processes through which we erroneously come to conceive of the deity in anthropomorphic terms. If we ask why so many natural law theorists held that our natural rights are specified and guaranteed by divine command, part of the answer is clearly cultural. On the whole, people in seventeenth-century Europe were taught to think of God as a legislator, and all the evidence at their disposal pointed in this direction. But Spinoza traces the social pressures that sustain this view to deeper metaphysical

---

[10] James 2012, 54–65.
[11] Hobbes, 1994, ch. 14.3. On Hobbes's and Spinoza's accounts of natural law see Matheron 1985; Curley 1991; Malcolm 2002.

and psychological dispositions, rooted in the principle of self-preservation that he calls the *conatus*. As discussed in Chapter 2, the essence or *conatus* of an individual thing is its striving to persevere in its being (E IIIp6; II/146), and in human beings this striving manifests itself in our efforts to live joyfully and avoid sadness (E IIIp11; II/148–9).

It is worth pausing to observe that the natural law theorists Spinoza is challenging are sympathetic to this view. In Grotius's account of the axioms of which his readers only need to be reminded, we find the claim that God has endowed every part of nature with the capacity to preserve itself. 'Since God fashioned creation and willed its existence, every individual part thereof has received from Him certain natural properties whereby that existence may be preserved and each part may be guided for its own good, in conformity, one might say, with the fundamental law inherent in its origin... For all things in nature, as Cicero repeatedly insists, are tenderly regardful of self, and seek their own happiness and security.'[12] Thus far, Spinoza and the natural lawyers agree. But whereas they treat the urge to self-preservation as an aspect of a law of nature commanded by God, Spinoza turns the argument around. Our striving to persevere in our being, he claims, commonly manifests itself in the mistaken conviction that the law of nature takes the form of a set of commands imposed by an anthropomorphic deity.

For the most part, our efforts to persevere in our being are informed by our limited experience of the world. Sometimes we form desires in the light of our experience and then try to satisfy them; but in other cases our experience is shaped by our desires. We view the world through the lens of individual or collective fantasies in which our desires are already wholly or partly satisfied, and we make them the basis of our strivings to live joyfully (E IIIp12). This is how we come to form anthropomorphic conceptions of God—we strive to persevere in our being by positing a deity who answers to our wishes and aspirations. At one level, images of a quasi-human deity arise from a metaphysical desire to understand the world by grasping the nature of its first cause. At another level, they answer to our desire to be cared for, and posit a God who is loving and benevolent. At yet another level, we attempt to satisfy a yearning for social and political order by representing God as the author and enforcer of a law that binds us all to a single standard of justice. With this last image comes a familiar account of divinely ordained laws together with the specific rights and obligations that flow from them. Internalizing this imaginary conception of their own condition, individuals come to think of themselves as bearers of divinely decreed claims and duties, and build their convictions into a range of social practices. Thus understood, the law of nature is analysed by philosophers or theologians and

---

[12] Grotius 2006, 22. See Cicero 1913, I.4.

adjudicated by courts of law whose decisions can have momentous consequences. But although this process integrates the notion of divinely guaranteed rights and duties into our interpretations of ourselves and our relationships with other people, and makes them in that respect real enough, there remains a crucial sense in which they are fictional. Rights conceived as divinely authorized claims or entitlements are in fact products of human imagination, and reflect a profoundly inadequate understanding of God. Just as a triangle would imagine a triangular God, Spinoza jokes, so humans imagine an anthropomorphic one who issues commands.[13] However, although the idea of natural law to which this image gives rise can serve pedagogical and political purposes, it has no place in a philosophical analysis of the right of nature.

In rejecting the first of Grotius's axioms, Spinoza distances himself from a widespread view of the relationship between God and the laws of nature. But he does not intend to discredit the underlying idea that natural laws can be attributed to God, and uses his critique to articulate a different sense in which the laws of nature can properly be characterized as divine. By 1670, when the *Theological-Political Treatise* was published, Spinoza had already worked out much of the philosophical system delineated in the *Ethics*, and draws on it in his discussion of law. Human beings, he argues in the *Treatise*, are insignificantly small aspects of an infinite universe, who strive to persevere in their being in accordance with laws of nature that determine things 'to exist and produce effects in a determinate way' (TTP IV.3; III/58). Viewed from our everyday perspective, nature contains many distinct individuals, each with its own *conatus*; but if we think of it as a whole, encompassing everything that exists and exercising all the causal power there is, we begin to get an idea of a Spinozist God, far removed from the anthropomorphic deities of Judaism and Christianity. This God is not a creator who exists apart from nature. Nor is he a providential deity. Rather, the regular, law-governed course of natural events is his activity and the expression of his infinite power.

Spinoza's treatment of Grotius's second axiom—that the law of nature requires us to act justly—is hard to grasp in the absence of an understanding of his account of the process of state formation, an issue to which I shall turn in Section III. Meanwhile, Spinoza aims to reject Grotius' third axiom—that the law of nature reflects God's 'will, plan and purpose'—by showing that the assumption that 'God himself directs things to some certain end' and 'has made all things for man' is nothing but a deeply held prejudice (E I App.; II/78). Although the laws that express divine power determine what happens to all individual things, they do not realize any plan and are not adapted to human needs. Instead of thinking of ourselves as subject to a deity who commands us to act in accordance with his design, we therefore need to recognize that God manifests his power in natural

---

[13] Letter 56 to Boxel, Spinoza 2016, IV/260.

laws that govern every aspect of everything we do. The possibility of disobeying them, as one might disobey a command, therefore does not arise (TTP IV.2–3; III/57).[14]

Assuming that any defensible conception of our individual right must be derived not from a fanciful idea of laws made by a commanding deity who works according to a plan, but rather from an impersonal law that governs all things, Spinoza confronts a problem as old as the natural law tradition itself. According to Cicero, so Grotius had reminded his readers, natural right must be grounded on 'the law sprung from nature'.[15] But if this law is simply, as Spinoza claims, 'the rules according to which all thing happen' (TP II.4; III/30), it remains to ask what sense we can make of the idea of a right that belong to us *by nature*. When we consider ourselves as tiny elements of the natural universe, each striving to persevere in our being in accordance with laws that do not sit in judgment over us or take account of our wellbeing, is there any sense in which we can be said to act by the right of nature?

Spinoza's answer is self-consciously austere. From the fact that 'the power of natural things, by which they exist and have effects, is the very power of God', he argues, 'we can easily understand what the right of nature is'. Since God has right over all things, and God's right is nothing but his power, 'it follows that each natural thing has as much right by nature as it has power to exist and have effects' (TP II.3; III/30).[16] To put the point another way, God's power is manifested in the power of each individual thing to persevere in its being, and since nothing in nature stops individuals from exercising this power, they can be said to exercise it rightfully or in accordance with natural right. The supreme law of nature (that everything strives to persevere in its being) therefore gives each individual, human or otherwise, the right to maintain itself as far as it can by doing anything in its power. The argument brings Spinoza to an arresting conclusion: 'it follows that the right and established practice of nature, under which all men are born and for the most part live, prohibits nothing except what no one desires and no one can do; it does not prohibit disputes, or hatreds, or anger, or deceptions, and it is absolutely not averse to anything appetite urges' (TP II.8; III/31).

This claim is among other things a provocation, a challenge to confront the implications of the view that our most fundamental rights and duties are natural.[17] While civil rights come and go with time and jurisdiction, natural ones endure, deriving their authority from unchanging features of our life and situation. But what rights answer to this requirement? Taking the question seriously, Spinoza answers that the only right we possess by nature is our power to do what

---

[14] On Spinoza's theory of law see Chapter 6. Also Rutherford 2010, 143–8; Garret 2003, 360–2; James 2012, 83–110.

[15] Grotius 2006, 19.   [16] On the validity of Spinoza's argument see Grey, forthcoming.

[17] Garrett 2003, 641.

we can to persevere in our being. How this power is expressed will vary from person to person and from time to time, depending for example on whether an individual is wise or foolish, sick or healthy. But any action they perform will be an expression of the only natural right they possess, namely the right to exercise their *conatus* by doing anything in their power.

The philosophical weight of this analysis is carried by the notion of a power to act; but what does such a power amount to? Thinking about our own case, it comes easily to us to conceive of our powers to act as liberties or standing capacities that belong to us even when we are not exercising them. Once we have learned to walk, for example, the power remains with us, ready to be used as the situation requires. However, although Spinoza allows that this interpretation is acceptable in everyday contexts where philosophical standards of truth are not at issue, he denies that it is philosophically coherent. In order for an individual to walk down the street, a ramifying constellation of determining conditions must be satisfied. The power to perform even such an apparently straightforward action depends on a vast web of material, psychological, and social circumstances, and it is only because we are largely unaware of these conditions that they rarely figure in our estimations of our powers.[18] Working with an incomplete grasp of the causes and effects in play, we come to believe that we can form desires and act on them at will, like the drunkard who 'believes that it is from a free decision of the mind that he speaks the things he later, when sober, wishes he had not said' (E IIIp2s[ii]; II/143). Most people maintain that the human mind was not produced by natural causes, but is 'so independent of other things that it has an absolute power (*potestas*) to determine itself and to use reason properly. But experience teaches all too well that it's no more in our power to have a sound mind than it is to have a sound body' (TP II.6; III/30–1). Desiring to be more powerful than we are, we satisfy the wish by imagining that our capacity to determine our actions is greater than it is, and mistakenly conceive of ourselves as possessing a level of autonomy that humans rarely attain.

Spinoza's attack on the freedom of the will is not designed to induce a deep scepticism about the very possibility of self-knowledge. Rather, it is an attempt to remind us how little we know about ourselves and how readily we exaggerate our power to persevere in our being. By imagining that we are equipped with steady capacities to decide how to act, we overlook the fact that what we do is ultimately determined by complex laws governing nature as a whole. Overestimating our individual power, we misunderstand our own agency, or to put the point another way, misunderstand our natural right.

Once we strip away this illusion, Spinoza contends, we are forced to acknowledge that our individual power counts for so little that it can barely be said to

---

[18] Balibar 1998, 61–3.

exist. '[A]s long as human natural right is determined by each person's power, and belongs to that person, there is no human natural right. It consists more in opinion than in fact, since there's no secure way to maintain it' (TP II.15; III/32–3).[19] Here we have moved a long way from the reassuring conceptions of natural right on which most seventeenth-century theorists relied so heavily. Far from endowing individuals with fixed and fruitful rights to life, liberty or property, the right that nature bestows on us is puny and inconstant. Formally, it licenses us to do anything in our power, but the ways in which we can actually exercise the right of nature are painfully limited.

If this is correct, one might wonder why so many mainstream theorists of natural law have failed to see it. What has led them to portray the law of nature in such misleading terms? Part of the answer, Spinoza implies, lies in the fact that, when people live in states, the quality and scope of their natural right is transformed. Instead of acting solely on their own power, they are sustained by the power of the community as a whole, and this dramatically alters what they have the natural right to do. Theorists such as Grotius who contend, for instance, that rights to property are guaranteed by divine command, mistakenly attribute the benefits of life in the state to states of nature where the only law in operation is the law of nature. By confusing the benefits of civil law with those of natural law, they fail to recognize the degraded character of states of nature, a character that can only be remedied by the formation of the state. 'The right of nature which is the peculiar property of the human race can hardly be conceived except where men have common rights and are jointly able to conceive for themselves lands they can inhabit and cultivate, are able to protect themselves, fend off any force, and live according to the common opinion of all' (TP II.15; III/33).

A state is formed, Spinoza argues, when 'each person transfers all the power he has to the social order (*in societatem transferat*), which alone will retain the supreme right of nature over all things' (TTP XVI.25;III/193–4). The right of the state, represented by a sovereign, is then 'nothing more than the right of nature, determined not by the power of each person, but by the power of a multitude, led as it were by one mind' (TP III.2; III/284–5). Although this is how Spinoza formulates his position, his account is in a way misleading, because individuals can never transfer all their natural right to the state or anything else.[20] 'No one', he reminds us, 'will ever be able to transfer to another his power, or consequently his right, in such a way that he ceases to be a man. And there will never be a supreme power that can get everything to happen just as he wishes' (TTP XVII.2; III/201). While individuals transfer particular powers to the sovereign, such as their power to break contracts with impunity, they cannot give up their overarching right to strive to persevere in their being. On the contrary, they continue to exercise it in

---

[19] Armstrong 2009.   [20] Hobbes 1994, ch. 26.44.

the state, albeit in a different way, by adapting their manner of striving to take account of the rights or powers created by the sovereign. In the process, these powers acquire a dual status. Insofar as they are validated and secured by the civil law they are positive civil rights; but insofar as they are individual or collective powers to act, they remain natural rights. States therefore do not remove or replace our natural right. As the *Political Treatise* emphasizes, 'a person's right of nature does not cease in the civil order' and each of us continues to act 'according to the laws of his own nature' (TP III.3; III/285).[21] Rather, the powers to act that the civil law creates are now among our natural rights. When we obey the civil law, we continue to exercise our natural right to do anything in our power.

A striking feature of this analysis is Spinoza's refusal to draw a sharp distinction between the natural and political realms, or between natural and civil right. By contrast with Hobbes, for whom states are artificial things, Spinoza views them as natural entities subject to natural laws, and construes the civil rights to which they give rise as expressions of the right of nature. Nature gives us the right to exercise the powers we have and does not praise or condemn us for being what we are. But it also gives us the right to alter and extend our power to act by creating political communities whose members share 'one and the same cause of security and principle of living' and cooperate in order to maintain it (TP III.3; III/285). The civil law enables subjects to exercise their natural right and persevere in their being in ways that are possible only within the state.

III

Implicit in this account of state formation is an attack on Grotius's second axiom, that the law of nature requires us to act justly. Before the civil law was established, Grotius argues, everyone was 'at liberty to right himself by force', but only if it was just to do so.[22] Spinoza, by contrast, countenances no such qualification. Following Hobbes's lead, he argues that normative standards of justice and injustice have no place in states of nature and 'can only be conceived in a state'. Justice is 'a constancy of mind in apportioning to each person what belongs to him according to civil law'; but since nothing in nature 'can rightly be said to belong to one person and not to another', justice can only take hold once the state exists (TTP XVI.42; III/196: TP II.23; III/284). States of nature may of course contain individuals who recognize the advantages of treating others justly and try to put their convictions into practice; but under the law of nature their efforts may rightly be

---

[21] Although Hobbes does not explicitly endorse this view, it is arguably implicit in his analysis. Individuals who have transferred their natural right to a sovereign do not just passively submit to its orders, but also play a part in enforcing the law. In doing so they can be said to be exercising their individual right.

[22] Hugo Grotius, 2005, 17–18.

thwarted. Until shared standards of equity are embedded in legal and social institutions, our individual conceptions of justice have no force. They do not bind us,
because there is nothing to stop us violating them when it suits us, and they do
they bind others. Their effect on the way we exercise our natural right can therefore only be *ad hoc*, and will not result in the consistently equitable treatment that
constitutes justice.

Pressing this line of argument, Spinoza goes out of his way to point out that
religious norms are no more rooted in the law of nature than civil ones. Just as the
state of nature is without justice, it is 'without religion or law and hence without
sin or violations of right' (TTP XVI.54;III/198).[23] In itself, the law of nature cannot serve as a moral yardstick for assessing how we treat one another, and until
people form states or political communities there are no shared standards to
which we can appeal.

With this rejection of Grotius's second axiom, however, Spinoza leaves himself
with a difficulty. If he is going to abandon the contention that natural law ante-
cedently binds us to respect certain moral norms, he must explain how a commitment to justice gains such a hold over us that it seems to orthodox theorists to be
part of the furniture of the universe. Since the law of nature does not bequeath us
any values, how do we develop the complex norms under which we live?[24]

A first point to bear in mind as we address this question is that Spinoza's conception of the state of nature is not as starkly non-normative as it initially appears.
Despite his emphasis on the gulf between his own view and that of the natural
lawyers, there is a sense in which the exercise of natural right as he conceives of it
is always a normative undertaking. This is because, when we strive for things we
think will make us joyful and avoid those we think will make us sad, we are
already implicitly employing a standard of good and evil. 'By good', Spinoza
explains, 'I understand every kind of joy and whatever leads to it, and especially
what satisfies any kind of longing, whatever that may be. And by evil I understand
every kind of sadness and especially what frustrates longing. For we have shown
that we desire nothing because we judge it to be good, but on the contrary, we call
it good because we desire it. Consequently, what we are averse to, we call evil' (E
IIIp39; II/170). To want something is already to view it as good in the sense of
conducive to the joyfulness that is a mark of persevering in one's being, and to be
averse to a thing is to view it as bad in the same terms. Moreover, all our actions
express this normative orientation. When we exercise our natural right by pursuing states of affairs that answer to our desires (E IVp19;II/223–4), we operate with
a conception of the difference between good and evil and strive to attain ends that
are by these lights good. To be sure, good and evil as they have so far been

---

[23] As St Paul confirms when he claims that 'there is no sin without a commandment and a law'
(TTP III.44; XVI.6). This point is also emphasized in TP 2.
[24] Pfersmann 2003, 644–5; Rutherford 2010, 148–56; Lenz 2013.

delineated are subjective qualities and only track our individual desires for sadness and joy. We may desire things for their novelty, sublimity, sensuousness, or moral worth, or indeed for the pain they cause others, and our attitudes to objects or states of affairs may also be idiosyncratic or deluded. Nevertheless, our fundamental disposition to evaluate—to assess things as good or evil—is always at work as we exercise our natural right by doing things that are in our power. It forms the basis of our capacity to distinguish values of different kinds and develop common normative standards.

A second point to bear in mind is that we are not in Spinoza's view dispositionally antisocial. While we can imagine people whose assessments of good and evil are indifferent to the desires of others, we humans are psychologically disposed to persevere in our being by cooperating with each other, and are led to do so by our affects. It is part of our nature to try to relate to at least some of our fellow human beings in ways that sustain and increase the joyfulness of our lives, and although, as the *Ethics* explains at length, we suffer many saddening failures, we also have some success. With few exceptions, most of us attach value to some powers to act that depend on the way others exercise the right of nature, and try to accommodate our actions to their desires. The benefits are obvious: 'if two men make an agreement with one another and join forces', Spinoza claims, 'they can do more together, and hence, have more right over nature than either does alone' (TP II.13; III/290).

When we strive for mutual empowerment, we are guided by a consensus of opinion about the desirability or goodness of particular patterns of action, and thus of particular powers to act; and the more we are guided in this fashion, the more we act in the light of shared normative conventions about what it is good or bad to do. In Spinoza's view, moreover, the desire for effective conventions of this kind is what gives rise to the state. To enhance their ability to cooperate, and thus extend their power to act, a group of individuals endows a sovereign with the power to make and enforce laws in the name of the community as a whole. Using its own right, the sovereign then alters its subjects' individual powers to act, whether by limiting what they can do or by enabling them to do things they could not do before. At the same time, it vastly extends their power or right by creating conditions in which they can act collectively. There is of course a straightforward sense in which the resulting distribution of powers expresses the right of the sovereign who determines and imposes the civil law; but the sovereign's right is at the same time 'defined by the power of the multitude' (TP II.16; III/281).[25] Unless a community has the collective right or power to comply with the law and is capable of doing what it demands, the decrees a sovereign issues will merely reflect its lack of right as it struggles to impose them on its uncooperative subjects. 'To

---

[25] Matheron 1969; Balibar 1994; Negri 1982; Bove 2012.

look out for their interests and retain their sovereignty, it is incumbent on [the supreme powers] most of all to consult the common good and to direct everything according to the dictate of reason' (TTP XVI.29; III/194).

For a state to survive, then, the law must answer to the natural right of its subjects by reflecting values and promoting forms of cooperation they are able to accept and have the power to put into practice. To put the point another way, it must embody enough of their existing conceptions of justice to ensure that they exercise their natural right by doing what the law demands. Although, as Spinoza clearly states, justice only exists within the state and has no place in a state of nature, states do not articulate norms of justice in a vacuum. If the civil law is to guarantee peace and security, the norms it articulates must reflect, and continue to reflect, a community's sense of what is just and unjust.

Once a state comes into existence, this consensus is in turn shaped by the civil law itself. Legal standards inform our understanding of what is just and endow particular powers to act with evaluative meaning, so that the manner in which communities and their members exercise their natural right is always informed by their legal commitments. Once our powers to act are determined by civil laws and other social conventions so that we exercise the law of nature by doing what they dictate, the law of nature as we practise it embodies a commitment to norms such as justice. As well as shaping what we have the power to do, these norms inform the way we strive to make our lives joyful.

In one respect, then, Spinoza radically opposes the orthodox assumption that justice is integral to the law of nature. The natural law does not command us to live justly, as Grotius and others assume, any more than it requires this of lions or tables. Nevertheless, there is a sense in which the law of nature as Spinoza conceives of it recommends us to practise justice. Given that our individual power to sustain a joyful way of life is negligible, that harmonious relationships with other people are one of our greatest sources of empowerment, and that the best way to sustain such relationships is to treat others equitably, we benefit from a just way of life. Whether or not we realize it, exercising the right of nature by living justly immeasurably increases our individual and collective natural right. While nothing constrains us to take advantage of these benefits, they are nevertheless there to be understood and put into practice. They reflect the way things are, or as Spinoza puts it, 'the rules according to which all things happen' (TTP II.4; III/277).[26]

Evaluative norms such as the ones Grotius posits are therefore not so alien to Spinoza's law of nature as his account initially suggests. They are implicit in it, not as commands, but in the form of naturalized prescriptions that are in principle accessible to reason. 'Whether a man is led by reason or only by desire', the

---

[26] Rutherford 2010, 165.

Political Treatise reminds us, 'he does nothing except according to the laws of nature, i.e. in accordance with the right of nature' (TP II.5; III/277). The better we understand the benefits of living in accordance with values such as justice, and put them into political practice, the more empoweringly we are able to exercise the right of nature and the more joyfully we are able to live.

IV

Despite these continuities between Spinoza's conception of the law of nature and more orthodox interpretations of it, the two remain radically opposed. Where Grotius, for example, claims to articulate an obligatory and divinely guaranteed framework of rights and duties that defines the terms of a moral way of life, Spinoza's law of nature merely gives us the right to do anything in our power. Many of his original readers would consequently have found his account of natural right unrecognizable, and it is not immediately clear whether it has anything to offer us. Arguably, as Theo Verbeek contends, Spinoza dismantles an emerging conception of universal moral rights but fails to put anything in its place.[27] There is, however, a more positive way to interpret his achievement. As I shall now go on to propose, Spinoza articulates a series of insights into the character of rights that we would do well to take seriously.

It is true that, from a contemporary perspective, the Spinozist outlook suffers from at least four major deficiencies.[28] The first, which can be quickly dealt with, is that it fails to distinguish natural rights from legal or positive ones. Unlike those contemporary theorists who view natural rights as universal moral entitlements and separate them from the positive rights we acquire within the state, Spinoza classifies all our rights as natural. Whether we find ourselves in a state of nature or a political community, we express the right of nature in everything we do. Here, it seems to me, Spinoza simply concedes the objection; since positive rights are also natural, the two classes are not distinct. I shall therefore move straight on to the three remaining problems that seem to afflict his view.

Like the orthodox interpreters of the right of nature whom Spinoza opposes, contemporary philosophers usually reserve the language of rights for types of action that are regarded as morally permissible, and use the notion of a power to act to cover anything people are capable of doing. According to this view, there are many things we have the power to do but no right to do, as for example when a man has the power but not the right to rape. Spinoza, however, eradicates this distinction. To say that an agent has a natural right to perform an action is just to say that they have a power to do it, regardless of whether they act for good or ill.[29]

---

[27] Verbeek 2007, 260, 274.   [28] C.f. Balibar 1998, 59–63; Verbeek 2007, 262.
[29] Barbone 1999, 91–2.

Spinoza's analysis also undercuts the assumption, equally deeply embedded in current rights discourse, that in respect of our natural rights we are equal.[30] Rather than endowing us with equal entitlements to life, liberty, or property, our natural rights as he defines them vary with our individual powers. In principle, one person's natural right may vastly exceed that of another, and ten years later their situations may be reversed.

The final problem concerns the status of natural rights. If, as the orthodox tradition maintains, natural rights stand above the civil law and limit what it can legitimately require, we can criticize states for violating the rights bestowed on us by the law of nature. Again, however, Spinoza's account blocks off this possibility. Since the law of nature does not give us any specific entitlements other than the right to do anything in our power, and since this right belongs to states as much as to their subjects, nothing in the natural law rules out the legitimacy of any action the state can manage to take.

We may feel that, if Spinoza's analysis of the right of nature is to have any contemporary relevance, it must be able to respond to these objections. Somehow, it must recoup the losses from which it seems to suffer and vindicate the existence of equal, moral rights of nature, to which discontented subjects can appeal in order to criticize their rulers. As we have seen, Spinoza acknowledges the benefits of living in a community where values such as justice are firmly entrenched and rationally defended, and he is also alive to the benefits of a degree of political equality. But his responses to the three criticisms I have identified are not direct. They emerge from his philosophical system, and are part of his attempt to disabuse us of what he sees as a series of philosophical misunderstandings. Instead of continuing to imagine that the protections we desire are somehow guaranteed by nature in the form of claims that other agents are bound to respect, we need to face up to the true character of the natural law and admit that it is indifferent to our welfare. Spinoza's deepest defence of his position therefore lies in the alternative outlook he offers, and in his claim to have shown it to be true. Since, as he claims, the only philosophically defensible notion of natural right is the one he identifies, we have the best possible reasons for adopting it; and although the gains this involves are not unequivocal—we do not get back everything we have to give up—its benefits nevertheless far outweigh those of the fiction that orthodox theorists cling to and some contemporary theorists continue to uphold.

Before we try to assess the balance sheet of gains and losses, it will be helpful to stay a little longer with Spinoza's notion of a right. As the first and second objections point out, the individual natural rights with which he endows us do not even approximate to our usual understanding of rights as specific, stable claims.

---

[30] Verbeek 2007, 264.

Insofar as we acquire steady powers to act, we only do so by collectively transforming our fluctuating individual powers into rights that are civil as well as natural. But this is precisely Spinoza's point. Rather than presupposing the existence of stable claims with specific contents, we have to ask how rights with these qualities can be brought into being. We may be inclined to suppose, for example, that a law designed to protect fishermen's rights of ownership by allowing them to prosecute anyone who steals their nets bestows a specific and well-defined right on each individual fisherman. But Spinoza asks us to emancipate ourselves from this picture by considering what it takes to give a fisherman the relevant power to act. Passing a law is not enough. We must also consider whether the fisherman has the confidence and determination to initiate a prosecution and see it through. Can he pay the lawyer's fees? Do the officials he has to deal with have the power to interpret his demands with some sympathy and do what it takes to meet them, regardless of his accent, lack of legal knowledge or bodily comportment? Instead of presupposing that we can distribute legal rights to just treatment, Spinoza draws our attention to the difficulties involved in creating the kind of powers to act that answer to our image of rights as secure entitlements.

In part, the issue is a practical one. Designing institutions and reinforcing conventions that make the fisherman's powers to act accessible requires experience and skill. But the problem also has a conceptual dimension. A right, as Spinoza sees the matter, is not a distinct entitlement that can simply be conferred on an individual or collective agent. Like a knot in a fisherman's net, it is an element in a set of interconnected powers from which it cannot be separated. Seen in this way, rights are not even clearly attributable to individuals; instead, the many powers to act on which they depend are dispersed through a set of related entities, human and otherwise. To endow an agent with a stable power to act, we consequently have to do more than give them a legal entitlement or permission; we also have to create and maintain the ramifying rights and conditions that together bring that particular right into being.

To recoup the benefits that the orthodox view claims for itself, we therefore have to work with this ontologically fragile conception of a right. Turning to the first objection, we have to consider how, given that rights are complex relations, we can construct a way of life in which the difference between mere powers to act, and powers to act in ways that sustain important values, is respected. Turning to the second objection—that Spinoza's natural rights are unequally distributed—we have to ask how we can construct a way of life in which certain powers to act are equally and stably accessible. Put like this, it may seem that we are bent on taming a radical position by showing that it is not so radical after all; despite appearances, Spinoza can accommodate the moral demands that modern conceptions of natural rights tend to take for granted. But this would be to underestimate the philosophical demands his position makes on us. Spinoza never ceases to reject the view that our natural rights impose certain moral standards on us, and consistently maintains that they entitle us to do anything in our power. At the same time, however, he acknowledges the value of the patterns of action that constitute collectively empowering rights to justice, property or liberty. We all live more joyfully in conditions where we possess, for example, a stable power to contribute to a just community by acting justly. The question is how we can create the conditions that will generate and sustain this right.

Whereas Spinoza's critics and opponents take it that this work has already been done—we are already endowed with and bound to respect certain natural rights—Spinoza makes the labour all our own. Among the resources at our disposal, he argues, the most powerful is our rational capacity to understand our own predicament and use our understanding to find out how we can live as joyfully as possible. In part, this is a matter of learning what we humans are like and what kinds of relationships typically empower and disempower us; but it is also a matter of finding out how, and how far, a given community can create the stable entitlements whose existence and force contemporary rights theorists tend to presuppose. The extent to which a state can build an effective culture of stable rights, and secure the particular rights it values most deeply, will vary with its history and circumstances.

The process of using our understanding to create and defend a range of normative rights is always, in Spinoza's view, blended with and dependent on our imaginative powers. Just as the orthodox theorists and their contemporary equivalents get ahead of themselves by positing stable natural rights that do not yet exist, even the best informed philosophers must imagine the rights they are trying to create and the benefits that will flow from them. At one level, we are to think coolly and hypothetically about what we want to achieve; but at another, the scenarios we imagine already straddle the porous barrier between fantasy and reality. They are simultaneously represented as powers we would like to have and powers we have already been given. Moreover, as soon as we begin to use these ideas in political debate, or appeal to them to inform social policy, we alter the way we exercise our power to act and shift the complex balances of power that constitute our rights. By demanding a universal right to justice, for example, a group may inspire a state to change its laws or provoke a revolution. But the change does not depend on, and is not validated by, the existence of a right or power to act in the ways justice demands. Instead, it flows from the various rights or powers to act that the shared image of that right help to create.

Armed with the dual resources of reason and imagination, Spinoza is able to answer two of the objections levelled against him. First, by understanding and imagining what is involved in living joyfully and how we might put these insights into practice, we distinguish the valuable powers to act that we usually describe as natural rights from the insignificant or destructive ones that we usually designate as powers. They are all natural rights; but within the state it becomes possible to differentiate rights or powers that individuals happen to have, such as the right or power of a particular man to rape a particular woman, from rights that are collectively valued and protected. Although differently formulated, the distinction between rights and powers is available and indeed essential to political life. Secondly, the process of giving individuals some equal rights is in Spinoza's view an integral part of creating conditions in which a community can live peacefully and securely. The specific rights a state aspires to equalize, and the extent to which it manages to live up to its aspirations, will vary; but the more we understand ourselves, the better we will appreciate the value of ways of life in which we are equally well placed to act justly and freely. While our natural rights are not naturally equal, there are in some cases irrevocable reasons for trying to equalize them.

Without betraying his philosophical commitments, Spinoza can therefore articulate the contemporary distinction between rights and powers, and support the equalizing of certain rights. In these respects he does not give up on the values that modern theorists associate with rights of nature. Turning now to the third objection, can he accommodate the provision that, when a state violates our natural rights, we are justified in resisting it? Here Spinoza is more equivocal. Since subjects who act in ways that are contrary to the law are always exercising a right to resist it, there is undoubtedly a sense in which this right exists. In addition, it is commonplace for groups to resist the state by imagining the benefits of opposing the sovereign and appealing to these benefits to advocate political change. Whether or not the resulting shifts of right are enough to threaten the existence of the sovereign, the right or power to introduce imagined ideals into political debate has consequences for the way communities manifest their natural right.

The exercise of rights of resistance is therefore not so much an exceptional measure as an integral part of ordinary political life, and is one of the everyday problems that states have to deal with. By appealing to imagined rights as grounds for resistance, subjects spell out what they regard as endurable, and in Spinoza's view sensible sovereigns will listen to them. But while he does not doubt that eloquent advocates of resistance can work on the imagination of a community, and alter the balance of rights or powers to act within it, he is less willing to allow that resisting the right of the state is rational. People undoubtedly do it, and their actions may sometimes help to produce more empowering forms of government; but the dangers of undermining an existing sovereign and risking a collapse into a state of nature loom large in Spinoza's imagination (TTP XVI.51; III/197). The more we understand the fragility of political life, he implies, the less willing we shall be to give rights of resistance a secure place in our pantheon of valuable powers to act.

V

Of the three challenges we have been considering, the one Spinoza is least able to meet is therefore the last. Rationally understood, natural rights do not, in his view, provide a means of legitimating resistance to the state. In other ways, however, his analysis is less alien than it first appears, though in order to accept it we have to be willing to revise an entrenched vocabulary and reformulate a range of familiar claims in novel terms. Why should we make the effort? As I have indicated, some aspects of Spinoza's critique of the orthodox conception of natural rights continue to echo within contemporary rights discourse and cast light on its limitations. Chief among these is the tendency to view rights as separable claims that can be distributed to individual or collective agents. (A state, for example, can give more of its individual subjects the right to vote.) Spinoza challenges this view at the deepest ontological level. Rights, as he portrays them, are constituted by complex sets of relations—so much so that one might describe their ascription to individuals as a fiction. While the fiction can serve valuable social and political purposes, it also encourages us to ignore the hinterland of powers on which our individual rights to act depend, and leads us to misunderstand both what rights are and what it takes to create them. Attempting to short-circuit the laborious process of building stable and effective powers to act, we take refuge in an imagined political realm where they lie ready and waiting.

The most illuminating feature of Spinoza's analysis of rights is its ability to counteract this illusion. Even if we cannot fully grasp the implications of the relational ontology he defends, he nevertheless alerts us to the many conditions on which rights depend, and shows us how to change the ways we set about creating them. This task, Spinoza urges us to recognize, is up to us. It is up to us to understand how we can live more joyfully, and up to us to stabilize the powers to act on which a collectively joyful way of life depends. With Spinoza's help, we may be able to make some progress.

8

Democracy and the Good Life
in Spinoza's Philosophy

I

One of the features of Spinoza's philosophy that makes it attractive to many twenty-first-century readers is its defence of democracy as the constitutional form of an ideal state.[1] Although the *Political Treatise* breaks off before spelling out the details of a democratic constitution, other texts encourage the reader to envisage a free way of life as most fully realizable in an inclusive polity where subjects advance their understanding and liberty by following laws they have made themselves. The view that human beings have the potential to live most freely in democratic states[2] is exceptional among seventeenth-century writers, and Spinoza is the best-known of a small group of Dutch authors who are justly celebrated for defending it. Focusing on this claim, a range of commentators of various ideological persuasions have hailed him as the initiator or inspiration of the modern democratic tradition. According to Jonathan Israel, for example, 'Spinoza was the first major European thinker in modern times—though he is preceded here by Johan de la Court and Van den Enden—to embrace democratic republicanism as the highest and most fully rational form of political organisation, and the one best suited to the needs of men.'[3]

This is indeed one way to read Spinoza and, as I shall argue, it draws on a central and inspiring strand of his thought. There are, however, other strands, perhaps less straightforwardly susceptible to celebration, but equally pertinent to an understanding of his assessment of democracy. My aim in this chapter is to

[1] Originally published in Charlie Huenemann ed., *Interpreting Spinoza* (Cambridge University Press, 2008), pp. 128–46. Reprinted with permission of Cambridge University Press.
    I am especially grateful to Edwin Curley, Moira Gatens, Charlie Huenemann, Stephen Nadler and Theo Verbeek, for their comments on earlier versions of this essay.
[2] While many writers defended the view that one can only be free if one lives in a free state, i.e. a republic as opposed to a monarchical regime, comparatively few authors regarded democracy as a form of state conducive to freedom.
[3] Israel 2001, 259. Israel's claim is part of a broader debate about the history of democratic thought, which embraces not only Spinoza but also his predecessor Thomas Hobbes. See Matheron 1997. See also Tuck 2006, 171, where Hobbes is described as 'a sophisticated and deep theorist of democracy'. Perhaps the most influential advocate of Spinoza as a theorist of democracy is Antonio Negri, according to whom Spinoza develops a novel conception of the multitude, and articulates 'the democracy of the multitude as the absolute form of politics' (see Hardt and Negri 2000, 77). See also Negri 1997.

Spinoza on Learning to Live Together. Susan James, Oxford University Press (2020). © Susan James.
DOI: 10.1093/oso/9780198713074.001.0001

explore one of them, namely Spinoza's view of the role played by imagination in the exercise of sovereignty. Successful sovereigns, as he describes them, need to deploy the skills of prophets in order to devise legal systems that their subjects will obey. (All politics, one might say, is in this sense prophetic.) While Spinoza gives us reasons for concluding that the ends of the state are in principle most fully achieved under a democratic constitution, the art of creating and sustaining a democracy depends on the imaginative ability of sovereign and subjects to legitimate and realize a democratic way of life. To achieve this goal, they have to be able to interpret the bare definition of democracy as a state in which the law is made by the body of the people, by working out, for example, who is to be included in this body and what it takes for such a body to make laws.

As Spinoza himself allows us to see, these questions can be answered in a variety of ways. His own unfinished account of a stable, democratic constitution begins by listing several classes of people who are to play no part at all in government: aliens, on the grounds that they are not bound by the law; women, servants, children, and wards, on the grounds that they are not *sui iuris* or able to act on their own wills; and criminals and others on the grounds that they are dishonourable or lack *honestum* (TP XI.3; III/359).[4] In the context of seventeenth-century political thought, these exclusions are not surprising, and it would be pointless to criticize Spinoza for advocating them. Nevertheless, I shall suggest, they serve to draw attention to a limitation in his imaginative power—a limitation he would himself describe both as a lack, and as the effect of some obstacle standing in the way of his ability to imagine a fully inclusive form of political freedom. More generally, the gap between the democratic ideal Spinoza offers us and his own imaginative grasp of what a democratic society would be like inadvertently exemplifies one of the problems with which he is explicitly concerned. Because the pursuit of freedom is held back by the imaginative limitations of communities, part of the task of the sovereign is to cultivate the kind of insight possessed by prophets, and make a free way of life imaginatively accessible.

II

Sovereignty, according to Spinoza, can be held equally well by an individual or a collectivity, and to make it easier to keep this fact in mind I shall always refer to the figure of the sovereign as 'it'. However, regardless of whether the sovereign is an individual or a group, its task is always the same: to promote peace and security by ensuring that its subjects obey the law; and to counteract vices which, whilst they are not contrary to law, nevertheless diminish the state. For example, when a long-lasting peace makes citizens slack and slothful, sovereigns must find

---

[4] For a fuller discussion of *honestum* see Chapter 2.

ways of redirecting their energies into activities that enhance security (TP X.6; III/355–6). A sovereign therefore bears responsibility for creating a legal structure and a broader way of life that successfully reconcile the diverse desires of individuals, and for inducing its subjects to promote harmony and cooperation within the state.

In the *Political Treatise*, Spinoza seems to suggest that sovereigns need only concern themselves with guaranteeing security (TP I.6; III/275). Elsewhere, however, he is adamant that security is so closely intertwined with liberty that the one cannot exist without the other. As the *Theological-Political Treatise* is largely designed to show, states are most secure when their subjects are not coerced into obeying the law, but obey willingly because they realize that it is in their interest to do so (TTP XX.8; III/240). Furthermore, subjects who understand the benefits of cooperating by obeying the law are freer than those who do not. The ultimate end of the republic 'is not to dominate, restraining men by fear and making them subject to another's control but on the contrary to free each person from fear so that he can live securely as far as possible...It is not, I repeat, to transform men from rational beings into beasts or *automata*, but to enable their minds and bodies to perform their functions safely, to enable them to use their reason freely, and not to clash with one another in hatred, anger or deception, or deal inequitably with one another. So the end of the state is really freedom' (TTP XX.12; III/240–1).[5] Sovereigns should therefore aim to cultivate circumstances in which individuals have enough security and freedom to appreciate the advantages of a cooperative form of existence and are in a position to enhance it. Although it would be too much to hope that such a policy will eliminate conflict completely, it can nevertheless minimize threats such as faction, corruption, and civil war, any of which can undermine the sovereign's power and ultimately destroy the state.

Abstracting from the merits and disadvantages of specific constitutional forms, Spinoza provides a general account of the problems a sovereign confronts and the means by which it can ameliorate them. The root of its difficulties lies in the inadequate ideas that constitute human imagination, and specifically human passion (E IVp37s1; II/236). Affects such as desire, sadness, and joy are part of our everyday way of responding to the world; but because they reflect our disposition to imagine ourselves as singular things, and obscure our understanding of the extent to which we depend on other parts of nature, they give us a partial and sometimes distorted view of what will damage or benefit us. Furthermore, it is hard to recognize and avoid the harms to which our affects expose us. For one thing, the phenomenology of freedom—the sense that, when we experience and act on our

---

[5] Against this interpretation, Balibar believes that there is a marked shift in Spinoza's view. Whereas Spinoza argues in the TTP that the end of political society is freedom, in the TP 'freedom is no longer the declared "purpose" of the state. The central preoccupation now is civil peace or security'. See Balibar 1998, 116.

affects, we are in control of ourselves and what we are doing—obscures the need to take stock of individual passions and get some critical distance on them. In addition, we are in Spinoza's view naturally prone to certain patterns of feeling and action which have a strong hold over us. Some of these patterns dispose us to productive affects such as love and compassion; but others incline us to negative passions such as hatred or fear, which tend to inhibit cooperation (E IIIp55s; II/183). Together with the causal sequences in which they are embedded, these latter passions habitually feed insecurity, and left to themselves are liable to undermine the effectiveness of the state. The first task of the sovereign is therefore to contain them.

One way to achieve this end is to terrorize subjects into obedience. But while threats and force are essential tools of government, Spinoza joins many of his contemporaries in urging that they should be used sparingly. Quoting Seneca, he repeatedly reminds his readers that sovereigns who resort to strong-arm tactics rarely survive for long, because subjects who obey the law only out of fear will do what they can to resist (TTP XVI.29; III/195). However fiercely they are oppressed, they always constitute a formidable threat.[6] Sovereigns therefore do better to ensure that their subjects' devotion to the law is stronger than their desire to pursue illegal goals. Even when this strategy succeeds, individuals may still find themselves torn between an inclination to obey and a desire to break the law, or between a desire to conform to standards of civic virtue and a longing to satisfy their private interests. But the mixture of encouragements and threats implicit in legal and other institutions and practices will on the whole guarantee that cooperation wins out. Passion will counter passion, and subjects will experience the decision to abide by the law as a choice they have made willingly, albeit sometimes reluctantly (E IVp7; II/214).

Where this level of cooperation has been achieved, individuals have already begun to identify their interests with those of the polity. In doing so, they have simultaneously begun to think of themselves not merely as singular things, but also as members of a community that is, 'as it were, one body and one mind' (E IVp18s(iii); II/223). To realize that the best way to serve one's own interests is to play one's part in maintaining and strengthening the security of the community is, according to Spinoza, to understand an important truth, which in turn strengthens one's desire to resist affects that undermine cooperation. Once one appreciates the social damage that envy can do, one has a reason for trying to control it in oneself and others by understanding how it comes about and what can be done to prevent it. Equally, once one understands that fear tends to breed

---

[6] In the Latin *Leviathan* of 1668, Hobbes brings this general point to bear on the history of the Netherlands. 'For the common people are the strongest element of the commonwealth...The sedition of those in Holland, called the Beggars, ought to serve as a warning how dangerous it is in the commonwealth to scorn citizens of modest means' Hobbes 1994, ch. 30.17.

hatred, which in turn brings a string of debilitating effects in its train, one has a reason for trying not to cause fear in others, and trying not to succumb to it one-self. Modifying one's passionate dispositions is, however, a complex project and cannot be undertaken in isolation. It depends on the guidance and support of other individuals, and on standards of cooperation encouraged and enforced within a society. Part of the sovereign's task is therefore to use its power to sustain an environment in which subjects can, so to speak, cooperate in increasing their ability to cooperate. As they do so, they protect themselves from the destructive effects of their own passions, thereby increasing the security of the state.

This process is an eminently practical one, requiring not only a more or less philosophical understanding of the laws of nature, but also a flair for applying them to particular situations. A sovereign may know, for example, that one passion can be used to control another, and have a rough grasp of our disposition to imitate one another's affects. However, while general knowledge of this sort is helpful, it will not be enough. To motivate its subjects to obey its commands, a sovereign will also need to take account of their own particular affective dispositions, and will need to pose questions such as 'Are these people susceptible to shame, or are they too alienated to care what others think?' or 'Will fear of divine anger weigh with these subjects, or are they so scared that they will break the law to worship a golden calf?' (E IIIp39s; II/170). To arrive at answers, sovereigns must possess the sort of local knowledge that Spinoza classifies under the heading of imagination, and must be able to enter into the imaginative business of devising laws with which their subjects will be in sympathy. In the process they may make use of education, civil associations, or religion to create a climate of cooperation, but it is up to them to find effective ways of deploying these resources.

This imaginative aspect of the sovereign's task bears comparison with the role of the prophet. As I showed in Chapter 2, Spinoza characterizes prophets as individuals whose exceptional powers of imagination enable them to perceive the vital importance of a cooperative way of life, and to express their insights in a manner accessible and persuasive to a particular community (TTP I.42–3; III/27–8). When philosophers explain the value of cooperating with others by arguing from premises about the nature and circumstances of human beings, their audiences may or may not be convinced. Individuals or groups who are wrapped up in their own passionate interpretations of themselves will not always find this kind of reasoning persuasive. By contrast, the genius of a prophet lies in the ability to employ images or stories that appeal to the situation and temperament of a specific people, thus offering them a compelling account of the benefits of living cooperatively, or of resolving a current problem in a cooperative fashion. In giving meaning to a situation, a prophet suggests a way of dealing with it that is both acceptable and more or less within reach.

There are, Spinoza stipulates, no longer any prophets to whom the divine law is revealed (TTP I.7; III/16). Nevertheless, the integrity of a political society depends on civil laws that re-enact the precepts of their divine counterparts in the form of commands imposed by the sovereign. Like the God of the prophets, the state commands obedience, and the need to make its laws acceptable remains as pressing as ever. Communities still need to build harmonious ways of life, and subjects still have to be encouraged to resolve the tensions between their civic and private interests in favour of the law. In the state, the task of achieving these ends falls to the sovereign. Like prophets, sovereigns must offer subjects empowering accounts of their situation and prospects, so that the courses of cooperative action specified by the law will strike them as desirable and attainable. However, whereas the narratives of prophets centred on the relation between a community and God, a sovereign's narrative focuses on its own law. Explicating and justifying the law is therefore a means of explaining a community to itself by interpreting its needs and possibilities in terms that it can accept and put into practice.

The parallel between sovereign and prophet is confirmed in a note to the *Theological-Political Treatise* which points out that, rather as a prophet's authority rests on a revelation that an audience cannot experience for itself but has to accept, so the sovereign's authority cannot be derived from the law but must be accepted as its source (TTP I n. 4 [ADN.II]; III/16). In each case authority stems from the very act of giving meaning, whether in the form of revelation or law, and in each case survival or power depends on the ability to perform this action in a way that is compelling and practically efficacious. The prophet who cannot convince his people that the divine law has been revealed to him, thereby persuading them to do as he says, ceases to be a prophet; and the sovereign who cannot impose his authority by getting subjects to obey the civil law ceases to be a sovereign (TTP XVII.2; III/201).

In many states, past and present, politics largely proceeds in imaginative terms. Sovereigns legitimate the law by means of narratives and images that they and their subjects find compelling, thus uniting individuals whose passions are otherwise conflicting and disparate. Spinoza evidently believes this strategy can work extremely well; for example, the success of the Jewish state under Moses was primarily due to his imaginative power, which far outstripped his understanding of nature. However, there are also cases in which the efficacy of imagination and the demands of philosophical understanding conflict and have to be reconciled. This problem is explored at an individual level in Book IV of the *Ethics*, where Spinoza outlines the characteristics of the free man. He is someone who does his best to live as his understanding dictates, and cultivates the two key virtues of *animositas* (the determination to preserve his being) and *generositas* (the determination to cooperate with others) (E IIIp59s; II/188). Nevertheless, in the course of his everyday life he has to deal with people whose understanding is less extensive than his own, and who are therefore apt to engage with him in passionate and potentially destructive ways. Building on Spinoza's own account of this predicament, we can imagine a free man who has been given special treatment by a merchant and expects the favour to be returned. The free man knows that partiality can generate envy and suspicion, and wishes he had been able to avoid the favour; but since it has been incurred, he has to decide how to respond. If he refuses to reciprocate, the merchant will feel angry and resentful, and cooperating with him will become more difficult. So, taking account of what is *utile* as well as what is in line with *ratio,* the free man concludes that the best course will be to return the favour in some way that is legal (and so does not undermine the authority of the law) yet acceptable to both parties (E IVp70; II/262–3).

In working out what to do, the free man does not insist on standards of behaviour he knows to be virtuous, bur bends to the passions he encounters. Rationality, and thus freedom, does not consist in sticking to the norms of virtue come what may, but lies in maintaining a cooperative way of life, thus keeping open the possibility of enhancing understanding. Although he feels the tension between the demand of understanding and the demand of his total situation, the free man resolves it by giving priority to maintaining harmony in the community of which he sees himself as a part (E IVp73;II/265). Moreover, his capacity to solve the problem in this way depends on his sensitivity to the imaginations of those around him, and on his appreciation of the passionate consequences of different courses of action. As individuals become more free, they lose some of their affective investment in practices that have grown up around passionate dispositions they no longer share, but they cannot turn their backs on the imagination. It is, after all, one of their objects of study, as well as an unavoidable aspect of their lives.

In the *Ethics,* Spinoza suggests that retaining a sensitivity to other people's passions while refraining from responding to them in passionate terms is a continual demand upon the wise. As he explains, 'It requires a singular power of mind to bear with each one according to his understanding, and to restrain oneself from imitating their affects' (E IV App. 13). Nonetheless, as he had earlier pointed out, it is a good rule 'to speak according to the power of understanding of ordinary people (*vulgi*), and to do whatever does not interfere with attaining our purpose. For we can gain a considerable advantage if we yield as much to their understanding as we can. In this way, they will give a favourable hearing to the truth' (TIE.17; II/9). Unless the wise accommodate themselves to the less wise by speaking and acting in terms the latter can understand, the less wise will not find the claims of reason appealing, and their reasoning will be held back. This in turn will impede their understanding of the value of cooperation, with the result that the freedom of the community as a whole will suffer. To avoid this outcome, the free man will do his best to enhance the understanding of those around him by cultivating the qualities of the prophet, and interpreting and implementing his knowledge in a manner that makes it attractive and accessible. Freedom, as Spinoza conceives it, is therefore always dependent on the extent to which particular individuals and communities are able to imagine ways of life that embody the general truths revealed by reasoning, thereby bringing cooperation within reach.

Spinoza's sketch of how the free man negotiates with others offers us an insight into the way that reason and imagination can work together to enhance cooperation and liberty. If we now return to the sphere of government, we see that a sovereign who has some understanding of the nature and purpose of the state needs to pursue a comparable policy. Just as free men aim to accommodate the passions of the people with whom they have dealings, sovereigns will do best to accommodate the passions of their subjects, while simultaneously doing all they can to encourage an appreciation of the benefits of obeying the law. As Gatens and Lloyd put the point, 'the best authority structures are ones which are realistic about the need to regulate human passions without cancelling the capacity for all to develop reason'.[7] There is, however, an important difference between the individual and political cases. Whereas a free man's pursuit of freedom is shaped by his obedience to the law, the main arena in which sovereigns aim to marry imagination and understanding is precisely that of legislation. In exercising their legal authority, they are guided by whatever knowledge of nature they possess; but they will only succeed in making the law acceptable and effective if they take account of their subjects' imaginative grasp of their own condition. For this, as we have seen, they need a share of the skills pre-eminently possessed by prophets.

III

If we accept this account of the sovereign's task, we can move on to consider whether there are reasons for thinking that democratically organized societies are better adapted to the cultivation of security and freedom than non-democratic states. To put the question in the terms we have been examining, is there any reason to think that, when sovereignty rests with the people, the law can be imaginatively represented in a way that is particularly compelling, and therefore moves subjects to obey it more willingly than otherwise? One way to reach an answer is to continue to pursue the implications of Spinoza's account of the free man. To begin with, we need to put aside the limiting case of a community made up of individuals who are so perfectly cooperative that they no longer have a use for coercion, and therefore in a sense have no need of the state. Following Spinoza's lead, we can view this condition as the unrealizable culmination of a schematically represented process in which human beings who are passionate and prone to conflict (and who therefore need a sovereign with power to coerce them) create ways of life in which they can be progressively more free. The question then is whether there is anything in this process that inclines them in the direction of democracy.

---

[7] Gatens and Lloyd 1999, 120.

We learn in the *Ethics* that freedom grows with rational understanding, which brings with it an appreciation of the need for cooperation. Free men cooperate or join themselves to others in friendship because they realize that this is the best way to foster a community capable of developing the kind of knowledge that enables individuals to limit the damaging effects of their passionate dispositions (E IVApp. xi; III/269). To some extent their undertaking is a matter of extending a community's shared grasp of universal laws of nature; but as we have seen, it is also a matter of creating circumstances in which local knowledge can be brought to bear on the task of harmonizing the desires of particular, historically situated individuals (TP III.3; III/285). What, though, are the political implications of this project? According to Spinoza, the only systematic way to moderate the destructive effects of passion, and harmonize individual interests, is to live under a sovereign in a state (E IVp73). So what sort of sovereign will free men favour? Since their ultimate aim is to include each individual in the collective enterprise of devising a cooperative way of life, and since an absolutely crucial element of such a modus vivendi is the law, free men will presumably regard as optimal a system that gives every member of the community a voice in making legislation. Democracy will have the benefit of allowing each individual to raise the quality of political debate by contributing relevant items of knowledge. Furthermore, it will enable each individual to play a part in the imaginative task of formulating laws that make sense, and are therefore effective.

Given that each embodied human being differs from every other and has a history of their own, each imagines to some extent in their own way, and can bring different experiences to bear on the collective project of creating a way of life that is secure and free. Under a democratic constitution, a state therefore increases its chance of devising laws, and indeed other institutions, that are responsive to the values and desires of its subjects and are consequently likely to be willingly obeyed. (To put this point the other way round, excluding subjects from the task of contributing to legislation endangers the security of the state by increasing the risk that its laws may turn out to be unacceptable to some sections of the population, who will therefore have to be forced to conform to them.) In addition, a democratic state can use the imaginative capacities of all its subjects to articulate the benefits of its own particular form of cooperation under the law, and to work out ways of extending the liberty of subjects. To settle for a less inclusive form of constitution would therefore be to deprive the state of the very insights it needs in order to sustain and develop a secure and harmonious way of life. Subjects who appreciate the force of this argument will recognize that democratically enacted laws reflect both the rational and imaginative resources of the community, and are liable to be well adapted to its needs. They therefore have a general reason for obeying them. Furthermore, as members of the community who share some aspects of its outlook and are comfortable with the terms in which law is justified and made intelligible, they are likely to find its particular laws relatively easy to accept and follow.

Spinoza encourages us to understand his account of the free man and the life he leads as an exemplar or model (E IV Pref.; II/206). While it sets a moral stand-ard that human beings may not be able fully to attain, it nevertheless provides a norm of perfection against which individuals and communities can measure and assess their own conceptions and enactments of the good life.[8] If we now consider what sort of political constitution would enable a community to approach this condition, we arrive at a complementary model of a democratic state. It holds out an image of a perfectly inclusive polity that is, like its moral counterpart, beyond human reach;[9] but in spite of this, it serves as a means of thinking critically and creatively about politics.[10]

Although Spinoza does not explicitly advance the view that we should think about democracy in this manner, his account of the free man's way of life undoubtedly incorporates a strong pull towards a democratic state. In addition, the *Theological-Political Treatise* contains a different argument for democracy, not as the kind of state consonant with the rich forms of freedom that emerge out of the collective pursuit of understanding and cooperation, but rather as the type of constitution it would make sense to choose if one were in a state of nature. This argument follows the lines laid down by Hobbes, who had contended in *On the Citizen* that 'when men have met to erect a commonwealth, they are, by the very fact that they have met, a *Democracy*'.[11] As soon as individuals in the state of nature come together to form a polity, they must agree to be bound by the will of the majority in choosing a sovereign to represent them; but in agreeing to this rule they have already in effect set up a democratic state. Echoing this thought, Spinoza explains that, when individuals in the state of nature transfer their right to the community, 'the right of such a social order is called a democracy', which can therefore be defined as a general assembly of men which has, as a body, the supreme right over everything within its power' (TTP XVI.25; III/193). Moreover, a democracy seems 'the most natural state, and the one which approaches most

---

[8] See Gatens 2012. The view that the image of democratic society implicit in the *Ethics* functions as an exemplar offers a response to Verbeek's claim that democracy is for Spinoza a nostalgic ideal. See Verbeek 2003, 141.

[9] See Matheron 1994, 164.

[10] This interpretation offers a way to understand Spinoza's claim that sovereignty is defined by the power of the multitude (TP 2.17; III/282). Compare Negri 1997. In keeping with the interpretation offered here, Balibar describes democracy as 'the "truth" of every political order, in relation to which the internal consistency, causes and ultimate tendencies of constitutions can be assessed.' Balibar 1998, 33.

[11] 'When men have met to erect a commonwealth, they are, by the very fact that they have met, a *Democracy*. From the fact that they have gathered voluntarily, they are understood to be bound by the decisions made by the agreement of the majority. And that is a democracy, as long as the convention lasts, or is set to reconvene at certain times and places. For a convention whose will is the will of all the citizens has sovereign power. And because it is assumed that each man in this convention has the right to vote, it is a Democracy...' Hobbes 1998, ch. 7, sect. 5. Kinch Hoekstra points out that Hobbes is talking here about the origin of 'commonwealths by institution' and not 'commonwealths by acquisi-tion,' and is therefore not claiming that all commonwealths start out as democracies. See Hoekstra 2006, 207–9.

nearly the freedom that nature concedes to everyone. In it, no one so transfers his natural right to another that in the future there is no consultation with him. Instead, he transfers it to the greatest part of the whole society, of which he makes one part. In this way everyone remain equal, as they were before, in a state of nature' (TTP XVI.36; III/195).

Here the emphasis is not so much on the collective benefit of giving all subjects a voice in the process of making the law as on the individual disadvantage of being excluded from this process. The argument invites us to address the issue in the light of our natural inclination to conceive of ourselves as separate individuals, and to focus on the question of how best to maintain our right or power. When we view ourselves in this light, we are led to see that democracy is in a sense the most minimal form of state, where individuals retain as much right as possible. And from the perspective of the state of nature, this is the state to choose. In a community where sovereignty is vested in all the citizens, and laws are sanctioned by common consent, each person can bind themselves to follow the law; and in a sense no one need obey it, since obedience consists in carrying out orders simply by reason of the authority of one who commands. If we put this argument together with the case for democracy as a political ideal, democracy emerges, conceptually speaking, as the first and last form of state. It marks the most natural transition from the state of nature because it best preserves our natural right; and it is also most consonant with the forms of freedom that emerge from the shared understanding and mutual cooperation of subjects.

Why, then, are there any non-democratic states? When Hobbes addresses this question in *On the Citizen* he outlines the various transfers of power through which democracies can be transformed into aristocracies or monarchies.[12] Spinoza approaches the problem from a different angle by dwelling on the gap between a principled defence of democracy and the qualities that are in practice needed to create and sustain a democratic sovereign. As we have seen, it takes a certain imagination and understanding to realize a democratic way of life, and in communities where this is lacking the form of life will be unsustainable. Even if we allow Hobbes's point that some political societies start out as democracies, a democratic constitution will only endure if a particular community is able to maintain it. Although the potential benefits of democracy militate in its favour, they do not by themselves ensure that a given political society will be attracted by them, or guarantee that existing democratic states will be successful. Everything will depend on the history and circumstances of the relevant community and its members.[13] Spinoza illustrates these points by appealing to various historical

---

[12] Hobbes, 1998, ch. 7, sects 8 and 11.

[13] Matheron argues that obstacles to democracy are always external to the power of the multitude. 'The existence of every non-democratic regime is explained by the conjunction of two factors: on the one hand, the power of the multitude, which desires to live in common agreement, which consequently attempts to find a terrain of understanding among all its members, which thus attempts to

cases. First, democracies are not always stable. For instance, when the Jews escaped from slavery they proved psychologically unequal to self-government and, out of fear, abandoned their attempt to form a democracy in favour of a kind of theocratic monarchy under the rule of Moses (TTP XVII.27; III/205). Or to take another example, this time mentioned in the *Political Treatise*, a democracy may turn itself into an aristocracy by deciding to exclude a class of aliens from government, as Venice did (TP VIII.12; III/329).[14]

In neither of these cases is it clear that Spinoza regards the movement away from democracy as a turn for the worse. He praises the Jewish state as exceptionally peaceful and long-lived; and, judging from the *Political Treatise*, he is also convinced that well-designed aristocracies can be stable and harmonious (TP VIII.7; III/326). Transitions from a more to a less inclusive form of constitution are therefore not necessarily to be deplored, and in some circumstances a non-democratic form of government may be better able to guarantee security, and thus a degree of liberty, than a democratic one. Equally, transitions in the other direction are, in Spinoza's view, not always beneficial. For example, he observes, when the English executed their king and set up a republic in 1649, they turned out to lack the understanding and imagination needed to make their new constitution stable, and after a short time reverted to a monarchy (TTP XVIII.33–4; III/227).[15] On the whole, then, 'the form of each state must necessarily be retained, and cannot be changed without a danger that the whole state will be ruined' (TTP XVIII.37: III/228).

In assessing a state of any type, we therefore need to consider how successfully its sovereign is fulfilling its task. (How far is it managing to make laws that are obeyed, and how lively is its subjects' sense of the benefits of cooperation?) As a claim about security, this view makes a certain amount of sense; but as a claim about the freedom with which security is supposed to be yoked, it may be harder to accept. Surely, one might object, the subjects of an absolute ruler such as Moses, who play no role in making the law, are bound to be less free than those of a democratic sovereign. Still worse, it might be argued that the prophetic basis of

---

organise itself into a democracy; and on the other hand, external causes that prevent it from directly realizing this tendency and obligate it to satisfy it by diverted paths and by resorting to a mediator' (Matheron 1997, 217). I think this interpretation underestimates the extent to which the obstacles that prevent states from moving towards a freer way of life can in Spinoza's view be constitutive of what Matheron calls the power of the multitude, rather than external to it.

[14] The Aristotelian view that different constitutions suit different societies was not uncommon in seventeenth-century Holland. For example, it was advocated in the 1640s at the University of Leiden by Franco Burgersdijk, who argued that, although democracy is by nature the most imperfect form of state, there can be conditions where it is preferable to the alternatives. The same view was defended a decade later by Boxhorn, who held that no particular form of government is the best in all circumstances. See Burgersdijk 1686, 189–90 (cited by Blom 1995, 97). See also Boxhornius 1657, 4 (cited by Wansink 1981, 100).

[15] The harm purportedly done by the English civil war is even more vividly portrayed by De la Court: 1662: Part III, Book III, ch. 6.

the Jewish state encouraged utter subservience to God and Moses, thus holding back the growth of understanding.

To appreciate Spinoza's response, we need to distinguish his model of ideal democracy from the particular democratic societies that have been, and might be, established in the course of human history. Subjects whose way of life approaches the standard of the first will indeed possess more freedom than is possible under an absolute monarchy or indeed any other form of non-democratic constitution; but Spinoza's examples, together with his warnings about the way that passions such as fear and the need for admiration can undermine political stability, remind us that democracies can also fail. Where a democratic sovereign and subjects cannot between them create basic forms of security, and therefore find themselves in a situation they experience as unacceptably precarious, they may as a matter of fact abandon their constitution for one that is less inclusive. Furthermore, it is possible that, under their new form of government, they may achieve forms of cooperation that were lacking earlier on, and that constitute an increase in freedom.

IV

A troublesome feature of Spinoza's argument is the implicit suggestion that the subjects of any state, however oppressive, can be said to be free. Is it, then, impossible to live under a sovereign, however dysfunctional, and be *unfree*? Drawing on a republican discourse stemming from Roman Law, Spinoza couches this question in terms of the difference between subjects and slaves. Will people say, he wonders, that subjects who are bound to obey the sovereign have in effect been reduced to a condition of slavery (TTP XVI.32; III/194)? A long line of republican writers had defined a slave as someone who is subject to the arbitrary power of another agent, and had argued that a sovereign exercises arbitrary power when it is in a position to enforce laws to which its subjects have not consented. For example, when a monarch makes use of prerogative powers it turns its subjects into slaves; but when the citizens of a republic are bound by laws to which they have agreed, including laws licensing punishment, they remain free men.[16] Spinoza both appeals to and modifies this position by implicitly reinterpreting its understanding of the distinction between arbitrary and non-arbitrary power. In order to determine whether subjects are free men or slaves, he argues, one must ask whether the law serves the common good. If it does, subjects remain free. Only when the law fails to meet this condition are they enslaved. By implication, then, a sovereign whose laws serve the common good does not exercise arbitrary power, and its capacity to coerce its citizens does not remove their liberty.

[16] See Pettit, 1997; Skinner 1998.

This argument is open to more than one interpretation. Concentrating on what they call the democratic *conatus* within Spinoza's philosophical system, commentators such as Negri and Matheron have inferred that only a democratically made law can serve the good of the community as a whole.[17] In order to be free, a man must play a part in making laws that bind each individual to act for the common good, and for his own good (TTP XVI.33; III/194–5). This reading accords with Spinoza's image of exemplary democracy, and helps to explicate the rich form of freedom that such a polity can guarantee. However, it neglects a crucial dimension of Spinoza's discussion. If it were the case that the common good is protected only when the law is made by a democratic sovereign, then the only way to escape slavery would be to live in a democracy. But this is not the conclusion Spinoza draws. Instead, echoing the Roman Law, he appeals to the analogy between a sovereign and a father to indicate how it is possible for subjects to be free while also being bound to obey laws they have not made. Fathers, Spinoza assumes, have a paternal duty to look after their sons by directing them to act in ways that will benefit them, and sons are correspondingly obliged to obey their fathers' commands. When a son fails to recognize that it is in his interest to do what his father tells him, his father may force him to obey, and in these circumstances he is subject to coercion. The son is not *sui iuris*; but as long as his father has his interests at heart, he is not enslaved (TTP XVI.35: III/195).[18] Similarly, a sovereign may have to coerce individuals into obeying the law; but as long as it enforces laws that protect the welfare of the people, it rules over subjects rather than slaves.

By setting a minimum standard for what is to count as liberty, this view secures the possibility that subjects can be free in nondemocratic states. It therefore offers a means to characterize the inhabitants of at least some aristocracies and monarchies as free. In addition, however, it provides a way to justify the view that some subjects should be prohibited from contributing to the business of legislation. Spinoza's analysis of the relationship between fathers and sons presumably also applies to the various classes of people who, even in the democratic constitution broached at the end of the *Political Treatise,* are held to be ineligible to play a part in making the law: servants, minors, wards, women, poor men, aliens, criminals, and other dishonourable persons.[19] Individuals who fall into one or more of these categories are excluded from politics. Yet as long as the law secures the common good and thus their own good, they remain free. Some of them,

[17] See for example Matheron 1997, 216–17, and Negri: 'In Spinoza the conception of the magistrate and the magistracy…is absolutely unitary…Just as each subject is a citizen, so each citizen is a magistrate—but the magistracy is the moment of revelation of the highest potential of unity and freedom.' Negri, 1997, 227–8:

[18] This argument rides on a Latin pun. Sons who are not enslaved remain *liberi,* which means both 'free persons' and 'children'.

[19] These exclusions are sometimes glossed over. See for example Israel 2001, 206. Their incongruity with other aspects of Spinoza's philosophy is powerfully illuminated by Matheron 1977, Gatens 1996, Gatens 2000, Montag 1999,83–6, Gatens and Lloyd 2009, Sharp 2012. See also James 2018.

such as married women and servants, have simultaneous duties to obey other authorities, such as husbands or masters; but although this gives them a distinctive legal status, it does not of itself turn them into slaves.

In defining the lower boundary of a free way of life, Spinoza offers sovereigns and subjects a guiding principle: if slavery is to be avoided, the law must uphold the common good. However, as we have come to expect, this principle stands in need of interpretation. In making the law, a sovereign relies on its imaginative capacity to envisage legal arrangements that it and its subjects can recognize and accept as a credible representation of the common good; and where it is success- ful, subjects will be able to conceive of themselves as free. Drawing on the *Ethics,* we can envisage an ideal democracy where the sovereign, constituted by the whole body of the people, guarantees its own common good. Not only does each subject participate in making legislation, but because the members of the com- munity appreciate the advantages of cooperation, they do all they can to devise laws that reconcile divergent desires and enhance their collective efforts to enrich their own freedom. In his other works, however, Spinoza offers a more cautious account of what it takes to satisfy his conception of political liberty. The *Theological-Political Treatise* defends the view that sovereign monarchs and aris- tocratic assemblies need not enslave their subjects, and may provide them with as much freedom and security as they are capable of attaining. The *Political Treatise* offers us an image of a democratic constitution where only a proportion of male subjects make the law, and represent the voices of politically invisible classes such as women and servants (TP XI. 3–4; III/359–60). Here, then, a sub- set of the population is exclusively invested with the capacity to determine the common good.

So while democracy functions for Spinoza as an exemplar or ideal on the basis of which we can try to enlarge our freedom, he also holds that it can only exist in certain circumstances. The secure freedom that states should aim to create depends on the understandings and imaginations of particular communities, and only some of them are in a position to sustain a democratic way of life. Where the resources needed to manage this are lacking, a community may maximize the freedom and security available to it under a non-democratic constitution. A sen- sitivity to the imaginative demands of politics therefore shapes Spinoza's view of constitutional forms such as monarchy and aristocracy. But in a different way it also moulds his treatment of democracy itself.

Against the inclusive spirit of his democratic exemplar, the *Political Treatise* defends what is to modern eyes an incomplete form of democracy. This limitation is worth examining; for although, as many commentators have pointed out, it is unsurprising that Spinoza should hold the view he does, his account of the demo- cratic state nevertheless provides a vivid illustration of the extent to which our freedom depends on our imaginative capacities. As we have seen, Spinoza's philo- sophical writings contain a subtle and suggestive exploration of the role of imagination in politics. Nevertheless, when he comes to envisage a democracy—a society in which the whole body of the people makes laws that answer to the common good—he excludes a large segment of the population. The body of the people, as he interprets it, just *is* a community of propertied men, and the implication that the common good can be upheld by the laws they make does not appear to cause him any disquiet. Viewed from the perspective of the democratic ideal, this interpretation embodies a grave imaginative failure; it falls short of envisaging the kind of truly inclusive democracy in which, as we learn from the *Ethics,* freedom and security are most fully realized. But it also illustrates one of Spinoza's most central claims: that successful democracies crucially depend on the imaginative abilities of their sovereigns and subjects, and that lack of imaginative power is among the chief factors that hold them back.

9

Freedom, Slavery, and the Passions

I

In the *Ethics* Spinoza offers us a model of the good life that we can use as a measure of human perfection: living well consists in conducting our lives as far as possible on the basis of a correct grasp of the abilities and weaknesses of human beings, together with a true understanding of the world they inhabit.[1] A person who achieves this form of existence becomes what Spinoza calls a free man, who lives 'according to the dictate of reason alone' (E IVp37s1; II/236). Although this ideal consists in the possession of reason or understanding, it is also characterized by the absence of something that Spinoza regards as an imperfection, namely the dominance of affects or passions, whether negative ones such as envy and hatred or their positive counterparts such as love and joy. The passions are therefore viewed as obstacles to freedom, and as long as we are unable to control and transcend them there is a sense in which we are enslaved. 'Man's lack of power to moderate and restrain the affects I call bondage [*servitus*]. For the man who is subject to affects is under the control, not of himself, but of fortune, in whose power he so greatly is that often, though he sees the better for himself, he is still forced to follow the worse' (E IV Pref.; II/205). Correspondingly, only insofar as we counteract our passions can we be said to be free.

In defending this alignment of reason with liberty and passion with slavery Spinoza is reiterating an outlook at least as old as Plato, for whom the mind is like a chariot pulled by two horses, one biddable and the other unruly.[2] The biddable horse obeys the charioteer's commands, but the unruly horse, which represents the passions, goes its own way. The charioteer struggles to control it, but when he is unsuccessful the unruly horse gets the upper hand and determines what happens to the chariot and its driver. Just as the charioteer is unable to govern the horse, so we are often unable to govern our passions and the actions that flow from them. They are things that happen to us rather than things we do; or, to put the point in Spinoza's terms, they enslave us by preventing us from acting virtuously in accordance with reason.

---

[1] Originally published in in Olli Koistinen ed., *The Cambridge Companion to Spinoza's 'Ethics'* (Cambridge University Press, 2009), pp. 223–41. Reprinted with permission of Cambridge University Press.

    I am grateful to Olli Koistinen for his helpful comments on an earlier draft of this essay.

[2] Plato 1997, 530–3, 253c–7.

Against this view, Aristotle had protested that some passions, such as fear of shame or righteous anger, are not in the least enslaving but are integral to a good life. The key to virtue is to be able to discriminate between morally appropriate and inappropriate passions, and to act as the former dictate. Aristotle's influential claim was accepted by many of Spinoza's contemporaries, and he himself recognizes its force. He allows that a man whose passions are based on inductively well-grounded judgments about the things he encounters is better off than someone whose judgments are fantastical; he recognizes that the passions play a vital role in the process of becoming free; and he agrees that a free life has an affective dimension. The passions are therefore by no means an unmitigated moral disaster. Nevertheless, he is adamant that an Aristotelian conception of virtue falls short in its failure to recognize that even the most constructive passions are manifestations of a lack of self-control and are thus obstructions to the kind of freedom he is advocating. As long as we remain subject to them we are not fully in charge of what we feel and do; and to the extent that we lack this form of control we remain slaves.

As its opponents have pointed out ever since antiquity, Spinoza's position is a perplexing one. To be sure, our passions can sweep us about, as Spinoza puts it, like waves driven by contrary winds (E IIIp59s; II/188). For example, when mired in depression or extremely angry we do indeed sometimes feel we have been taken over by something we cannot control, and in the face of which we are passive. However, not all our affects answer to this description. We cheerfully identify with many of our everyday loves, hatreds, and desires, and whether or not we regard them as morally virtuous they have a more active feel about them. Given this phenomenological diversity, is it not perverse to insist that whenever we experience a passion we are being controlled? A second line of objection stems from the moral significance we ordinarily attach to passions of different kinds. If, as Spinoza believes, the life of the free man is a life of virtue, will it not include passions such as the ones that Aristotle identifies? Surely the free man will, for example, fear shame, hate injustice, and love his friends? But if we then stigmatize these aspects of his character by classifying them as a form of slavery, do we not ride roughshod over a significant ethical distinction between virtuous and vicious affects, and condemn ourselves to an impoverished ideal of the good life?

In his *Ethics*, Spinoza confronts and answers these objections. With characteristic thoroughness, he offers us a way to understand the claim that the passions enslave, and sketches an ideal kind of freedom in which their power to determine our lives is overcome. In a sense, then, we are left with nothing to worry about. But despite the elegance and consistency with which he integrates his conception of slavery into his philosophical system, the system itself fuels a nagging doubt. As the *Ethics* explains, humans are essentially embodied, and their passions are their experience of the way that their bodies are acted on by external things (E IIIp3; II/145). Moreover, because their survival depends on numerous interactions such as with different foods or other people, passions cannot be avoided. 'Man is necessarily always subject to passions' (E IVp4c; II/213). To some extent, then, slavery is an inevitable part of human existence. The freedom that Spinoza recommends is not fully attainable, and the model of the good life that he holds out to us will always be offset by *servitus*.

At this point, Spinoza's readers may feel torn between competing responses. On the one hand, the conviction that perfect liberty is incompatible with human corporeality has a long history and a deep appeal. Perhaps this is the tradition of thought to which Spinoza is contributing, and nothing more need be said. On the other hand, there is something paradoxical and even sadistic about an image of the good life that will in practice always be at least in part a life of slavery. What drives a philosopher, one might wonder, so to define his terms that he is inexorably brought to this conclusion? Why must one accept slavery as the other face of freedom? The *Ethics* is of course designed to rule out and discredit such questions by presenting its conclusions as the fruit of incontrovertible inferences grounded on self-evident axioms and definitions. To feel the need to ask why the argument is set up in a particular way is to have failed to follow it. However, in spite of this internal discouragement, a reader may still be curious to know where Spinoza acquired the components of his philosophical armour, and what prompted him to assemble them as he did. The thinking that resulted in his extraordinary and path-finding system was, after all, partly about existing philosophical positions and the problems they created, and a grasp of these antecedents may enable us not only to reconstruct the intellectual milieu with which he was engaging, but also to enrich our understanding of his claims.

In this essay I propose that we can gain a fuller appreciation of Spinoza's reasons for conceiving freedom and slavery as he does by considering the definitions of these terms that drive the argument of the *Ethics* in the light of an early modern conception of *political* liberty. Spinoza holds that a true knowledge of the principles of ethics and politics can be deduced from knowledge of God (TTP IV.10–12; III, 59–60), and this is indeed the direction of argument he follows in his *magnum opus*. However, we do not have to assume that this order of exposition is the only one capable of revealing how his system hangs together, and we may find it equally fruitful to argue in the other direction, from the political to the ethical and metaphysical. By starting with the political, I aim to show, we can gain a fuller appreciation of what it is about the passions that enslaves and what it takes to escape from slavery. In addition, we can gain a better understanding of why Spinoza needs to address this conception of slavery at all. The *Ethics*, I shall argue, brings together a view of political slavery that played a major part in seventeenth-century Dutch political debate with a broader conception of the passions as impediments to freedom. One of Spinoza's projects is to show how these two views can be integrated into a single, overarching conception of slavery and its positive counterpart, freedom.

II

In the European republics of the seventeenth century, the notion of slavery had strong political connotations. As the Dutch had occasion to argue during the period of their subjection to Spain, conquest could turn a free nation into a nation of slaves.[3] Moreover, it was widely assumed, individual subjects could be enslaved by their own government when it ruled for its own good rather than for that of the people. Sustaining both these claims was an enduring conception of slavery that had been influentially articulated in the *Digest* of the Roman law.[4] According to this account, a slave is someone who is subject to the power of another and is thus unable to act in accordance with his own will or *arbitrium*. By contrast, a free man is not subject to the power of anyone else and can therefore live *sui iuris*, in accordance with his own will. In the case of an individual slave who is subject to a master, one way for the master to exercise his power is to coerce the slave into doing his bidding. However, the *Digest* assumes, the presence of coercion is not what makes the slave unfree. While it may make him unfree to act, it is not what makes him an unfree person. His status as a slave rests on the fact that he is at his master's mercy, a situation that continues to obtain even if the master does not choose to exercise his power. A happy slave, for example, may never have to act against his own interests; but his ability to do what he wants nevertheless remains conditional on his master's will and pleasure, and this is what reduces him to slavery.

In the works of the Roman moralists and historians, this conception of servitude was applied to the relationship between subjects and rulers. When rulers possess enough power to make and enforce laws as they please, their subjects are at their mercy in just the way that the individual slave is at the mercy of his master. A ruler may or may not choose to oppress his subjects; but in either case, the ability of subjects to pursue their interests depends on his discretion. They therefore satisfy the conditions of slavery, and are in fact enslaved. Among Roman writers, this contention gave rise to a debate about the kind of state that can best uphold the free status of subjects, and due to the ready availability of the works of authors such as Livy, Sallust, Seneca, and Tacitus, the issue remained central to political discussion in early modern Europe. Moreover, the controversy surrounding it received a new lease of life from the writings of Machiavelli, who used the Roman view in his *Discorsi* on Livy's history to rework and reiterate the claim that it is only possible to be a free man as opposed to a slave if one lives in a free state.[5]

What exactly is a free state? Although there was no agreement, in the Netherlands or anywhere else, about the precise form of constitution that answered to this

---

[3] See van Gelderen 1992, 117.   [4] Mommsen and Krueger 1985, I. v. 4 (1).
[5] Machiavelli 1996, 129–30.

description, the tradition of thought originating in Roman moral and legal theory bequeathed an account of the essential features of a polity made up of free men. As we have seen, the main predicament to be avoided was one in which a ruler could enslave a community of subjects by virtue of possessing the power to subject them to his arbitrary will. Most authors who took this requirement seriously were of the view that freedom is incompatible with government by an absolute monarch, or by a monarch who holds prerogative and hence discretionary powers. This antimonarchical position was in turn taken up in Holland during the latter part of the seventeenth century and used against pro-Orangist defenders of mixed constitutions, notably by the De la Court brothers, with whose writings Spinoza was familiar.[6] Even after monarchy had been put aside, however, there remained a question as to what sort of constitutional checks and balances could ensure that sovereigns could not rule in accordance with their arbitrary will. If we again consider the individual slave and remember that his servitude consists in his subjection to a power that is not constrained to take account of his interests, we can see that becoming free is for him a matter of becoming subject to his own power as opposed to that of his master, whether through manumission, escape, or revolt. So what we are looking for in the case of political freedom is a form of state in which individual subjects retain the power to act in accordance with their own wills, while at the same time living under the law. The traditional solution to this problem proposes that one can remain a free man within the state as long as one plays a part in making the law, thus ensuring that it reflects one's will. When the law is to this extent made in accordance with one's will, one can willingly obey it. The constraints it imposes on one's actions are consequently not imposed by a ruler, or indeed by anyone else, and therefore do not reduce one to servitude.

How can this kind of freedom be achieved? According to its defenders, political liberty can exist only where there is some form of popular sovereignty. Although there is still plenty of room to argue about the pros and cons of different types of constitution, the two essential requirements for any kind of free state are that the law alone should rule (and hence that there should be no discretionary powers) and that all citizens should in some sense participate in making the law. Only where these conditions are met can they properly be described as free men rather than slaves.

III

In the *Theological-Political Treatise*, Spinoza argues that freedom is the paramount value of political life. The ultimate purpose of the *res publica*, he writes, 'is not to dominate, restraining men by fear and making them subject to another's control,

---

[6] De la Court 1972. See also Scott 2002, Prokhovnik 2004.

but on the contrary to free each person from fear so that he can live securely as far as possible...It is not, I say, to change men from rational beings into beasts or automata, but to enable their minds and bodies to perform their functions safely, to enable them to use their reason freely; and not to clash with one another in hatred, anger or deception, or deal inequitably with one another. So the end of the Republic is really freedom' (TTP XX.5; III/241). Furthermore, political freedom can be achieved only when individuals are governed by a sovereign power that is prevented from acting arbitrarily. When a person is bound to obey commands that are concerned only with the advantage of the person issuing the command, Spinoza explains, then 'he is a slave, useless to himself'. However, 'in a Republic, and a state where the supreme law is the well-being of the whole people, not that of the ruler, someone who obeys the supreme power in everything should not be called a slave, useless to himself, but a subject' (TTP XVI.34; III/195).

Political freedom, as Spinoza presents it here, depends on two separable conditions, one of them necessary and the other highly desirable. First, in order to be free, one must live in a state where the law upholds the common good; or, as the *Theological-Political Treatise* puts it, where the supreme law is the well-being of the people. Within the tradition we have been examining, many authors argue that this requirement is satisfied only when the subjects of a free state *make* the law, because this is the sole means of ensuring that the law expresses their will. Spinoza, however, does not share this opinion. The important thing, in his view, is that the law should avoid arbitrariness by upholding the good of the people as opposed to that of the ruler, and the good of all the people as opposed to that of a particular faction. A free state will therefore need institutions capable of guaranteeing that this requirement is satisfied. Giving subjects the responsibility of making the law is certainly one mechanism for achieving freedom, and there is evidence that Spinoza regards it as optimal. 'Obedience has no place in a social order where sovereignty is in the hands of everyone and laws are enacted by common consent' (TTP V.25; III/74). But because other institutional mechanisms may do the same job, no single type of constitution is essential to the existence of political liberty.[7]

The subjects of a state therefore cannot be free unless the law upholds their common good; but the quality of freedom that this alone yields is comparatively thin. Inserting a second condition, Spinoza adds that, in order to make their liberty more resilient, subjects must grasp the opportunity that this kind of law presents by obeying it willingly. Here again, his approach is cautious. It is perfectly possible, he concedes, to be a free subject whilst being made to obey the law against one's will, as long as the law does in fact protect the interests that one shares with other subjects. 'An action done on a command—obedience—does,

---

[7] For example, in the TTP (17.26–40; III/205–6) Spinoza allows that the Jewish theocracy lifted the Jews out of slavery.

in some measure, take away freedom. But that isn't what makes a slave.' (TTP XVI.33; III/194). However, even though a subject who obeys the law unwillingly (for example, because he fears punishment) is not actually enslaved, his unwillingness is nevertheless an obstacle to the development of a stronger type of liberty. First, his grudging obedience may endanger or undermine the institutions essential to the freedom of the state. If his attitudes or behaviour make it difficult or impossible to enforce the common good, the law itself may become the creature of the sovereign or of a faction, in which case subjecthood will degenerate into slavery. Second, a subject who obeys out of fear is *like* a slave. As Spinoza puts it, 'he who acts from fear of evil is compelled by evil, acts like a slave, and lives under the command of another' (TTP IV.38 III/66).

This latter claim draws on a further classical argument to the effect that living as a slave has predictable psychological consequences, so that slaves tend to be slavish. An individual who is under the command of a master and subject to his will is in a position of dependence, and lacks the power effectively to protect his own interests. At the limit, a master may have the legal right to kill him on a whim. In circumstances of such insecurity, slaves will as a rule fear their masters and do their best to placate them by any available means. Cringing, flattery, and deception consequently become their stock in trade, and form the elements of a character type that had been explored by Roman moralists and playwrights, as well as by their early modern followers. Echoing this discussion in both the Preface to the *Theological-Political Treatise* and the *Ethics*,[8] Spinoza, too, condemns the superstition and hypocrisy that arise from fear and threaten the liberty of the state. Acting from fear of evil does indeed make us slavish. So although a man who is forced to obey a law that upholds his interests may possess a degree of liberty, his character is liable to reflect the fact that he does not yet have the fuller form of freedom attained by those who obey the law willingly.

Why, though, is willing the law thought to have such a transformative effect? The answer rests on the assumption that, in order to consistently and voluntarily obey the law, one must understand why it is in one's interest to do so. Even if particular laws are not to one's liking, life under a law that upholds the common good is the best of the available options because it is the only effective protection against slavery. A subject who recognizes this fact will therefore see that it is in his interests to obey, and his understanding of his situation will move him to obey willingly.

Becoming free by coming to appreciate the benefits of conforming to the law's demands also brings about further attitudes and affects that are characteristic of free men. Where the law guarantees subjects the independence and security that slaves lack, they are not subject to arbitrary powers over which they have no

---

[8] 'Flattery also gives rise to harmony, but by the foul crime of bondage, or by treachery' (E IVApp. xxi; II/272).

control, and consequently have no need to resort to flattery or hypocrisy in their dealings with one another. As long as they respect legal limits, they can act as they wish and speak their own minds. Thus sustained, they can live well. They can be just and honourable and can play a constructive part in maintaining the free state with which their individual liberty is inextricably bound up.

When these two conditions of political liberty are met, subjects are independent both in the sense that they are not subject to arbitrary power, and in the sense that obeying the law does not limit their individual freedom to act as they think best. This latter point is important. A subject who so internalizes the reasons for obeying the law that he would act as it dictates even if he were not commanded to do so is held to bring about a fundamental change in his situation. Instead of submitting to a command, and thus to the will of the sovereign as represented by the law, he acts in accordance with his own will. Instead of allowing the law to determine his action, he determines the course of events for himself. So although the legal command is still in place, there is a sense in which it has become powerless, because it no longer determines his actions. And because being a free man is, by definition, not being under the will of another, the subject is a free man with respect to the law.

If we now return to the earlier case of the man who obeys the law out of fear of punishment, we can see that the quality of his liberty does not approach that of the free man. From an institutional point of view he is free as long as the law upholds his interests, but from an individual point of view his course of action is determined by the force of the law. In this respect, then, he remains subject to the power of another, and is to this extent like a slave.

This argument implies, as Machiavelli had insisted, that it is possible to be fully free only in a free state in which the law upholds the common good.[9] Human beings are, in Spinoza's view, incapable of desiring states of affairs that they regard as fundamentally detrimental to their advantage. So a law that fails to protect the shared interests of those subjects who are bound by it cannot win their whole-hearted, collective consent. Whether a sovereign forces them to act against their interests, or merely has the power to do so, their obedience will be accompanied by dissatisfaction or anxiety. In these circumstances they cannot release themselves from subjection to the law by obeying it out of a justified confidence that it can be relied on to uphold their interests, and thus cannot live as free men.

IV

If the two claims set out in the previous section capture the crucial elements of what it is to be a slave and what it is to become a *liber homo* or free person, we can go on to ask whether this model has a wider application. This is one of the

---

[9] Machiavelli 1996, Book II.ii.

questions Spinoza implicitly sets out to answer in the *Ethics*. Taking up the analysis of political liberty that he and many other supporters of Dutch republican government had advocated, he aims to show that, as well as illuminating the relationship between a subject and the law, it can cast light on what it means to stand in a free relationship to all external things. The account of political liberty on which we have so far been concentrating thus becomes a single application of a more comprehensive theory of human freedom, which spells out the general principles underlying the political case.

This project is guided by a sensitivity to the peculiar blend of dependence and independence that characterizes political liberty. Because it is only possible to be free when one lives in a free state, the freedom of individual subjects is inevitably dependent on a feature of their external circumstances: the existence of legal institutions of a certain type. These institutions create a form of independence that is sufficient to defeat the threat of slavery by ensuring that subjects are not at the mercy of the arbitrary exercise of sovereign power. In addition, they contribute to the conditions for achieving a further type of independence, which comes from obeying the law because one understands that one has good reason to do so. In order to extend the model to cover not just our relationship with the law, but also our relationship with the whole of our environment, Spinoza therefore needs to identify some analogue of these forms of dependence and independence.

Initially, it seems extremely unlikely that such an account will be forthcoming. Throughout much of the *Ethics*, Spinoza emphasizes the numerous ways in which human beings are dependent on (or as he puts it, acted on by) external things in ways that are beyond their control. We are surrounded by things that are much more powerful than ourselves and are often unable 'to adapt things outside us to our use' (E IVApp. xxxii; II/276). It is true that we can to some extent modify our natural environment in order to diminish the threats it poses; but we can never completely overcome its capacity to act on us in ways that may or may not be to our advantage, and whose effect on us is in this sense arbitrary. It is because our ability to live securely and healthily lies outside our control and is always to some degree precarious that the goods of health and security are referred to gifts of fortune (TTP III.13; III/47). So although we are at least potentially capable of creating legal systems that enable us to live freely by guaranteeing the social and political interests that we share with others, we cannot eradicate our vulnerability to death, disease, and other natural threats. To this extent, we are bound to be dependent on the power of nature, and insofar as its effects may or may not serve our interests, they are arbitrary (E IVp4; II/213).

Furthermore, this form of dependence is in Spinoza's view constitutive of our passions. When an external body acts on the body of an individual human being, it has an effect on their body that is determined partly by the nature of the external body and partly by the nature of the human body (E IIp16c2; II/104). The nature or essence of each body is to be conceived in Spinoza's view as its *conatus* or striving to persevere in its being (E IIIp7; II/146). As one body acts on the other, each strives to maintain the pattern, of motion and rest by which it is constituted, and in this process the human body's capacity to maintain itself may be increased or reduced. For example, an encounter with a cluster of bacteria may diminish the body's power by causing a bad sore throat, whereas digesting a food that is rich in vitamins may enhance its ability to ward off infection.

Such changes are always experienced by one's mind, which has ideas of everything that happens to one's body, including the ways it is empowered or disempowered by interactions with external things. Like the body, the mind strives to persevere in its being, and its ability to do so is shaped by its ideas of the body's interactions with other things. When the body is affected in a debilitating way, as in the case of the sore throat, the mind experiences a parallel reduction of its power to persevere in its being and feels this as some kind of sadness. By contrast, when an interaction with an external thing empowers the body, the mind is also empowered and experiences some kind of joy. Its attempts to relate to its ideas of external things in ways that are empowering therefore manifest themselves as passions or affects, organized around the fundamental categories of desire, sadness, and joy (EIIIp11; II/148).

In registering the way our bodies are affected, the passions chart a form of dependence. We experience affects, Spinoza insists, when we are acted on by external things. However, the mere fact of dependence is not enough to enslave us to our passions. As we have seen, political slavery is not constituted by the mere fact that we are subject to the law; rather, it comes into being when the law is arbitrary. In Spinoza's analysis of the passions as manifestations of our dependence on external things, we find that arbitrariness is once again a central theme. As human beings, we strive to put ourselves in situations that empower us and make us joyful and to avoid situations that disempower us and make us sad. However, insofar as we are unable to control the way we are acted on by external things, we are also unable to control either our own power or the passions in which it is manifested. As Spinoza puts it, 'the man who is subject to affects is under the control, not of himself, but of fortune' (E IVPref.; II/205). Things may or may not go well for him; but whatever course they take he is at the mercy of external events, and this is what makes him a slave.

Here, then, we have an initial explication of the claim that our passions enslave us, and an initial answer to the question of why Spinoza should say such a thing. But our appreciation of this phenomenon is not yet complete because, as well as *charting* our enslavement to external things, the passions contribute to it. In the *Ethics*, Spinoza takes pains to show how the psychological laws to which our passions conform introduce an element of arbitrariness into our affective responses. First of all, our disposition to form associations between ideas enables a passion to be transferred from one object to another. Suppose, for instance, that as a result of a recent encounter I both hate and fear A, and then come across B, whom I already hate. Because the two encounters have something in common (I hate both A and B), the second will reactivate the passions involved in the first. And because my hatred of A was accompanied by fear, my new experience of hatred will also make me afraid. I shall fear as well as hate B, whether or not I have any independent grounds for doing so (E IIIp14; II/151). In addition, we form associations on the basis of resemblance. For example, if I love A and A reminds me of B, I shall also love B, regardless of her other qualities (E IIIp16; II/153). This pattern of feeling determines some of our responses to individuals; but it also governs our feelings about social groups. As Spinoza explains, if a member of class A loves or hates a member of class B, she will feel the same passion for all members of the latter class (E IIIp46; II/175). Laws of association thus shape our passions on the slenderest of pretexts. Moreover, they are not the only mechanisms to have this kind of impact, and are joined by a different, imitative process. When we encounter people for whom we do not yet have any particular feeling, we are liable to imitate their affects (E IIIp22; II/157). If they are sad, we shall become sad, and if they desire some object, we shall come to want it (E IIIp27: II/160).

As these cases indicate, and as Spinoza explicitly observes, the laws governing our nature ensure that 'anything can be the accidental cause of joy, sadness or desire' (E IIIp15; II/151–2) and 'anything whatever can be the accidental cause of hope or fear', E IIIp50;_II/177). Our passions are often grounded on accidental associations and resemblances, and arise from processes of which we may not be aware. In these respects they contribute to the arbitrariness of the way that external things affect us, and thus to our slavery.

The kind of bondage that Spinoza has now identified presents a formidable challenge to the project of showing how human beings can become free. What we were looking for was a way of defeating the arbitrary control that external objects exercise over us. But what we have come to appreciate is just how dependent we are on external things. By virtue of the laws of our own psychology, we cooperate in ensuring that they have arbitrary effects on us, so that our subjection to them can fairly be described as internally as well as externally caused.

It is not easy to see how we could escape this kind of slavery while remaining human. Worse still, its depth and pervasiveness cast doubt on our ability to achieve the kind of liberty from which our discussion began. Political liberty depends, as we have seen, on two sorts of independence: independence from subjection to arbitrary civil laws; and, in its fullest form, independence from the coercive force of even non-arbitrary laws. But if the individuals posited in the political model are subject to the more general form of arbitrariness manifested in the passions, it is not obvious that they will be able to sustain a free way of life. Among the feelings that will be generated by the combination of their own psychological dispositions and their encounters with external things are hatred, envy, and fear; but these very passions are liable to undermine their capacity to maintain a system of non-arbitrary laws. It is difficult to be fair to people whom we

hate, and fear is, in Spinoza's view, incompatible with completely willing obedience (TTP 17.8; III/202). Legislators will therefore tend to make arbitrary laws,
the judiciary will tend to arbitrary enforcement, and subjects will view the law
with suspicion or downright contempt (TTP 17.3; III/201). A form of slavery that
is an aspect of our very situation as human beings will, it seems, undermine our
attempts to create free states and condemn us to a double form of servitude.

V

Spinoza is not prepared to accept the conclusion we have arrived at, and sets out
to show what other resources we can use to attain not only political freedom, but
also a more comprehensive form of liberty. As the *Theological-Political Treatise*
explains, he intends to show that the happiness that comes with a free way of life
depends on our internal virtue rather than on the course of external events (TTP
4.46; III/68). Once again, moreover, his discussion mirrors the structure of his
model of political liberty.

   To see how he now proceeds, it will be helpful to focus on a feature of his model
for which we have so far identified no analogue in his more general analysis of the
relations between human beings and the rest of nature. As we have seen, a political subject becomes fully free by obeying the law willingly, and in doing so
defeats the law's capacity to determine what he does. Rather than being determined to act by a legal apparatus that is external to him, he takes control. Spinoza
is careful to point out that the language of will and volition in which this description is couched is liable to be misleading. We need to appreciate that the ideas we
describe as volitions are themselves caused by antecedent ideas, so that we are not
'free' in the sense of being undetermined (TTP 4.3–4; III/58; E I App. [III]; II/81–2).
But this in turn gives rise to a problem. If all our ideas are determined, as Spinoza
believes, we need some way to explicate the sense in which a man who willingly
obeys the law can be said to control what he does. If his action, just like that of the
man who obeys unwillingly, is determined by antecedent conditions, in what
sense does he act freely? As we have noted, Spinoza takes over a longstanding
view that the free man is able to obey willingly because he understands that it is in
his interests to do so. For example, when a new law increases his taxes and
unsettles his finances, he may feel anxious and tempted to cheat; but on rational
reflection he will conclude that the benefits of upholding the legal system on
which his liberty depends are greater than the financial gains of cheating, and will
pay his bill in full. Nevertheless, we still need to ask how his understanding gives
him a capacity to control what he does, and thus to sidestep the determining
power of the law. To put the point in Spinoza's terms, it is still not clear why we are
said to act when we obey the law because we understand the reasons for doing so,
but are said to be acted on when we obey because we are afraid of being punished.

The *Ethics* resolves this puzzle by distinguishing the causal processes at work in each type of case, and its discussion of this point is grounded on the claim that ideas can be sorted into two categories: some are adequate or true, whereas the rest are inadequate or confused. As we have seen, some of the ideas in the human mind are ideas of the way the body is acted on by external things. These affects are inadequate and do not provide us with true or accurate ideas either of the human body or of the body acting on it. At the same time, however, the mind contains some adequate ideas. According to Spinoza, we possess, for example, an adequate idea of bodily extension. Because the extendedness of the human body does not depend on its interactions with external bodies, there is an idea of the body's extension in the mind that does not depend on the mind's ideas of external bodies. Here he introduces a crucial sense in which our adequate ideas are not the register of, and do not depend on, our bodily interactions with other things. They are not determined by these interactions, as our inadequate ideas are, and this gives them a kind of independence.

Adequate and inadequate ideas provide the material for two kinds of thinking: imagining, and reasoning or understanding. The first deals in the inadequate ideas we gain via our interactions with external things; but the kind of thinking Spinoza describes as reasoning or understanding is a matter of clearly and distinctly perceiving how adequate ideas presuppose and follow from one another. Reasoning therefore relies on an ability to distinguish the various ways in which ideas are interrelated or, as Spinoza prefers to put it, the various types of causal relations between them. In particular, a competent reasoner must be alive to the difference between cases where one idea is the adequate or complete cause of another, and cases where the first idea is only the inadequate or partial cause of the second. For example, the inadequate idea that constitutes a passion is caused both by an idea of the human body and by an idea of an external body, and because each of these ideas is only a partial or inadequate cause of the passion, the passion cannot be conceived through (or understood as an effect of) the idea of the body alone (E IVp2; II/212). At least two ideas must be in play. The situation is different, however, when we clearly and distinctly perceive how one adequate idea follows from another. In this type of case, the first adequate idea is the complete or adequate cause of the second. Moreover, the capacity to reason from one adequate idea to another is, in Spinoza's view, a power of the mind that does not essentially depend on its causal relations with anything outside it. Reasoning is a manifestation of the mind's own power and is something that the mind does.

Both in his analysis of adequate ideas, and in his account of what it is to reason with them, Spinoza makes space for a conception of reasoning as an independent activity of the mind. At first sight, this is an odd position to hold, because our capacities to acquire adequate ideas and reason with them depend at least in part on the way we interact with external things, and thus on the inadequate ideas that constitute our affects. For example, our ability to extend our understanding will be determined by our education, our desires, and our physical circumstances, and to this extent will not depend solely on the mind. Spinoza agrees that this is the case. The power to reason is a manifestation of an individual's *conatus,* and will therefore vary with the constitution of his or her body and the particular conditions under which he or she lives. Equally, reasoning has to be learned. We are all born ignorant, 'and before men can know the true principle of living and acquire a virtuous disposition, much of their life has passed, even if they have been well brought up' (TTP XVI.7; III/190). However, these features of the capacity to reason can be separated from reasoning itself. When we clearly and distinctly perceive the relations between one adequate idea and another, the mind exercises its own power and acts (E Vp3; II/282). Equally, to act from reason 'is nothing but doing those things which follow from the necessity of our own nature, considered in itself alone' (E IVp59; II/254).

It is not immediately obvious why Spinoza should be concerned to separate what he regards as the active aspect of reasoning from the external conditions on which it always depends; but if we look back to his model of political freedom we can see what is at stake. To gain the fullest form of political liberty, one must occupy a position where one is not dependent on the arbitrary power of the law, but can act independently of it in accordance with one's own desires. The way to achieve this, so the political model claims, is to obey the law because one understands that it is in one's interests to do so. When Spinoza seeks to vindicate his conception of freedom by spelling out the framework of adequate ideas and causes that distinguish reasoning from imagining, one of the features he needs to capture and explain is the association between reasoning, independence, and liberty around which the model is organized. A satisfactory account of reasoning or understanding must elucidate the sense in which it unleashes us from our dependence on the coercive force of the law and allows us to think and act for ourselves. The political model therefore embodies a number of requirements to which Spinoza is responding when he characterizes reasoning as a power to act that depends on the mind alone. Part of his project is to assimilate the model of political freedom that is so central to the *Theological-Political Treatise* into a broader conception of a life in which the ability to live freely under the law is just one of a wide range of liberties that understanding makes possible.

Understanding or reasoning empowers us, as Spinoza sees the matter, in two intermingled ways. It allows us to see how we are situated by providing us with true ideas of ourselves and the things around us, and it gives us reasons for acting on our knowledge of how things stand. In some cases, it enables us to act in a manner that is also dictated by some external thing. For example, just as the free man willingly does what the law also commands, you may find that you can defeat the effect of a bout of flu that is acting on you, and giving you a passionate desire to go to bed, by way of understanding that in such circumstances going to bed is the best thing to do. Your action takes account of features of the situation that you do not control, such as the feeling of having a high temperature. But it is nevertheless said to be caused by your rational appreciation of your situation rather than by your passionate desire to lie down, so that you act rather than being acted on. In other cases, however, this type of concord between internal and external determinations does not obtain. An external thing may produce passions that prompt you to do one thing, while your understanding moves you to do something else. It is then an open question whether your understanding or power to act will be great enough to overcome the power of the external things that are acting on you, and thus whether you will be able to act freely (E IVp59; II/255).

So far we have been considering the role of reason in releasing us from the power of external things. There is, however, a further way in which reasoning can liberate us, this time by altering the power of our own psychological impulses. 'The more an affect is known to us, then, the more it is in our power, and the less the mind is acted on by it' (E Vp3c; II/282). As we gain a more adequate understanding of ourselves, we come to recognize how the psychological laws governing our passions contribute to their arbitrariness, and thus to our enslavement. In addition, once we come to see this as a disempowering state of affairs, we shall strive to resist it; and one of the resources to which we shall appeal in order to do so is our capacity for reasoning. The more we understand the operations of the *conatus* that manifest themselves in our passions, the better placed we shall be to use this understanding to free ourselves from the bondage that the affects impose. Moreover, in the process, we shall increase our power to act.

To some extent, then, reasoning or understanding provides a means to resist the arbitrary power that external things exercise over us, as well as the psychological laws that contribute to our dependence. But how far can this process go? In the political case, liberty depends on external and internal conditions; on the existence of a certain type of law, and on the capacity of subjects to act in accordance with it. Although the first condition lies within human reach (it is possible, though difficult, to devise laws that successfully protect the common good), the second will in practice only be partially realized. Because the relevant kind of understanding is hard to achieve, at least a proportion of subjects will not attain it. They will obey the law out of some passion such as fear of punishment, and will thus fail to become fully free. Turning now to Spinoza's broader conception of liberty, the situation appears to be still more bleak. On one side, at least some external things continue to exercise arbitrary power over us and thus continue to enslave us. Because we are not sufficiently powerful to create an environment in which we are totally protected from arbitrary interference, it seems that Fortune cannot be altogether vanquished, and we cannot hope to be entirely released from this aspect of our bondage. On the other side, our power to act is only as strong as our capacity to understand, and in practice this capacity is limited. Many people in many circumstances will therefore remain enslaved to the way that things act on them, and thus to the passions that these interactions engender.

Spinoza does not deny that the kind of freedom he envisages is largely unattainable. 'All things excellent', he remarks in another context, 'are as difficult as they are rare' (E Vp42s; II/308). But he is confident that, just as a group of subjects can enhance their political freedom by devising the right kind of law, freedom in the broader sense can be nurtured by a particular kind of community, which he describes as one of free men (E IVp71–p73; II/263–5). Like a constitution that protects subjects from the incursions of arbitrary political power, a community of free men devotes itself to the pursuit of the understanding through which the arbitrary power of nature can be defeated. By sustaining and encouraging its members' efforts to extend their active control over themselves and the natural world, it reduces both external dependence on the arbitrary power of nature, and, still more importantly, internal dependence on the way that things affect us. It thus generates a level of collective freedom far greater than anything an individual can attain alone, and concomitantly diminishes slavery.

The success of this enterprise depends, in Spinoza's view, on distinctive features of reasoning or understanding. Insofar as people grasp the world by means of the passionate kind of thinking known as imagining, they are bound to experience disempowering affects such as hatred and envy; and these in turn are liable to disrupt and degrade the quality of social life. In particular passionate people are prone to compete for things they regard as empowering, such as love or money. In the marketplace, for example, the success of one merchant will excite the envy of another, and businesses that go badly will come to be held in contempt. Furthermore, any or all of these outcomes can split a community, thus reinforcing the passionate struggle for power (E IVp32; II/230). By contrast, the understanding that free men strive to acquire is proof against envy and other forms of sadness. Unlike the objects of our passions, it is not a scarce good, and the fact that one person understands the causes of a phenomenon does not prevent others from understanding it as well (E IVp36; II/234). On the contrary, the more the members of a community pool their rational insights, the more powerful each of them becomes. People who are guided by these insights can consequently be depended on not to undermine each other's efforts to extend understanding and the form of independence that it brings. The more they understand, the more they are able to resist the arbitrariness that the passions manifest and intensify, and the more free they become. Once again, then, freedom can only be realized under certain conditions. A community of free men provides a bulwark against the arbitrary incursions of the passions, and in doing so minimizes our vulnerability to the arbitrary incursion of nature. It provides an environment in which freedom can grow.

VI

Throughout the *Ethics* Spinoza builds up an increasingly ambitious conception of liberty, which eventually transcends even the limits imposed by human embodiment. This edifice is partly founded on his conviction that, although the passions enslave us, we can to some extent throw off our servitude and become free. In working out this view, I have suggested, he produces a theory that mirrors the central features of a more limited conception of political liberty, to which he was also committed. In doing so, he unites a political conception of independence with a broader account of the passions, by showing that each is underpinned by a single interpretation of freedom and slavery. In both cases, slavery consists in subjection to an arbitrary power, and only if we appreciate this fact can we understand what it is about the passions that makes them inimical to freedom. Spinoza is not the only seventeenth-century author to link political liberty with its more general counterpart. Other defenders of republican government, such as Pieter De la Court's correspondent James Harrington, also point to the interconnections between political servitude and the slavery that the passions impose.[10] However, this evidence of a general interest in the relationship between the two allows us to speculate that one of Spinoza's many aims in writing the *Ethics* may have been to produce a rigorous analysis of the ideas on which the political conception depends, and to show that its ideal of political liberty can only be fully realised by a community dedicated to the more general pursuit of understanding, and thus to a more wide-ranging type of freedom. To put the point in terms of the debates in which Spinoza was involved, a republican style of government can only be reliably sustained where the pursuit of philosophical understanding is encouraged and protected. Although Spinoza defends this conclusion in the *Theological-Political Treatise*, it is in the *Ethics* that he provides his readers with a comprehensive account of his reasons for holding it, and fully explicates the extent of the arbitrariness or slavery against which human beings struggle. Political freedom then emerges as a special case of a more general kind of freedom, through which we can to some extent release ourselves from bondage.

[10] Harrington 1992, 10.

10

Freedom of Conscience and Civic Peace

Spinoza on Piety

Seventeenth-century European struggles about the extent to which people should be free to express their religious convictions were generally grounded on the assumption that, if individuals are left to decide this for themselves, discord will inevitably follow.[1] The limits of free expression therefore need be set by some recognized authority. But who should exercise this power? Should the right to determine the extent of religious liberty lie with the church or the state? The question was made more urgent by an influential conception of the relationship between two systems of law, divine and civil. If, as was widely accepted, theologians possess the authority to interpret the divine law revealed in Scripture, while sovereigns can legitimately make and enforce civil law, what are people to do when the two laws clash? As Hobbes sums up the dilemma, one might 'either by too much civil obedience, offend the divine majesty, or through fear of offending God transgress the commands of the commonwealth'.[2] More specifically, when church and state disagree about the proper extent of religious freedom, how is the deadlock to be broken?

An obvious way to resolve the problem is to award one party legal priority over the other. The church must give way to the state or vice versa. Faced with these options, Spinoza stands firmly on the side of the state. The only way to maintain peace and freedom, and thus to secure the proper ends of political life, he argues, is to give the civil sovereign sole jurisdiction over religious matters. As the agent with responsibility for preserving and protecting the state, a sovereign must have 'the supreme right to maintain whatever it judges concerning religion' (TTP XVI.63; III/199). In advocating this view, Spinoza was aligning himself with the supporters of the Estates of Holland and opposing the Dutch Reformed Church's aspiration to control certain aspects of religious institutions and practice. At the same time, he was distancing himself from the demand for freedom of conscience pressed by various nonconformist sects.[3] His view was consequently contested. As he complains in the *Theological-Political Treatise*, many people 'assume for themselves a licence to censure [civil rulers], expose them to scorn, and even

---

[1] I am grateful to Ed Curley, Edit Dobbs Weinstein, Willi Goetschel, Stephen Nadler and Michael Rosenthal for their comments on an earlier version of this essay.

[2] Hobbes, 1994, 31.1.

[3] Quakers and Anabaptists, for example, defended the separation of church and state. On the history of Dutch efforts to find a basis for religious peace see van Gelderen (2007).

Spinoza on Learning to Live Together. Susan James, Oxford University Press (2020). © Susan James.
DOI: 10.1093/oso/9780198713074.001.0001

excommunicate them from the church' (TTP XIX.1; III/228). Spinoza is not prepared to engage with the arguments marshalled in favour of this stance, and dismisses them as too frivolous to merit refutation (TTP XIX.34; III/234). But the
prevalence of opponents who radically disagreed with him obviously threatens
the success of his proposal. As long as institutions are divided about where the
authority to limit religious expression lies, it is not clear that any party will be able
to impose a stable and lasting peace.

This difficulty is surely endemic to any attempt to resolve the problem in the
manner that Spinoza so far seems to defend. In the persistent conflict between
church and state, giving one side legal precedence over the other will only secure
peace if the preferred side has the power to impose its will.[4] A sovereign will only
be able to enforce its interpretation of religion if it has enough power to do so,
and as long as this right is seriously contested the sovereign's authority will remain
vulnerable. So while Spinoza's solution is viable in theory, it will often be unstable
in practice. States, churches, and their respective supporters will continue to
struggle for power to determine the limits of free religious expression.

The contest can be resolved, Spinoza argues, once the right of the state is properly understood. Anyone who fully grasps the nature of sovereignty will recognize
that subjects have no adequate justification for contravening the civil law, whether
on religious or any other grounds. Churches and other religious parties who
appreciate this truth will therefore be willing to submit to laws made by a civil
sovereign. But first they must be persuaded. Partly with this goal in mind, Spinoza
couches his argument for the supremacy of the civil sovereign in terms that religious as well as civil parties might in principle accept. Drawing on the Bible, and
on a classical conception of *pietas*, he aims to bypass the traditional conflict
between religious and civil law by dissolving the distinction between them.
Instead of conceding that there are two kinds of law that can pull in different
directions, he sets out show that they cannot be separated; when sovereigns
impose the civil law they also impose its divine counterpart, and when religious
authorities defend the divine law they defend the civil law as well.

Within early-modern Dutch debates about the proper extent of sovereign
power, it was sometimes argued that the constitutional organization of the United
Provinces should mirror that of the ancient Hebrew Republic.[5] What could be
more perfect, after all, than a state ordained by God? But while various groups
were sympathetic to this aspiration, they radically disagreed about what it
implied. On the one hand, a number of anti-Arminian theologians contended
that the Jewish state set a precedent for independent religious authority, because
priests rather than kings were responsible for directing spiritual life. On the other
hand, Arminian sympathisers rejected this interpretation of the Old Testament.
Citing Josephus's claim that the Hebrew Republic was a theocracy in which civil

---

[4] Levene (2004), 155.   [5] Nelson 2010, 88–111.

sovereignty lay in the hands of God,[6] and in which there was no distinction between civil and divine law,[7] they argued that religious authority had always rested with the civil sovereign. Under Moses there was no independent ecclesiastical authority; and even after his death, supreme power to make and enforce law lay with a civil sovereign rather than with priests. In states modelled on the Hebrew constitution, a supreme civil magistrate must therefore control religious as well as civil affairs.

Writing in the early decades of the seventeenth century, the jurist Hugo Grotius and his Hebraist colleague Petrus Cunaeus had both defended this Arminian line of argument, and a generation later Spinoza followed their lead.[8] Although his interpretation of Hebrew history does not entirely coincide with those of either Grotius or Cunaeus, he agrees with them about the *locus* of sovereignty. People who hold the seditious opinion that Hebrew sovereignty lay with the priests, he claims, 'are wretchedly deceived' (TTP XIX.35; III/234). They fail to recognize that, in the first phase of the Hebrew state, Moses possessed the right to command 'absolutely all things to all people' (TTP XVIII.4; III/222). By contrast with the ambitions of the Dutch Reformed Church, it was as a civil sovereign that Moses 'taught the people religion, ordained sacred ministries and chose ministers'.[9] It is true, Spinoza goes on, that after Moses's death, priests became interpreters of the law and gave civil rulers advice; but 'it was still not their function to judge the citizens or excommunicate anyone'. This power lay with the leaders of the tribes and the judges they appointed—in short with the civil authorities. 'Though no one after Moses's death had absolute sovereignty, still the ruler...had the right to make decrees about sacred matters and about all others' (TTP XIX.55; III/237).

The Jewish Republic therefore offers no precedent for dividing priestly authority over religious law from sovereignty over civil affairs. In fact, according to the Josephan view that Spinoza and his Arminian predecessors took up, it did not even acknowledge the existence of such a division, because its civil and religious laws were united. Obedience to the fundamentals of the law was simultaneously a matter of religious and civil duty, and any decree articulated a civil as well as a religious requirement. 'In this state, civil law and religion were one and the same thing. The doctrines of religion were not teachings but laws' (TTP XVII.31; III/206). Writing in the *Theological-Political Treatise*, Spinoza goes on to explain how such a crucial insight came to be lost. Originally, Christianity was practised

---

[6] Josephus 1926, 358. Cited in Nelson, 2010, 89–90.

[7] Josephus, 1930–65, vol. 3, 214–24. Cited in Nelson 2010, 91.

[8] Grotius develops this view in *De republica emendanda*, written between 1600 and 1610, and again in *De imperio summarum potestatum circa sacra*, completed in 1617 and published after his death in 1647. Cunaeus defends it in his *De republica Hebraeorum*, published in 1617. See Nelson 2010, 98–104, 107–9. On the dispute between Arminians and their opponents see Nobbs 1938. The argument I develop here can be seen as a fourth origin of Spinoza's theory of toleration, in addition to the three identified in Rosenthal 2003, 320–1.

[9] In the United Provinces during Spinoza's lifetime, the Dutch Reform Church and the Estates struggled over who should possess the right to appoint ministers and teach religion. See Rowen 1978, 427–30; Israel 1995, 697; James 2012, 290–4.

by groups of private citizens who made laws for themselves 'without any consideration of the sovereign'. When their religion was first introduced into the state, it was taught to civil sovereigns or *imperatores* by ecclesiastics, who consequently came to be seen as interpreters of divine law and deputies or *vicarii* of God (TTP XIX.51; III/237). The conviction that civil sovereigns have limited authority and must bow to theologians or priests in matters relating to religion is consequently no more than a local prejudice, inculcated by the development of Christianity.

For many Dutch theorists, the original Jewish constitution served as a model.[10] Grotius, for example, proposes that a republic founded by God must surely be the one to imitate, and the same sentiment is echoed by Cunaeus; 'The Hebrew commonwealth', he claims, 'is the holiest and best of states.'[11] By contrast, Spinoza often seems to distance himself from this stance. In the first place, he argues, the law of the ancient Republic was the law of a particular state, and bound the Jews only while the state existed (TTP III.47; III/55). Once they transferred their right to the King of Babylon, it no longer applied to them (TTP XIX.13; III/230). Moreover, because the ancient law was adapted to the outlook of the Jews at a particular stage of their history and is unsuited to the demands of a seventeenth-century state, it would be fruitless to try to revive it as the legislative code of a modern polity (TTP IV.53; III/56). However, although Spinoza emphasizes that the ancient constitution cannot be reinstated in its entirety, he does not deny that it may be possible to learn from it, and here, once again, he is in agreement with Grotius and Cunaeus. As all three suggest, it may be possible to revive some features of the constitution, and among the positive lessons to be drawn from it is the wisdom of unifying the civil and religious laws. Building on the work of his Arminian predecessors, the question Spinoza poses is therefore whether this aspect of the Jewish Republic can be replicated in a modern polity. Instead of trying to divide power between two legal authorities, with all the risks this involves, would it not be better to create a republic in which, as Spinoza describes the Jewish state, civil and religious law are the same, and piety is identified with justice (TTP XVII.30–31; III/206)?

This approach is one of the guiding inspirations of Spinoza's defence of civil sovereignty. It aims to validate a major theoretical shift in Dutch debate about the reconciliation of civil and religious power, and is among his most innovative contributions to early-modern political philosophy. Although, as we have seen, there had been a number of earlier appeals to Josephus's account of the Jewish theocracy as a state where civil and divine law merged, Spinoza's attempt to work out the implications of this view and explain what it would be to realize them in a modern state is exceptionally rigorous and unblinking.

---

[10] Nelson traces this view to a work by Erastus published in 1568: 'I do not see why the Christian magistrate ought not to do the same [as] at this time in the Jewish commonwealth, he was commanded by God to do. Do we think that we can constitute a better form of Church and Commonwealth?' Erastus 1599, 60. Quoted in Nelson 2010, 93.

[11] Grotius 1984. cited in Nelson 2010, 98. Cunaeus 2006, 6.

The Jewish constitution, as Spinoza describes it, was a work of collective imagination. It reposed on the Jews' imaginary conception of God as a legislator and judge, and on the exceptional imaginative powers of Moses, whose prophetic insights took the form of commands issued by an anthropomorphic deity. Reconstructing the story of the origins of the state, Spinoza enters the imaginative world of the Jews shortly after their escape from Egypt. Unable to rule themselves, they asked Moses to communicate with God on their behalf and convey the laws God revealed to him. As God's representative, Moses pronounced and enforced the divine law in God's name, so that, in obeying the law, the people obeyed both Moses and God. In one sense, Spinoza explains, 'this form of government could be called a theocracy, since its citizens were only bound by such law as was revealed by God' (TTP XVII.32; III/206). At the same time, since Moses was the only human being with authority to articulate God's commands, his position resembled that of a sovereign monarch (TTP XVII.37; III/207). In this second sense, the theocratic status of the republic was 'a matter of opinion rather than fact' (TTP XVII.32; III/206);[12] it reflected the way the Jews and Moses imagined their relationship with God rather than the way it truly was. But this did not prevent the constitution from unifying divine and civil law into an effective legislative system. Since there was no gap between obeying the civil law and obeying the deity, every act of civil obedience was an act of worship and every violation of the divine law an act of sedition.

While the Jewish Republic exemplifies the kind of unity Spinoza is seeking to defend, he is adamant that modern states must find a different basis for unifying the duty to obey God with duty to obey the sovereign.[13] Here, he contends, the content of the divine law revealed to Moses provides a vital source of insight. Although Moses imposed an extensive system of laws governing every aspect of his subjects' lives, the vast majority of these commands were not revealed to him by God. They were merely his implementation of the core doctrines of the divine law, revealed, in Spinoza's naturalistic sense of the term, not only to Moses but to other prophets as well. Taken on its own, this law is simple. All it demands of us is that we should love God by obeying his law, as opposed to stubbornly resisting it (TTP XIV.2; III/176); and all it takes to obey the divine law is to love our neighbours as ourselves. 'The whole law consists only in this: loving one's neighbour. So no one can deny that one who, according to God's command, loves his neighbour as himself is really obedient and, according to the law, blessed. But one who hates or fails to care for his neighbour is a stiff-necked rebel' (TTP XIV.9; III/174). Since loving one's neighbour is in turn a matter of consistently practising justice and *caritas*, people who manage this, and in doing so obey the divine law, do

---

[12] See Levene 2004, 218; Armstrong 2009, 291–3; Hammill 2012, 67–99; Fraenkel 2012, 240–4.
[13] Garver (2006) describes Spinoza's solution as 'the discovery of morality'. I think the elision of *pietas* with morality distorts our understanding of the former.

everything necessary to a pious and faithful life. The most pious and faithful person is thus the one 'who displays the best works of justice and loving-kindness' (TTP XIV.33; III/179).

To obey the divine law by loving our neighbours, Spinoza goes on, we need a common understanding of what justice and charity involve. If private individuals abide by standards of their own, disagreements and resentments will arise and spiral into conflict. In Spinoza's view, however, shared standards of justice can only be imposed within the state, where a sovereign has enough power to deter-mine what they are and impose them on everyone alike (TP II.23; III/284). To put the point another way, we can live justly only by living under civil law, and justice as a social practice only comes into existence once there is a civil law that subjects are obliged to obey (TTP XIX.9; III/230). To live in accordance with the divine law by treating one's neighbours justly, one therefore has to commit to maintaining the conditions in which this is possible by obeying the civil law. As the *Theological-Political Treatise* sums it up, no one can practise piety nor obey God unless he obeys all the sovereign's decrees (TTP XIX.25; III/233).

Spinoza's attempt to align the divine with the civil law therefore initially aims to show that it is impossible to obey the first without also obeying the second; but it seems a weakness of this Hobbesian piece of reasoning that it reduces piety to living by the standard of justice that the civil law embodies.[14] If piety amounts to obeying the sovereign, it loses any independent religious content. To offset the criticism, Spinoza offers a further argument, this time designed to show that, just as creating a secure civil society is part of what is involved in creating a religious way of life, so creating a religious way of life is part of what it takes to secure the ends of the state. In order to uphold peace and security, the ends of the civil law, the sovereign must bring it about that its subjects live in accordance with the divine law, and thus live religiously. This side of Spinoza's case rests on his claim that the divine law requires us to practise piety by treating our neighbours with justice and *caritas*. Unless the members of a community treat one another in this way, the state will not be able to guarantee their security. If they are to live peace-fully and securely, they must commit themselves to loving their neighbours; and this is what it means to live religiously in accordance with the divine law.

Combining the arguments we have so far considered, Spinoza reaches the con-clusion that civil and religious obedience coincide. One cannot obey the divine law without obeying the civil law, and vice versa. Despite this symmetry, however, there is a sense in which the state retains the upper hand. The divine law can only be implemented, so that it is possible for us to obey it, by a civil sovereign who imposes certain terms of cooperation and uses the civil law to articulate and enforce them. 'Since it is the duty of the sovereign alone to determine what is

---

[14] See Matheron 1985, 149–76; Curley 1999, 327–35; Gatens 2009b, 455–68.

necessary for the well-being of the whole people and the security of the state, and to command what it judges to be necessary, it follows that it is the duty of the supreme power alone to determine in what way each person must devote himself to his neighbour in accordance with piety, i.e. in what way each person is bound to obey God' (TTP XIX.24; III/232).

It is important to Spinoza's position that the sovereign's power over religion is a power to *interpret* the divine law rather than a power to determine its content. Reason and revelation both confirm that the law enjoins us to love our neighbour, and this is not a fact that anyone can change. All a ruler can do is to fill out this divine injunction by specifying how subjects are to love their neighbours, and enshrining these judgments in law. Using its legislative powers, the sovereign imposes a civil law that is simultaneously an interpretation of the divine law. By these means, a sovereign makes it possible for its subjects to live religiously by giving them a shared and enforceable account of what—for them—loving their neighbours involves, and in doing so, it closes the gap between the civil and the divine laws. As in the ancient Hebrew Republic, the requirements of one law mirror the requirements of the other. The sovereign's task is to enable its subjects to live peacefully and securely, and at the same time piously and obediently. So although the divine law is not revealed to modern sovereigns as it was to Moses, they inherit his duty to interpret and enforce it. Like Moses, their job is to make it possible for their subjects to love their neighbours or obey the divine law by imposing standards of justice.

In principle, Spinoza's analysis provides the theoretical basis for a modern analogue of the ancient Jewish theocracy by showing how the civil and divine laws coincide. But because many of his contemporaries rejected the interpretation of piety on which his argument rests, they were hardly likely to be persuaded by his account. Whereas Spinoza appeals to a relatively thin account of piety as a matter of treating one's neighbours justly and charitably, they defended thicker senses of the term. While he insists that piety does not, for example, require us to worship in any particular fashion or hold more than a few specific religious beliefs, they disagreed. Seen from their perspective, Spinoza's minimalist interpretation stripped piety of its religious content and distorted its meaning to a point where the term became unrecognizable. Moreover, once what they regarded as its proper meaning is restored, Spinoza's argument fails. Since the demands of piety are not exhausted by the edicts of the civil law, but also impose particular religious constraints, the sovereign's laws can indeed deviate from, and violate, the requirements of a pious way of life. Once again, we find ourselves staring into the gulf between the demands of civil and divine law.

Disputes about the nature of piety ran deep in early-modern Dutch society, and Spinoza is of course aware that his own account contradicts those favoured by many of his opponents. Judged by the standards of Dutch religious debate, his interpretation is idiosyncratic; but it would be wrong to accuse him of simply redefining the notion of piety to suit the theologico-political goals we have been tracing. His analysis draws on a classical conception of piety that would have been familiar to many of his readers and remained current in early-modern Europe. *Pietas*, as Roman authors habitually interpret it, encompasses one's duties to God, to one's country, to one's parents and to one's other relatives. Cicero, for example, defines piety as 'doing justice to the gods',[15] but also as 'respecting our duties to our parents and other kin'.[16] In a similar vein, Tacitus describes an episode in which Tiberius commends the *pietas* of an assembly which voted to punish Clutorius Priscus for disloyalty to the emperor. To criticize the sovereign, and by implication the *patria* he represents, is impious.[17] The same breadth of meaning is echoed in the *Theological-Political Treatise*, where Spinoza claims that the greatest form of piety is piety to one's country (*patria*), and by implication to one's sovereign, because once sovereignty is destroyed nothing good can survive (TTP XIX.22; III/232). Here, living piously is no longer confined to the performance of specifically religious duties, but encompasses a range of obligations to the community of which one forms a part. As a result, our duties to the state and our kin acquire theological overtones, while our duties to God carry the connotations of our responsibilities for family and country. As Spinoza repeatedly emphasizes, the project of living piously is therefore not focused on specific religious beliefs or forms of worship. Rather, in accordance with the classical conception, it is a matter of upholding a collective way of life in which, under the aegis of the state, we are able to reap the theologico-political benefits of living justly and cooperatively.[18]

While Spinoza's interpretation of piety therefore reflects an established meaning of the term that his readers would have recognized, it nevertheless draws attention to an aspect of his sensibility that may strike us as strange. For him, the fact that an individual holds a particular set of religious beliefs, or has a deep theological commitment to a certain mode of worship, is not a ground for allowing them to express their beliefs or worship as they believe they should. We first need to know whether their commitments are consistent with piety and peace; but even if they are , it does not follow that they are entitled to these forms of religious self-expression. In practice, Spinoza believes, attempts to impose uniformity of religious belief or worship tend to strain social relations to breaking point, so that the only effective way to maintain conditions in which people can treat one another justly and charitably is to allow people to worship freely. Wise sovereigns will therefore permit as much religious diversity as they can; but neither the civil nor the divine law put them under any obligation to do so. Instead, 'external religious worship and every expression of piety must be accommodated

---

[15] Cicero 1933, I xli–xlii.   [16] Cicero1968, II.23, 65–7.   [17] Tacitus 1931 *Book* III, li.

[18] For the view that Spinoza is best understood as reinterpreting Christian religion, see Fraenkel 2013, 377–407.

to the peace and preservation of the republic if we want to obey God properly'
(TTP XIX.21; III/232).[19]

The fact that freedom of conscience is not of any intrinsic political or religious
value, and consequently imposes no normative pressure on the argument we are
considering, becomes clear from Spinoza's discussion of two familiar dilemmas.
One concerns the conviction that, when a man asks for my shirt, piety requires
me to give him my cloak (TTP XIX.23; III/232). The structure of this problem
would have been familiar, not only from the Bible,[20] but also from the legend of St
Martin, who divided his cloak with a beggar. The scene is shown, for example, in
a relief over the door of the Domkerk dedicated to the saint in Utrecht, and was
illustrated by a number of painters.[21]

Spinoza agrees that, as long as the civil law does not forbid it, individuals are
free to part with their cloaks, and indeed their shirts. But he adds a qualification.
If, for example, the law classifies such an action as theft and requires subjects to
report it to the authorities, piety constrains them to obey. When the law holds
that giving away one's cloak is harmful to the preservation of the republic, a pious
state will call a St Martin to judgment, and even condemn him to death (TTP
XIX.23; III 232). As long as the people involved in the case act in the spirit of justice, the individual who reports the miscreant, the magistrate who judges and sen-
tences him, and the sovereign who signs his death warrant, all act piously (E
IVp51s; II/248). So, contrary to widespread opinion, piety is above all a duty to
obey the state, and we should not reproach ourselves for behaving impiously
when we do what the state decrees. Instead of admiring saints, prophets, or rad-
icals who break the law in the name of their religious convictions, we should learn
to regard them as impious people who, by acting unjustly, fail to obey God.

The purported problem posed by St Martin is therefore easily solved. We may
think we face a conflict between our duties to god and the state, but this is because
our everyday conception of piety is inadequate or confused. Once we have properly understood it, apparent conflicts between the divine and civil laws will turn
out to rest on a misunderstanding. This does not mean, of course, that it will
always be easy to do what the divine and civil laws demand. A Saint Martin may
find it impossible to refrain from giving away half his cloak, regardless of the law,
because the strength of his concern for the beggar and his desire to help him banish all other considerations from his mind. Indeed he may be quite unable to see
the situation in what Spinoza regards as the correct light.

---

[19] As in the case of justice, there may be a gap between an individual's understanding of what piety
might ideally demand, and the social practice of piety, which must be authorized by the civil law
(TTP xix.3; III/229).

[20] Matthew 5.40; Luke 6.29.

[21] See for example the paintings by Anthony van Dyck (c. 1620, Royal Collection, London) and
Pieter de Bloot (c. 1650, Victoria and Albert Museum, London).

Illustrating this kind of tension yet more graphically, Spinoza turns to the celebrated example of the Roman consul Manlius Torquatus, who condemned his own son to death for disobeying military orders. Torquatus's case had been discussed by Livy, taken up by Machiavelli, and was familiar to Spinoza's Dutch contemporaries.[22] In the early 1660s, for instance, the artist Ferdinand Bol was commissioned to paint the scene for the headquarters of the Admiralty in Amsterdam, as a reminder of the price of insubordination. Bol depicts the enthroned father, surrounded by an assembly of counsellors and soldiers, overseeing the beheading of his son.[23] But while we may find the scene horrifying, Spinoza is adamant that Torquatus managed to do what the greatest form of piety requires. Putting his patriotism ahead of his paternal duty, 'he valued the wellbeing of the people more than piety towards his son' (TTP XIX.23; III/232).

In both these examples Spinoza aligns piety unswervingly with the law, and thus with justice. An overwhelming commitment to justice that spans the civil and divine laws is what prevents them from diverging. At the same time, piety rules out the possibility of legitimate civil disobedience and puts strict limits on freedom of conscience.[24] Although, as Spinoza concedes, no one can prevent an individual from holding a seditious belief (TTP XX.1; III/239), the sovereign can rightfully use the law to prevent people from expressing or acting on their convictions, and is under no obligation to hold back, however deeply its subjects care about the belief in question. Unless the civil law allows it, there is no right to freedom of religious expression.

Faced with this potentially harsh outlook, one may wonder whether Spinoza has any means of softening his conclusions. Must the unified civil and divine laws invariably give such pride of place to justice, or is there any way to temper its decrees? The answer lies in the divine law itself. As well as requiring us to live justly, it demands that we treat our neighbours with *caritas* or, as Curley translates it, lovingkindness. Where, though, does this quality fit into Spinoza's picture of a pious life? A first possibility is that *caritas* may limit the scope of the civil and divine justice we have so far been examining, so that in some circumstances it need not be imposed. However, in keeping with the republican tradition to which he belongs, Spinoza's commitment to the law brooks no exceptions. Unless it is uncompromisingly upheld, he contends, the ends of the state will be jeopardized, and both security and piety will be endangered. *Caritas* therefore cannot demand anything contrary to justice, as the examples of St Martin and Manlius Torquatus indicate. A further possibility is that *caritas* can only be expressed in relation to matters on which the law does not pronounce. This is certainly part of Spinoza's

---

[22] Livy 1926, Book VIII, ch. 7; Machiavelli 1996, III.22–5.

[23] Heinrich Bol, 'Manlius Torquatus orders the Beheading of his Son' (1664, Rijksmuseum, Amsterdam).

[24] See Rosenthal 1999.

argument. As long the law does not forbid it, people are free to treat one another with as much lovingkindness as they choose. In addition, however, Spinoza makes space for *caritas* within the law, so that a civil code itself can reflect the divine requirement to practise it. In the first place, the divine law can be said to impose a requirement on sovereigns and their officials to dispense justice with *caritas* by avoiding brutality, terror or torture, and by punishing proportionately. Viewed like this, *caritas* is an aspect of justice as well as piety. In addition, the divine law arguably requires sovereigns to exercise *caritas* in interpreting the divine law. Civil laws themselves must embody lovingkindness.

The importance of this point is rather obscured by Spinoza's use of the example of Manlius Torquatus. The law Torquatus is called on to obey makes an unimaginably heavy demand, so much so that one may think it asks more than anyone should be expected to give. It is true that the story is set in the context of a war where Torquatus's son has disobeyed military orders, where it is his father's job to dispense military discipline, and where his commanders and troops are watching to see what he will do. If he makes an exception for his son, his authority will be undermined and the military costs to Rome may be disastrous. He will face the prospect of public shame, whether for partiality or military failure. In these circumstances Torquatus manages to do what piety demands. But sovereigns clearly cannot count on such unswerving fortitude and loyalty. As Spinoza acknowledges, even people who understand and agree with the outlook we have been reconstructing will often be unable to obey laws that contradict their passionate apprehension of the good (TTP XX.44; III/247), and many individuals will find the outlook itself unintelligible. If ordinary subjects are to be capable of living piously, the demands that justice imposes on them must be ones they have a reasonable chance of living up to, and sovereigns will need to take account of this constraint. When they express the divine law in their civil legislation, they need to practise *caritas* by assessing what their subjects can manage.[25]

Sovereigns therefore have a delicate task. As the *Theological-Political Treatise* reminds us, even Moses intermittently endangered the Jewish Republic by demanding levels of obedience that his people could not meet, and successful sovereigns will do their best to avoid this risk by adapting their laws to the temperament of their subjects. However, states can also help subjects to become more capable of obeying laws that stretch their powers of cooperation. Some of Spinoza's illustrations of this process are drawn from the Bible. By teaching the law to the Jews, for example, Moses increased their ability to meet the demands of piety. Other examples refer us to seventeenth-century practices. By rehearsing maxims in calm circumstances, the *Ethics* suggests, people can strengthen their resolution to obey a taxing law when the situation requires it (E Vp10; II/287).[26]

---

[25] See Bijlsma 2017.

[26] For further discussion of this issue see Steinberg 2014, 54–7; Steinberg 2018, 156–62.

Sovereigns practise *caritas* when they acknowledge that their task is not merely to decide what justice commands, but to make the corresponding way of life livable for a particular group of people by taking account of their strengths, vulnerabilities, commitments, and convictions. To meet the demands of the divine law, sovereigns must temper their determination to impose legislation with a kindly sensitivity to what their communities are capable of. At the same time, they can try to ensure that *caritas* is practised by individuals and groups within the state. Judges, for example, show it when they sentence defendants without anger or vengefulness. Private citizens exercise it when they avoid self-righteousness in their dealings with others, or help their friends to work through conflicts of loyalty that make it difficult for them to do what the law requires.

Unless civil sovereigns cultivate and practise *caritas*, their subjects will be unable to live as the unified civil and divine laws require. But although this gives sovereigns a reason to avoid legislation that stifles conscience, a tension remains. When the law conflicts with one's religious convictions, piety still demands that one obey the law, and this, Spinoza implies, may be a state of affairs one simply has to live with. In societies where religious groups are strongly and aggressively committed to diverse and contradictory forms of life, it is quite likely that a sovereign will use the law to limit freedom of conscience in the name of piety. To sustain conditions in which people can treat their neighbours with justice and lovingkindness, the expression of some religious beliefs and practices may have to be suppressed. Which beliefs and practices are outlawed will of course ultimately depend on the sovereign; but sovereigns who exercise *caritas* will also take account of what the community can tolerate. Where subjects are unable to rise (or descend) to the standards of piety that the law demands of them, both minorities and majorities run the risk of losing some rights to free expression, and each may have to live in ways that are at odds with their convictions.

People whose freedom of expression has been restricted are of course liable to feel that they have suffered a painful reduction of liberty, and are more likely to try to resist the law (TTP XX.29; III/244). But while Spinoza acknowledges this danger as a political problem, he does not think that laws limiting our rights of expression always reduce our freedom. True freedom, he contends, is not a matter of living as you happen to want to live, in the light of the beliefs you happen to have, but of living cooperatively with others as the divine law requires; and where our beliefs or preferred ways of life stand in the way of this project, expressing them may decrease our liberty. There is, of course, a perfectly intelligible sense in which being prevented from denouncing a rival religion as the work of the devil, for example, makes me less free. It prevents me from acting as I desire. But true freedom, as Spinoza conceives of it, lies in gaining as full an understanding as possible of what it takes for communities to live piously, and in living harmoniously with others on the basis of that understanding.

In an ideal community of the kind Spinoza describes as rational, the sovereign and its subjects work with a shared and empowering conception of what peace and piety demand, and unequivocally commit themselves to realizing it in their way of life. Because individuals discipline themselves to do only what loving their neighbours allows, they are able to live as they want to live; and because the civil law reflects their understanding of piety, it does not violate their consciences. The demands of the law merge with the urgings of conscience, and the problem of how to resolve conflicts between them does not arise. But in states that fall short of this ideal, part of the sovereign's task lies in limiting freedom of expression in the name of strengthening a community's longer-term commitment to peace and piety. Rather than letting these values deteriorate by licensing antagonism and the expression of hatred, successful sovereigns will use the law not only to prevent conflict, but to help people overcome it; and where they use these powers wisely, they will increase rather than sacrifice liberty.

In states such as the one Spinoza lived in, where religious differences were a source of entrenched, existential conflict, the view he defends imposes extremely heavy demands on sovereigns and subjects. Sovereigns must live up to the demands of piety as they coax warring parties towards a peaceful way of life, while subjects must piously exercise patience and restraint when the law rubs against their consciences. This process of negotiation will take different forms in polities with different kinds of constitution; but in none of them will it be straight-forward. What, then, will persuade a community to hold fast to Spinoza's outlook? The most conclusive reasons for doing so, he argues, lie in his own philosophy. The surest way to live in accordance with one's conscience is to understand the philosophical truths he sets out and, by internalizing them, become committed to living as the unified civil and divine laws dictate. As the *Ethics* puts it, the more one desires to do good by living in accordance with the guidance of reason, the more pious one becomes (EIV p37s; II/236). At the same time, however, Spinoza seeks to make his view of the state persuasive by present-ing it as a re-enactment of the constitutional principles of the ancient Hebrew republic. This is partly an attempt to make his outlook appealing to people whose conception of piety is rooted in the Bible. But Spinoza's view is also indebted to Josesphus's interpretation of theocracy. By working out the implications of the claim that there was no distinction between the Jews' religious and civil laws, and adapting this model to the conditions of early-modern states, Spinoza makes a radical intervention in seventeenth-century debate about the significance of reli-gious freedom. Piety, he argues, does not require us to break the civil law in the name of conscience. On the contrary, it requires us to obey it.

PART III
PHILOSOPHICAL COMMUNITIES

11

Freedom and Nature

A Spinozist Invitation

I

Greenhouse gases accumulate.[1] Sea levels rise. Weather patterns become more violent. Some of the gravest threats to our way of life, and even to the survival of humanity, are undoubtedly environmental, and have at least in part been brought about by our own activities. Yet, as our individual and collective attitudes attest, we are finding these threats difficult to confront. As individuals we cannot see what to do about them. (Small differences are differences, to be sure, but how can our efforts to recycle or switch off the lights measure up to the scale of the problem?) Still worse, we have so far been unable to address them collectively. Even modern states, with all their power, have not managed to implement policies that might make our ways of life sustainable.

These familiar anxieties pose urgent political challenges, but also set us a philosophical test, since our capacity to deal with them will partly depend on how we view the threats themselves, and thus how we assess any remedies we are offered. Among people who live in the wealthier parts of the world, an unwillingness to embrace environmentally friendly measures is sometimes grounded on the conviction that they demand an unacceptable sacrifice of liberty—our liberty to choose to travel, to shop without regard to air miles, to live in brightly lit cities, and so on in a seemingly endless list of potential privations. The costs of an environmentally sustainable way of life appear to be exceptionally damaging to our freedom. No surprise, then, that we drag our feet.

As long as we view the problem in these terms we face a stark dilemma: we either continue to put our ways of life in danger or try to reconcile ourselves to diminished levels of liberty. But we may also wonder whether this is the only way to characterize our options. Is the conception of freedom presupposed in this account the only one available to us? Must we envisage an environmentally friendly way of life as one in which we lose freedom, or might we somehow come to see it as liberating? Even posing the question is liable to make people sigh, as images of living in yurts and growing vegetables swim before their eyes.

[1] Originally published in *Proceedings of the Aristotelian Society* CXVI, 2015–16, 1–19. Reprinted with the permission of The Aristotelian Society and Oxford University Press.

Spinoza on Learning to Live Together. Susan James, Oxford University Press (2020). © Susan James.
DOI: 10.1093/oso/9780198713074.001.0001

Nevertheless, if our attachment to a view of freedom puts our way of life in danger, it may not be a bad idea to consider whether we are working with our fullest and most productive understanding of liberty.

Following this line of thought, I shall offer a Spinozist defence of the claim that learning to live within the constraints imposed by our natural environment is an integral aspect of living freely and that, insofar as we fail in this task, we become subject to a form of servitude. Rather than damaging our freedom, the process of struggling to release ourselves from the destructive powers of natural forces can make us more free. Needless to say, the Spinozist position I shall explore does not provide immediate solutions to our environmental problems. How could it? Rather, it provides us with an opportunity to investigate an ambitious picture of what freedom can amount to, and of the traits we need to cultivate in order to enjoy it. It is, in effect, an invitation to try to put this vision to work and see if we can use it to ameliorate the dilemma I have outlined. According to Spinoza, people can be so deeply mistaken about the nature of liberty that they will fight for their servitude as if for their survival (*salus*) (TTP Pref. 10; III/7). The question is whether we, too, may unwittingly be falling into this trap when we resist efforts to accommodate ourselves to nature on the grounds that doing so will render us less free.

II

Spinoza's analysis of liberty shares the central commitments of the broadly republican conception of freedom that was popular in the United Provinces during his lifetime, a conception that in turn drew heavily on Roman Law.[2] At the heart of this view lies the assumption that one lives freely when one is not subject to the power of other agents who can treat you as they choose. To take the stock example, a master possesses the freedom to do what he likes with his slaves, and it is the fact that they are subject to his power that makes them unfree. Their vulnerability constitutes their servitude, regardless of whether the master treats them well or badly. Thus conceived, freedom and servitude come in degrees; for example, a chattel slave will be less free than the citizen of a democracy who is largely well protected by the law, but remains in certain ways subject to her employer. Equally, some forms of freedom may be more valuable than others; freedom from chattel slavery is normally far more valuable than freedom from a limited dependence on one's employer. Yet again, some forms of unfreedom are less present than others; the chattel slave whose master treats her well is as unfree

---

[2] Spinoza's interest in the contribution of the natural environment to a free way of life is arguably indebted to the work of his fellow republican Pieter de la Court, who dwells on the relation between a state's natural features and its liberty. De la Court, 1972.

as a fellow-slave who is beaten every day, but the quality of her servitude is not as oppressive. Through all these variations, freedom consists in being able to sustain the capacity to live as one wants, rather than as someone else wants one to live.

Because republican theorists have traditionally been concerned with political liberty, their interests have tended to focus on the relations between individual people, and between individuals and states. Furthermore, this set of concerns is reflected in their formulations of what freedom is. For example, republicans standardly claim that the distinction between freedom and servitude lies in the difference between being able to act according to your own *arbitrium* or will and being subject to the will of another. What renders an agent unfree is subjection to the will of someone who can, with impunity, treat them as they choose. This formulation makes freedom a function of relationships between agents who possess wills, and it is implicitly assumed that, at least among finite things, this condition restricts the domain of liberty. Putting aside non-human animals (who are sometimes held to be capable of volition) we are left with individual humans, and with entities such as states in which law or convention determines how the wills of individuals are to be collectively expressed. Living freely or in accordance with one's own will is thus mainly construed as a capacity of human beings.

The same assumption is implicit in an associated aspect of the republican position, this time to the effect that one is free insofar as one is *sui iuris* or able act in accordance with one's own right (TP II.9; III.280).[3] In this case, freedom only extends to things that possess *ius*, and once again it is widely agreed that this is primarily a feature of human beings. By contrast with rocks, waves or rabbits, humans are bearers of rights and, since they also possess wills, are capable of exercising their rights voluntarily or for themselves. One person can therefore render another unfree by arbitrarily suppressing the right of the second person to act in accordance with their own will, and the same applies to human associations such as states or households. Beyond this, however, few if any natural things are capable of living *sui iuris* or freely.

Republicans therefore mainly regard freedom as a human trait; but one feature of their analysis sits uneasily with this outlook. To live freely, they repeatedly argue, one must be protected from the arbitrary power of other agents, and when one loses this protection one loses liberty. One way of being unfree is to be vulnerable to another person who can treat you as they wish, and here we return to familiar figures such as the slave master, the tyrant, and the patriarchal father or husband. However, if we focus on this interpretation of liberty, there seems no reason to assume that humans and human associations are the only things that

---

[3] According to Spinoza, being *sui iuris* or living in accordance with your own *ingenium* or temperament is contrasted with being *sub alterius potestate*, being under the power of another. The capacity to live *sui iuris* can be limited by bonds, by being disarmed and by having no means of self defence, but also by fear, and by being so beholden to a benefactor that you'd rather please him than yourself.

can reduce it. After all, the world is full of viruses, torrents, and hurricanes, which exercise their power over us with impunity. Why should we not describe our vulnerability to them as a form of servitude?

In this respect, then, the republican view invites us to envisage freedom as dependent on our relationships with non-human as well as human things. To live freely, it suggests, is to be protected against all arbitrary power, regardless of its source, and the more we fail to meet this condition the less free we are. Reflecting on this proposal, one may feel that it sets the bar too high; as well as making unalloyed freedom impossible to attain, it points in the direction of a way of life so cautious and risk averse as to be the very opposite of free. Perhaps these presumed implications help to explain why few writers within the republican tradition attempt to theorize nature as the domain of freedom, and why most concern themselves only with civil or political liberty. In Spinoza, however, we find an exception. The arguments of his *Ethics* and his two political works (the *Theological-Political Treatise* and the *Political Treatise*) provide a metaphysical basis for a more expansive conception of liberty that nevertheless retains the essential features of the republican view.

Nature, Spinoza argues, contains an infinity of finite individuals, yoked together by an overarching system of causes and effects, and continually interacting with one another. This pattern of relationships is determined by the power of each individual to maintain itself in existence. As the *Ethics* puts it, 'Each thing, as far as it can by its own power, strives to persevere in its being.' (E IIIp6; II/146). *How* an individual perseveres in its being or exercises its power varies from one kind of thing to another, and indeed among individuals of a single kind. But despite these variations, we can think of nature as a field of interacting individuals, where the powers through which they maintain themselves are constantly at work. Each individual does what it can to remain in existence as its environment alters, until something external destroys it. To cite the *Ethics* again, 'No thing has anything in itself by which it can be destroyed, or which takes its existence away' (E IIIp6;II/146).

Among republican theorists, the ability to exercise one's own power is, as we have seen, traditionally identified with the notion of being *sui iuris* or able to act according to one's own right, just as being dependent upon the power of another is identified with being subject to their right. Reiterating a version of this position, Spinoza claims that 'the natural right of each individual extends as far as its power does' (TTP XVI.3; III/189). Once we allow that individual things continue to exist by exercising their power to persevere in their being, it is a short step to the claim that, in exercising this power, an individual exercises its right. For example, 'whatever each man does according to the laws of his nature he does with the supreme right of nature. He has as much right over nature as he has power' (TP II.4; III/277). In the human sphere, this conclusion has startling implications. 'Just as the wise man has the supreme right to do everything that reason dictates,...so also the ignorant and weak-minded have the supreme right to do everything appetite urges...' (TTP XVI.6; III/190). But the equation of right with power has a no less striking effect on the way we think about non-human things, since they too can be said to exercise their power to persevere in their being by right. If a plant, for instance, exercises its power to continue to exist by moving towards the sun it does so rightfully, just as a stone exercises its right when it resists being broken by a hammer. Adopting the republican formulation we have already explored, we can say that each of these things acts *sui iuris* and this is what it is to act freely.[4] Insofar, then, as an individual of any kind strives to remain in existence or exercises its own right, it acts freely; and since any individual strives in this fashion for as long as it exists, any existing thing must be at least somewhat free.

We have here the beginnings of a comprehensive analysis of freedom and servitude that extends to all finite things, but it is still not clear what the notion of acting in accordance with your own right amounts to. What sort of power qualifies a thing as active and hence constitutes its own right? We act, Spinoza explains, when 'something happens, in us or outside us, of which we are the adequate cause...By contrast,...we are acted on when something happens in us, or something follows from our nature, of which we are only the partial cause' (E III def. 2; II/139). In the *Ethics*, these definitions are introduced to throw light on the character of human freedom, but they apply quite generally. The more a thing affects the external things it encounters, the more it acts or exercises its right and the more free it is; correspondingly, the more it is affected by external things, the more it is acted on and the greater its unfreedom or servitude. An individual's power to act is therefore constituted by its own causal efficacy, though this in turn is a complex phenomenon. It has a quantitative dimension, as when one kind of stone has a greater power than another to resist the blows of a hammer; and a qualitative one, as when a plant has the power to turn to the sun but not to survive a hard frost.[5] Furthermore, as Spinoza repeatedly emphasizes, an individual's power to act may be more or less sustainable. Short-lived plasma cells, as they are known, have less power to persevere in their being than long-lived plasma cells; or to take one of Spinoza's examples, 'the virtue of a free man is seen to be as great in avoiding dangers as in overcoming them....In a free man, a timely flight is held to show as much tenacity (*animositas*) as fighting' (E IVp69; II/262).

Because an individual's power to act has these various dimensions, it is not always clear when one thing acts on another. 'No one has yet determined', Spinoza reminds us, 'what the body can do' (E IIIp2s; II/142). Perhaps we can hazard that

---

[4] 'I call a man completely free just insofar as he is guided by reason, because to that extent he is determined to action by causes which can be understood adequately through his own nature alone...' (TP II.11; III/280).

[5] On this distinction see Gatens 2009b, 455–68.

a plant is acted on when it is killed by a frost, and a child is acted on when weakened by a virus. But even if these particular examples are not persuasive, Spinoza has given us an analysis of freedom and servitude that, by contrast with most republican interpretations of liberty, extends throughout the realm of nature. The continual interplay of individuals' rights or powers expresses their changing levels of freedom and servitude, and this is as true of plants or electricity grids as it is of human beings.[6]

III

Despite the broad applicability of his account of liberty, Spinoza shares with his fellow-republicans a special interest in human freedom, and thus in what it is for humans to act and be acted on. As he explains, the character of our human power to persevere in our being reflects the kind of thing we are, and consequently has an intellectual dimension. 'Insofar as our mind has adequate ideas it necessarily does certain things [acts], and insofar as it has inadequate ideas it necessarily undergoes certain things' (E IIIp1; II/140). Implicit in these claims is the idea that what gives us our distinctive power to affect external things is our grasp of the relationships at work within the natural domain of which we are a part. In our human case, it is by understanding the powers of individual things, and the pattern of their interactions, that we become most active and best able to protect ourselves against servitude. Just as a plant has a particular way of manifesting the power that belongs to it, so do we. The more we are guided by adequate ideas, as opposed to being guided by things outside us, the more we act for ourselves.

Developing this strand of argument, Spinoza describes the process of acquiring and using adequate ideas as reasoning, so that it is through reasoning that we manifest our power to act.[7] This already indicates where we should look in order to get a better grasp of the nature of human freedom. But what is it, exactly, to reason or have adequate ideas, and thus to act in accordance with our own power or right? It is tempting to assume that Spinoza conceives of reasoning as a self-contained and self-validating kind of thinking. Suppose, for instance, you already have adequate ideas of certain premises and now go on to derive a set of conclusions from them. The causes of this operation—the adequate ideas that constitute the premises together with the exercise of reason that enables you to infer one conclusion from another—are in your mind, and your commitment to them is not indebted to the way that external things affect you. You see why the premises are true and how the conclusions follow from them, and actively derive each step of the argument from

---

[6] On electricity grids see Bennett 2010, 24–8.
[7] 'Only insofar as it understands does the mind act' (E IVp28; II/228).

its predecessor. When you reason in this fashion, you determine your own thoughts, and rather than being acted on by other things, you act.

The *Ethics* offers some textual support for such a reading (e.g. E IIp43–4; II/123–6). But if reasoning is construed in this fashion it is not obvious how it will make us more active and less vulnerable to the power of external things. For example, I may know that A follows from B, but not be motivated to do anything about it. To see how reasoning constitutes our power to *act*, we first need to take account of Spinoza's claim that our experiences of acting and being acted on are themselves affective, and that much of our everyday behaviour is determined by the way that external things act on us. In our ordinary encounters with external things, the way they act on us causes us to experience them as lovable, frightening and so on, and this in turn prompts us to respond to them. They subject us to their power, and in this sense render us passive.[8] When we reason, however, the situation changes. There is something satisfying or pleasurable about the process of coming to know more about ourselves and our environment which, as well as breeding intellectual conviction, is manifested in what Spinoza calls *fortitudo*—a desire or determination to do what reason dictates (E IIIp59; II/188). Reasoning or understanding is therefore not just a matter of seeing how one thing follows from another, but also of acting on our knowledge or putting it into practice. Furthermore, this is our characteristically human way of exercising our *conatus* or power to persevere in our being. When we act in the light of our understanding we act as opposed to being acted on, and this is what it is for us to manifest our freedom. As Spinoza sums it up, 'a free man lives according to the dictate of reason alone', and the more we reason the more freely we live (E IIIp67; II/261).

The process of becoming more active and free therefore has two inseparable aspects. On the one hand, it is a matter of extending our rational knowledge of the powers of individual things and their resulting patterns of interaction, a project that demands intellectual insight, together with the capacity to persevere in the face of intellectual obstacles and overcome prejudice. On the other hand, it is a matter of putting our knowledge into practice or extending our ability to live in accordance with it, and for this we need both the ingenuity to counteract passive affects and the resourcefulness to devise ways of life that protect us from arbitrary power. Since, as Spinoza points out, it is possible to be convinced of something without being attracted to it (EI App. [III]; II/81]), both aspects have to be worked at. Acting tests our theoretical and practical ingenuity, and only by cultivating both dimensions of our power can we succeed in enlarging our freedom.

If liberating ourselves is a matter of creating and sustaining ways of life that reflect our surest knowledge and enable us to secure ourselves against servitude, one of the first truths we need to grasp is that, as individuals, we have comparatively

---

[8] 'The actions of the mind arise from adequate ideas alone; the passions depend on inadequate ideas alone' (E IIIp3; II/144).

little power. Although we attribute power or right to individual human beings, the right we are referring to is so slight and fragile as to be almost a fiction. 'It consists more in opinion than in fact, since there is no secure way to maintain it' (TP II.15; III/281). The only way to significantly increase our power is to combine forces with other things, and the things that are most useful to us are, in Spinoza's considered opinion, other human beings. 'If two men make an agreement with one another and join forces, they can do more together, and hence, together have more right over nature than either does alone. The more connections they've formed in this way, the more right they'll all have together' (TP II.13; III/281).

At first glance, this seems an unpromising claim. People who live in communities often find themselves subject to factions or officials who reduce rather than extend their freedom, and shared ways of life can be oppressive and frustrating. Without denying the force of these objections, Spinoza responds in characteristically republican style. Although communities often fail to generate worthwhile forms of freedom, communal forms of existence are our only chance. The challenge is therefore to devise collective ways of life that do in fact protect us from arbitrary power and enhance our individual and collective liberty.

Picking up this gauntlet, Spinoza outlines two types of association. The first is an idealized and fictional community, whose members each possess an exceptional level of understanding, together with the virtues that allow them to live as their understanding dictates. Each recognizes that the optimal way to maintain and extend their power and freedom is to ensure that others have no reason to disempower them, and also recognizes that the way to realize this goal is to commit to a way of life that is equally advantageous for all. Furthermore, each knows how to treat the others with unfailing justice, honesty, kindness, and humanity, and refrains from exercising arbitrary power over anyone else (E IVp37s1; II/236). As a consequence, each is able to embrace the effects that others have on them as contributions to their own power or right and enhancements of their freedom.

Taken together, these wise people constitute a community that qualifies as an individual in its own right, a body politic whose power to act derives entirely from that of its individual members. Other than its members' commitment to upholding norms from which they all benefit, the collective has no further power to maintain itself, so that if the individuals who constitute it were to stop cooperating, it would collapse. As things are, however, their actions give rise to powers that none of them individually possess, including the power to sustain a maximally free way of life. They contribute to a free community, and the free community in turn upholds their individual liberty.

Spinoza is clear that the most powerful kind of association through which we can actually protect and enhance our freedom is the state. However corrupt our states may be, their goal is not 'to restrain men by fear and make them subject to another's control, but on the contrary to free each person from fear so that he may live securely, as far as possible, i.e. so that he retains to the utmost his natural right to exist and operate without harm to himself or anyone else. The end of the Republic, I say, is to enable men's minds and bodies to perform their functions safely, to enable them to use their reason freely, and not to clash with one another in hatred, anger or deception, or deal inequitably with one another. So the end of the state is really freedom' (TTP XX.11–12; III/240–1). However, while the members of an idealized community of the wise can, in the standard republican formulation, trust one another to make the safety of the people the supreme law,[9] the state is a different kettle of fish. No one, however well-intentioned, can be at the peak of their understanding the whole time (TP II.8; III/279), and many people have only a limited degree of understanding in the first place. The state is consequently an arena of agonistic conflict in which individual and collective agents, including the state itself, engage in unending struggle, in which these agents often try to subject one another to arbitrary power, and in which sovereigns and citizens have to be protected from the effects of their own powerlessness.

Various tools are needed to generate freedom in these circumstances, of which the foremost, Spinoza suggests, is institutional design. By this he means the creation of laws and political systems that both constrain individuals to uphold conditions in which they are protected from arbitrary power, and allow them to use their understanding to live increasingly freely. In the model republics he sets out in the *Political Treatise* these ends are largely achieved by means of political inclusion. The best way to protect a community from the state's arbitrary power is to ensure that constitutional and policy decisions are made by large and relatively diverse assemblies, in which many groups are represented and vested interests cancel each other out. Nevertheless, since the symbiosis between state and individual is always less than complete, so too is freedom. The threats to liberty that arise from within are never entirely or conclusively overcome, and the task of keeping them at bay requires continual attention and ingenuity.

Discussing these problems, Spinoza sometimes gives the impression that they can only be dealt with by a ruling elite, which uses the force of legislation to keep the mob at bay. For example, he sometimes speaks contemptuously of the *vulgus*, whose members are bent on flouting the law and exercising arbitrary power over one another, and who, when they join forces, can destabilize a whole community. However, as he elsewhere indicates, these deficiencies are ones that, to varying degrees, we all share. We all suffer from the insufficiency of our understanding. We do not know enough about the causes and effects of our interactions with one another to be sure when we are acting and when we are not, how far we are exercising our own power or right and how far we are being acted on by external things. Furthermore, even when we have a theoretical grasp of what is causing what, we may not know how to live by it. For example, we may not know how to

<hr>

[9] For Spinoza's use of this formulation see for example TP VII.5; III/310.

counter our passive affects, to how to make our shared knowledge collectively compelling so that it can contribute to our common way of life.

The task of the state is to offset the damaging effects of both these aspects of powerlessness. In some cases, states can make it possible for individuals to live as they would if they were more powerful than they are, by protecting them against the arbitrary power of other agents and curbing their capacity to exercise arbitrary power over others. The state, we could say, carries the burden of protecting its members from arbitrary power in the face of their own passivity. In one sense, it gives them more political freedom than they possess as individuals; but in another sense it constitutes their individual liberty, by creating circumstances in which they can become better acquainted with the boundaries of their own power or right, precisely because their collective way of life makes this knowledge available to them.

Spinoza also addresses a set of problems that arise when people suffer from the second aspect of powerlessness and cannot see how to live in the light of their understanding. For example, individual citizens who are subject to a badly designed law may foresee its enslaving effects and be able to envisage more liberating legal arrangements. They know how the law could be improved, and may find themselves torn between conforming to the status quo on the grounds that it is part of a legal system on which their freedom depends, and resisting it because it will increase the exercise of arbitrary power (TTP XX.29; III/244). While he is not a principled opponent of political resistance, Spinoza emphasizes its risks, reminding his readers of cases where revolutionaries were unable to implement their aspirations and destroyed more freedom than they created (TTP XVIII.33; III/227). Citizens need to remain alive to the difference between knowing how one could in principle produce a more active way of life, and knowing how to put this knowledge into practice by converting the arrangements they imagine into a political reality. Since the measure of their understanding is not what they can envisage in the way of a free life, but what they can do to realize it, their lack of practical know-how acts as a brake on their freedom. When the state coerces them into obeying the law, it protects its own freedom and may to some extent protect theirs. But the fact that neither is able to take advantage of their potentially liberating knowledge reveals the limits of each party's power. The state lacks the power to extend its freedom by drawing on the insights of its citizens, and its citizens lack the power to get their insights translated into policy.

As these cases indicate, freedom as Spinoza conceives it is a practical political achievement. In order to realize it, states and individuals must be alive to the demands of understanding; but they must also appreciate the need to compensate for, and adapt to, the lack of it. To live as freely as we can, we must learn to act together in a shifting social landscape, where the threat and reality of arbitrary power is never absent, and our power to combat it must continually take new forms.

IV

Spinoza's interest in political freedom is driven by his conviction that states and the individuals who live in them are mutually vulnerable. Nothing poses a greater threat to the power of a state than its own members, and nothing is better placed to reduce individuals to subjection than a state. At the same time, states and their members are mutually dependent. While their relations can be treacherous and destructive, their capacity to respond to one another gives them, in Spinoza's view, an unparalleled potential to create free ways of life. When he discusses the freedom of states, his thoughts are therefore mainly turned inward to those who live in them. He is of course aware that states also exist among other kinds of individuals whose powers outstrip their own and, as we have seen, is committed to the view that a state's freedom can be affected by its relations with non-human things. But to make his analysis of freedom complete, he needs to address the implications of these issues and explain how states can protect themselves from the arbitrary power of the natural environment.

A distinctive feature of many non-human natural things is that they are, as far as we know, unable to adapt to us. While states may be able to negotiate with other states, and by this means produce yet more powerful individuals, there is no negotiating with the sea or the weather. Confronted by forces such as these, a state must either try to master them, or alter its own way of life so that they no longer diminish its power or right to live freely. Following the first strategy, one might hold back the sea by building a dyke; following the second, one might move a city to higher ground.

As a firm exponent of the view that individuals of all kinds have the right to do anything in their power, Spinoza endorses the first of these strategies without blenching. Humans, he argues, have the right to use other natural things for their own ends, and are under no obligation to hold back. For example, they may eat animals when they can, and to refrain from doing so is to fall prey to unmanly compassion.[10] But this encouragement to subdue the earth comes with a warning. Since we are prone to overestimate our power to act, our efforts to consolidate and extend it are liable to backfire. We need to learn to appreciate the extent of our vulnerability and proceed cautiously, taking account of the limits of our understanding and of our physical weaknesses. In some cases we may be able to subject natural things to our power without endangering our freedom; but where we cannot, the only way forward is to adopt the second strategy, and try to defeat the arbitrary power of external things by adapting our way of life to the

---

[10] 'The law against killing animals is based more on empty superstition and unmanly compassion than on sound reason. The rational principle of seeking our own advantage teaches us the necessity of joining with other men, but not with other animals, or with things whose nature is different from our nature. We have the same right against them as they have against us' (E IVp37s1; II/236–7).

ineluctable forces of nature. Individually and collectively, we can either employ these two strategies to ensure as far as possible that we are not arbitrarily acted on, or else submit to a life of servitude.

It may seem that, in our own case, the second and more concessive strategy counsels nothing but resignation. To adapt ourselves to greenhouse gases, rising sea levels and so on, we shall after all have to give up the freedoms we care about and live in yurts. Spinoza does not rule out the possibility that this may turn out to be the most we can achieve; perhaps, in order to survive, we shall have to live in ways that now strike many of us as unacceptably impoverished. Nor does he deny that communities which have to live like this are liable to be comparatively miserable. Learning to counteract the negative passions that external things arouse in us by cultivating our active understanding is, he acknowledges, extremely difficult. Using the forms of training and self-discipline that Foucault examines in *The Care of the Self*, some individuals may acquire the power to remain active and unruffled in the face of a vastly more restricted and threatened existence, but many of us can be expected to suffer from regret and disappointment, together with the resentment, fear and anger that these passions are in turn liable to cause.[11] Living freely will consequently become harder, and the obstacles that communities have to deal with in order to sustain liberating ways of life will increase.

Whilst he acknowledges these sombre possibilities, Spinoza is not an advocate of resignation. Our freedom, after all, consists in exercising our power to live in the light of the surest knowledge we possess by cultivating our understanding in all the ways we can, and to abandon this task is to succumb to the power of external things. We should therefore continue to subdue the earth as long as we can safely do so; and where we need to adapt to it, we should use our understanding to create alternative forms of living that we can enter into cheerfully. If the prospect of life in a yurt fills us with a sense of desolation, we must exercise all our power to devise alternatives that answer to our knowledge of our environment, but are also within our collective power to embrace. Since there is no *telos* or limit to our efforts to persevere in our being (EI App [II]; II/80), and since we do not yet know what the body can do, nothing in our own nature gives us grounds for abandoning the attempt to live more freely.

It is helpful to recognize that, because Spinoza ties human freedom so closely to our knowledge, theoretical and practical, his notion of a free way of life is extremely fluid. The freedom of a community is constituted by what it knows and what it can do with its knowledge, and will therefore vary from case to case. For example (and here Spinoza uncritically echoes a widespread early-modern European view), in a despotism such as the Ottoman Empire the way of life that

---

[11] Foucault 1986.

sovereigns and subjects regard as free is premised on such a restricted level of understanding as to be, in fact, a form of servitude (TTP Pref. 10; III/7). By contrast (and here Spinoza's tongue is somewhat in his cheek), the inhabitants of the city of Amsterdam are able to live in a fashion that answers to their richer understanding and protects them from arbitrary power. As he puts it, 'we happen to have the rare good fortune to live in a republic in which everyone is granted complete freedom of judgment, and is permitted to worship God according to his mentality (*ingenium*), and in which nothing is thought dearer or sweeter than freedom' (TTP Pref. 12; III/7).

The underlying point here is that, as a community's knowledge grows, the demands that a free way of life imposes on it will alter, so that living freely requires a certain flexibility—an openness to the opportunities that new knowledge creates, a willingness to develop the practical expertise to adapt to it, and a wary sensitivity to the vulnerabilities that changing ways of life may generate. An active community, as well as guarding its current understanding of freedom, will foster its capacity to embrace changes to its way of life that flow from its evolving knowledge of its environment. Which adaptations it can make, and how successfully it can embrace them, will in turn reflect its existing understanding—its grasp of what is going on and its capacity to live accordingly. But the more it can resist ossification and rigidity, the better placed it will be to sustain its freedom.

One may feel inclined to object that this conception of liberty as a moving target is too demanding. Even if we accept Spinoza's claim that freedom consists in the absence of arbitrary power, and are willing to agree that, as our understanding of the arbitrary powers to which we are subject grows, the project of liberating ourselves changes shape, it may still seem that he places too much emphasis upon this single value. Living freely is important, but so is living comfortably within the bounds of tradition. Can we not allow that, despite being subject to the arbitrary power of various features of our environment, we have enough freedom to get along and do not need to stretch ourselves to increase it?

What we feel about this plea may of course depend on where we are living and who we are, but Spinoza's reply is intended to be comprehensive. As we have seen, existing things act or exercise their power in different ways, and humans are distinguished by the fact that their activity consists in understanding. This is our human way of persevering in our being, and it is only by exercising our power in this fashion that we live freely. It is of course possible for us passively to relinquish our freedom by becoming subject to the arbitrary power of other things. For example, the threats posed by our environment may make us so fearful that we lose all hope of finding a solution to them and give up the attempt to do so. In this scenario, however, we would not be exercising our own power. Our debilitating passions would mark the extent to which we were being acted on by external things, and had lost the power to act for ourselves. To abandon the project of persevering in our being by extending our understanding would be to give up being what we are, and this is not within our power. We are, as it were, condemned to live as freely as we can, by collectively adjusting ourselves not only to one another, but to our natural environment as well. Where we succeed we increase our liberty, and where we fail we lose it.

Returning to our current situation, Spinoza would urge us to see it not as one where many of our existing freedoms are threatened, but rather as one of increasing servitude. Our subjection to the arbitrary power of environmental forces, combined with our inability to overcome or offset this power, is a significant infringement of our liberty. Rather than worrying about how to keep such freedoms as we have, we need to ask ourselves how, in the light of our growing knowledge, we are going to become more free. How are we going to put our knowledge into practice and generate ways of life that will enhance our liberty by reducing our vulnerability to arbitrary environmental powers? In sum, then, the threat we face is not that we may have to abandon our current way of life for one that is not so free. The depletion of our liberty is already under way, and we are bound to resist it as far as we can. Our task is to make our resistance effective by engaging with nature in a fashion that manifests our understanding and sustains our power to live freely.

12

The Affective Cost of Philosophical Self-Transformation

I

We tend to accept that, over the course of our lives, we experience some pleasures and satisfactions at the expense of others, and sometimes regret paths we have not taken.[1] A politician who rejoices in her all-consuming profession may be sad not to have more time for her friends, and an immigrant who leads a fulfilling life in her adopted country may still yearn for the pleasures of home. Trade-offs of this kind seem unavoidable. Joy cannot but be mixed with sadness. Yet according to a long tradition of thought, negative affects can be completely transcended by philosophical understanding. The more we understand, the more the ordinary emotional costs of our lives pale into insignificance and ultimately disappear. Freed from affective ambivalence, the true philosopher is so absorbed in the joy of understanding that it encompasses all his feelings for individual things. Rather than regretting pleasures that fail to fit into his way of life, he takes delight in cultivating insights that entirely free him from sadness.

Distant as this philosophical ideal may be, our everyday experience lends it some plausibility. As we acquire fresh objects of desire or become committed to new values, we sometimes unequivocally lose the ones we had before. Food that once seemed delicious ceases to be appealing, the pleasures of adolescent passion no longer move us, and so on. Why, then, should the experience of philosophizing not generate a further, unequivocal transformation of our values that detaches us from those we previously held without affective loss? Why should we not become entirely and uncompromisingly committed to the pleasure that understanding is said to generate?

Many philosophers have embraced the view that philosophy is the only route to unalloyed joyfulness and have argued that, as we increase our philosophical understanding, we become more like God. But their vision remains clouded by the suspicion that it is delusory. Does it not represent a wish on the part of the philosopher rather than a real possibility? May it not be a form of compensation

[1] I am particularly grateful to Timothy Harrison for his generous suggestions about the structure of this essay. I should also like to thank Emanuele Costa, Evelyne Ender, Moira Gatens, Genevieve Lloyd, Yi-Ping Ong, Robert Pippin, Christopher Thomas and Anthony Uhlmann for their helpful comments.

Spinoza on Learning to Live Together. Susan James, Oxford University Press (2020). © Susan James.
DOI: 10.1093/oso/9780198713074.001.0001

or legitimation, designed to distract attention from philosophy's intellectual or affective limits? May it not be bombastic and even authoritarian to aspire to a form of existence so far removed from ordinary life and to surround it with an aura of divinity?

These doubts deserve a full-scale examination, but I shall restrict myself to considering the issue as it appears in the work of a single philosopher. According to Spinoza, the achievement of philosophical understanding produces a form of joy unmarred by any sadness or regret. But how persuasively does he defend this view? Within the confines of his philosophical system, I shall suggest, his defence is watertight. To suggest that the process of philosophical enlightenment involves any affective cost is simply to display a lack of understanding, and thus to fall short of the insight and joy that understanding ultimately yields. As I shall try to show, however, something nevertheless seems to be missing from this account, and a sense of its incompleteness hovers around the edges of Spinoza's thinking as well as ours.

II

According to Spinoza, our efforts to understand ourselves and the world culminate in a kind of knowledge in which our ideas merge with those of God. Our minds become, as he expresses it, part of God's infinite intellect. At the same time, this knowledge brings with it a supreme and indefeasible form of joyfulness, the so-called intellectual love of God that 'nothing in nature can take away' (E Vp37; II/303). In defending this transformative conception of philosophy, Spinoza inserts himself into a long tradition, stretching far back into Antiquity. According to David Sedley, it was Plato who first articulated the version Spinoza inherits. Whilst figures such as Pythagoras and Empedocles had conceived the process of becoming divine as a matter of passing through a series of incarnations, Plato proposes that we emulate God by learning to live a particular kind of life.[2]

The divine standards that the philosopher tries to practise are partly moral: since God is essentially good, we emulate him by exercising the virtues of justice, courage, moderation, and wisdom that together constitute goodness. Moreover, since this is what it is to serve God, we simultaneously practise the virtue of holiness, so that the philosopher's virtuousness also expresses his godliness or piety.[3] In addition, there is a more specifically intellectual aspect of a godlike existence. As Sedley puts it, 'a human being is a mixture of mortal and immortal parts... If you concentrate your concerns on one or other of the mortal parts of the soul, by devoting your life to acquisitive or to competitive pursuits, you will be making

---

[2] Sedley, 1999, 310.   [3] Sedley, 1999, 313–14.

your mortal soul your true self...Conversely, if you concentrate on developing your intellect, you will be identifying your true self with the immortal part of your soul. It is in that sense that someone who pursues intellectual excellence is achieving immortality, to the extent that this is possible for a human being.'[4] If we ask how we can develop our intellect, Plato answers that we should turn our minds away from becoming and towards being, and argues that the way to do this is to focus our thoughts on the eternal mathematical principles governing the heavenly bodies. We become more like God as we understand these principles and, as the *Timaeus* explains, harmonize the motions of our rational souls with the motions of the stars.[5]

Viewed in this light, philosophy enables us to emulate the divine, and those who know how to practise it progressively transform themselves into the kind of human beings whose way of life has four salient features. They strive for knowledge of eternal rather than temporal things. As they come to possess knowledge of this kind they think some of God's thoughts, and thus come to participate in the divine. Since they have to develop this kind of understanding for themselves, acquiring it is an active process requiring tenacity and skill. Furthermore, as Socrates explains, 'the divine standard is supremely happy, the godless one supremely wretched', so that the more the philosopher manages to emulate God by immersing himself in his knowledge of the eternal and living accordingly, the more joyful he becomes.[6]

Sedley contends that this interpretation of Plato's doctrine was largely taken for granted by Roman authors. When, in the *Laws*, the Athenian stranger opposes the view of Protagoras, arguing that 'It will be God who, par excellence, is the measure of all things for us, rather than a man, as some people claim', he concisely sums up what Romans regarded as the moral *telos* of Platonism.[7] However, because this Platonic image of the philosophical life was transmitted to early-modern authors by diverse routes, they do not always associate it with Plato. Spinoza, for example, dismisses Plato's authority as 'not worth much', and only mentions him in passing.[8] He defends Plato's use of definitions (PP I.301; I/235), but disparages his 'speculations' (TTP II.258; III/168) and criticizes his view of universals (ST I.86–7; I/42). But although Spinoza's position is antithetical to that of Plato in several crucial respects, his conception of what philosophy is able to achieve can justly be described as Platonic. For him, as for Plato, the pursuit of philosophical enlightenment requires dedication and skill; it is a matter of developing one's intellect or understanding. Moreover, it yields knowledge of the eternal, enables us to become more like God by participating in divine knowledge, and generates a level of joyfulness that transcends all others.

---

[4] Sedley 1999, 320.   [5] Plato 2016, 76.   [6] Sedley 1999, 312.   [7] Sedley 1999, 309.
[8] Letter 56 to Boxel, October/November 1674, Spinoza 2016; IV/261.

The process of cultivating philosophical knowledge can in Spinoza's view be divided into three overlapping stages (E IIp40s2; II/122). We start out with inadequate ideas derived from the ways we have been affected by external things, and with the passive affects that inadequate ideas incorporate. We strive to live joyfully and minimize sadness, but are hampered by our incomplete and confused grasp of what exists and what is good for us. The remedy lies in a second kind of knowledge—reason or understanding—constituted by adequate or true ideas. As we learn how to distinguish our adequate ideas and become adept at reasoning our way from one to another, we gain a fuller understanding; and because this kind of knowledge simultaneously generates active affects—a desire to live in the light of our understanding and an ability to take joy in doing so—it enables us to empower ourselves by living as our understanding dictates. Understanding therefore already has a transformative effect. In place of the unstable joys and sadnesses that characterize an imaginative way of life, we become increasingly able to secure our own joyfulness.

One might be inclined to suppose that this is as much insight as we need, but Spinoza goes on to posit a third kind of knowledge, intuition, which builds upon our rational understanding and 'proceeds from an adequate idea of the formal essence of certain attributes of God to the adequate knowledge of the formal essence of things' (E IIp40s2 [IV]; II/122). When we intuit how our adequate ideas of things follow from our adequate idea of God, and put this insight at the centre of our quest for a more empowering way of life, we experiences a further affect—the intellectual love of God (E Vp32c; II/300). God and everything that follows from him becomes the object of our love, and our affects are subsumed into the desire to increase the extent to which we share his ideas. At the pinnacle of philosophical enlightenment, our knowledge and love become focused on a single object, namely God, and our minds are, as it were, absorbed into his infinite intellect.

Spinoza's account of intuitive knowledge echoes Plato's view that, as we make philosophical progress, we come to share some of God's ideas and know that we are doing so. The mind, Spinoza tells us, 'knows that it is in God and conceived by God' (E Vp30; II/299). But intuitive knowledge—and to a lesser extent rational understanding—also possess the three further Platonic features we have identified: they are concerned with eternal things, they are active states, and they yield an incomparable level of joy. Whereas our everyday or imaginative thinking focuses on ephemeral things that come into existence and perish, understanding gives us knowledge of the eternal essences of things, and intuitive knowledge makes our ideas of these essences fully adequate by enabling us to appreciate how they follow from the divine attributes (E IAx. 4; II/46). As we acquire these levels of insight, we increasingly conceive things 'under a species of eternity'; and 'to that extent they involve the eternal and infinite essence of God' (E Vp29s; II/299). Furthermore, as we acquire understanding and intuitive knowledge, we become more active in the sense of becoming more able to think and act for ourselves. Whilst our imaginative conception of the world is assembled from a sequence of arbitrary encounters with external things, and yields ideas that are partial and confused, understanding and intuition manifest themselves in active thought processes of which we are the guarantors. We see for ourselves whether an idea is true and how one idea follows from another. We take control of our own thinking and in doing so gain power over the way that external things affect us, transforming the vulnerability to the world that is the mark of imagination into the ability to prevent our experience from disempowering us. As Spinoza sums it up, 'that mind is most acted on of which inadequate ideas form the greatest part, so that it is distinguished more by what it undergoes than by what it does. By contrast, that mind acts most, of which adequate ideas constitute the greatest part' (E Vp20s;II/293).

Because, in Spinoza's view, increases in our power manifest themselves in joy-fulness, and decreases manifest themselves in sadness, the growth of activity that understanding brings simultaneously enhances our joy. In our imaginative lives, we try to relate to external things in ways that are empowering and satisfying, but we remain vulnerable to the sadness with which they are capable of affecting us. The great advantage of understanding is that it frees us from this constraint. Insofar as joy flows from our understanding, it flows from something we control and can bring to bear on the passive affects that beset us. As our understanding grows, we increase our power to counter sadness with joy, and as our knowledge becomes intuitive, we reach a point where we become impervious to sadness. Nothing that happens to us diminishes our power or disturbs the joyfulness of sharing God's ideas (E Vp37; II/303).

In the *Ethics* Spinoza develops the metaphysical and psychological aspects of this position. On the metaphysical side, he construes the difference between the adequate ideas that constitute understanding and the inadequate ideas that belong to imagination in terms of lack or privation. 'Falsity', he tells us, 'consists in the privation of knowledge that inadequate, or mutilated and confused, ideas involve', so that the inadequacy of an idea is merely a lack of adequacy (E IIp35; II/117). Writing to Hugo Boxel, he spells out this view by describing what it is like to acquire an adequate idea of a triangle. 'When I first began to learn Euclid's *Elements*', he writes, 'I understood first that the three angles of a triangle equal two right angles. I understood this property of the triangle clearly and distinctly, though I was ignorant of many other properties of the same triangle' (Letter 56; IV/261). As he acquired clear ideas of more of these properties, Spinoza's idea of the triangle became more adequate; but this development was not fundamentally a matter of correcting what he already knew. Rather, it was a matter of filling what were previously privations or gaps in his knowledge of the triangle. The more gaps he filled, the better he came to know its essence or being, and the less his idea of it was characterized by lack. In place of an idea that was unreal to the extent that it failed to capture aspects of the being of a triangle, he arrived at an

eternal idea of its being that is also in the mind of God. In this process no knowledge is lost; on the contrary, overcoming the privations in our imaginatively
grounded knowledge is nothing but gain.

For a philosopher who adequately understands the being of a triangle, opting
for an inadequate over an adequate idea of it would therefore amount to opting
for nothingness over being and ignorance over knowledge, and in Spinoza's view
this is not a move the philosopher can intentionally make. Humans are of course
subject to many kinds of delusion, including the delusion that we have an unlim-
ited power to affirm or deny ideas; but understanding is nevertheless compelling.
Once you really understand Pythagoras's theorem you will affirm its conclusion,
and will be unable knowingly to affirm a claim that contradicts it. Once you
understand that a fly is a finite body, you will not be able to affirm the idea of an
infinite fly (TIE I.27; II/23). You may feign or fantasize about such a thing, but
you will not be able to take its existence seriously. Furthermore, the force of
reasoning has an even more powerful analogue in intuitive knowledge. To grasp
intuitively how the formal essence of a thing follows from an attribute of God is to
grasp an idea that is in God's eternal and unchanging mind. Once again, this kind
of knowledge makes it impossible to gainsay what one knows. The further we
progress towards intuitive understanding, the more intellectually inescapable our
insights become.

On the psychological side, this increase of intellectual conviction is matched by
an affective transformation because, as our understanding progressively excludes
our inadequate ideas, it diminishes our passive affects. Someone who is infatuated,
for example, but understands the causes of their passion, will feel differently from
someone who has no idea why the infatuation has occurred. The first person's
appreciation of the web of causes and effects to which the infatuation belongs,
and their correspondingly richer feeling of its emotional pros and cons, will colour
the affect and be reflected in their desires. In some cases this context may overcome the infatuation, but Spinoza returns several times to a popular seventeenth-
century trope, Ovid's portrayal of Medea, who 'sees the better but follows the
worse' when she abandons her familial duties to follow Jason.[9] Medea's predicament,
as Spinoza construes it, is that, while she knows enough to struggle with her
dilemma and conclude that she ought to stay at home, she does not know how to
act on her judgment. Lacking a more adequate understanding of herself and her
situation, she cannot stabilize her desire to relinquish Jason, and makes what proves
to be a tragic choice. If, *per impossibile*, her understanding had been greater, her
story would have had a different ending (E III p31c; II/164: E IV p17s; II/221).

The philosopher who has acquired a fair degree of understanding stands at a
different point in this process. Whereas Medea has a vacillating and inadequate idea

---

[9] Ovid 1955, Book VII. 1–150, 155–9.

of what she should do in order to live as joyfully as possible, the philosopher is fully committed to the pursuit of adequate ideas, and is familiar with the empowerment and joyfulness which result. His strongest desire is therefore to extend his understanding, and he knows how to counteract or dismiss conflicting desires for other ends. Furthermore, as his understanding grows, he becomes capable of acquiring intuitive knowledge and experiencing a further affective transformation. The more adequately he understands how his ideas of the formal essences of things follow from the mind of God, the more his affects focus on the cause of these ideas, namely the divine mind. The more actively he appreciates how his knowledge depends on God, the more he experiences an active or intellectual love for God, which in turn shapes his affective responses to everything that flows from him.

Is this transition accompanied by any regret for the passive susceptibilities and satisfactions that the philosopher leaves behind? Can he mourn the overwhelming sexual passions of his youth, for example, or the delight he once took in making more money than his peers? It seems not. As he cultivates his understanding, Spinoza argues, the philosopher becomes progressively less susceptible to ordinary forms of sadness and only esteems himself, as the *Ethics* puts it, for his rational part. His joys are integral to his adequate ideas, and his desires are focused on increasing them. 'He who knows things by this kind of knowledge passes to the greatest perfection', Spinoza tells us, and 'is affected by the greatest joy, accompanied by the idea of himself and his virtue. Therefore, the greatest satisfaction there can be arises from this kind of knowledge' (E Vp27; II/297).

Once the philosopher has achieved this perspective, any residual desire for the less powerful conditions he has surpassed is bound to manifest itself as a mark of imperfect understanding. Metaphysically, to give it weight would be to slip back into confusing being with lack of being. Psychologically, it would be to opt for what he understands to be a lesser joy, and this, Spinoza claims, he cannot knowingly do. For a philosopher who has steadily progressed towards greater understanding, the past does not contain anything worthy of regret. In Platonic vein, the *Ethics* holds out an ideal of an utterly secure and joyful way of life, free from sadness about what one has been and what one now is.

Spinoza does his best to make this ideal attractive. Philosophers, as he portrays them, are not reclusive or ascetic (E IVp35s; II/234: IVp45s; II/244–5). Nor do they entirely lose touch with the passive affects of those around them. They understand the transient joys and sadnesses that ordinary people derive from their changing relationships with one another, and feel some sympathy for them. But they do not share their passions, and stand at a distance from the patterns of affective exchange that are the stuff of everyday emotional life. For example, a philosopher whose neighbour does him a well-meaning but compromising favour understands that the neighbour is trying to benefit him, but does not feel the pleasure the neighbour expects him to feel and cannot give him the satisfaction of accepting or reciprocating his gift on the terms in which it is offered. He runs the risk that the neighbour will feel slighted or offended; but he will not do anything that contravenes his rational understanding of what, in the circumstances, justice requires (E IVp70; II/263). Equally, a wise man will stand back from friendships with people who want him to prioritize their desires over his own, or want to subordinate their desires to his. He will understand their passions, sexual or otherwise, and do his best to help give them some satisfying direction. But he will not be able to reciprocate them in the way these would-be friends or lovers desire; instead, he will strive to free them from their unrequitable desires 'from the dictate of reason alone' (E IVp50; II/247).

In their relationships with people who are less wise than they are, philosophers therefore adopt a pedagogical role. They use their understanding to protect themselves from saddening affects and to teach others to do the same, and because this process actively empowers them, it brings them joy. This, at least, is Spinoza's official story. But it remains to ask whether these distancing strategies are not in any way saddening, and whether the successful pursuit of a philosophical life is unequivocally joyful.

III

In the light of Spinoza's official doctrine, it comes as something of a surprise to learn that the philosopher who has so far achieved the greatest level of intuitive knowledge is, in his view, Jesus Christ. Only Christ, we discover from the *Theological-Political Treatise*, has fully understood how the eternal truths that he taught follow from the divine nature (TTP IV.31; III/64-5). Only he 'communicated with God mind to mind' (TTP I.24; III/21). More than any other human known to the historical record, his understanding enabled him to participate in God's mind and in this sense become like God. However, if Christ exemplifies the model of philosophical self-transformation described in the *Ethics*, we may wonder why his life as it is recounted in the New Testament was not more unequivocally joyful. The gospel Spinoza most often refers to in the *Treatise* is that of Matthew who, as its readers would have been well aware, dwells on Jesus's sadness in the Garden of Gethsemane. Jesus 'took with him Peter and the two sons of Zebedee, and began to be sorrowful and very heavy. Then said he unto them, My soul is exceedingly sorrowful even unto death; tarry ye here and watch with me.' Christ fears death, grieves for the imminent loss of his life, and reproaches his sleeping disciples for failing to comfort him. ('What, could you not watch with me one hour?')[10] The joy he derives from his intuitive knowledge and love of God

---

[10] Gospel according to St Matthew, 26.37–26.41.

is tempered by sadness, and his determination to try to live as his knowledge and love dictate is not without emotional cost.

Here we encounter a tension in Spinoza's position. On the one hand, he argues that philosophical understanding is incompatible with sadness; on the other hand, Matthew's account of Jesus' life suggests that even the greatest philosophers remain subject to sad passions. We seem forced to conclude either that Jesus' philosophical understanding was limited, so that he continued to be subject to passive affects, or that the account of the affective dimension of philosophical illumination given in the *Ethics* is oversimplified and leaves something out. Spinoza is not unaware of this difficulty and offers two ways of resolving it. Since the gospels are written for ordinary people and are adapted to their understanding, he contends, we should treat Matthew's description of Jesus' suffering as a fiction designed to arouse our feelings for his plight (TTP XI. 12–13; III/155). We do not need to regard it as evidence of a real affective burden attaching to the process of philosophical self-transformation, and the philosophical ideal described in the *Ethics* is therefore not endangered. A second line of argument is more concessive. It may well be, Spinoza sometimes implies, that not even a human being of Jesus' philosophical stature can acquire enough understanding to resist or counteract all disempowering affects. In practice, the philosophical transformation we undergo as we cultivate understanding is never complete and never entirely frees us from sadness (E IVp4; II/212–3). But insofar as we do achieve understanding and intuitive knowledge, we do not suffer any affective loss.

These are powerful replies, and Spinoza stands by each of them. But they leave an uncertainty as to why we are unable to live wholly in accordance with his philosophical ideal. Is the problem simply that external things sometimes affect us with such force that, however wise we become, we remain subject to passive affects? Or is it also that certain forms of sadness are an inescapable feature of the process of philosophical self-transformation, so that no philosopher, however powerful, can avoid them? Spinoza is comfortable with the first suggestion and can easily embrace it; but by making Jesus the exemplar of a philosophical life, he perhaps unwittingly raises the suspicion that some sadness or affective loss may be integral to self-transformation. If even Jesus suffered such a loss, why should we believe that any philosopher can avoid it?

The structure of Spinoza's philosophical position makes this worry difficult to articulate. As we have seen, developing our understanding is a matter of increasing our adequate ideas. As the philosopher cultivates understanding, he leaves behind his inadequate ideas and reduces the extent to which he confuses being with lack of being. He becomes able to distinguish things as they truly are in the mind of God from things as he merely imagines them to be. This process, Spinoza contends, increases his power, and since increases in his power manifest themselves in joyfulness, it also increases his joy. Furthermore, since sadness is an expression of decreases in his power, and power is never decreased by understanding, understanding cannot be manifested in sadness. Any residual sadness that the philosopher experiences as he pursues understanding can only be an expression of inadequate ideas and thus a lack of understanding.

Within this tightly organized argument there is no space for the possibility I have raised—that sadness or affective loss might be integral to understanding. Any attempt to articulate such a view emerges as a failure to grasp what understanding is, and becomes in Spinozist terms unintelligible. Once subjected to the power of reason, it ceases to make sense. This logical exclusion is undoubtedly an impressive feature of Spinoza's broadly Platonist conception of philosophy. But there is something strained about it that surfaces from time to time, for example in his account of the negotiations between more and less philosophically capable people such as the donor and recipient of the corrupt favour. By presenting relationships like these as staging posts on the way to a condition of greater understanding, Spinoza marginalizes the significance of the affective losses they involve. Yes, the donor, for instance, is liable to suffer some sadness, but it is temporary. As his understanding increases he will come to realize that this affect reflected a privation in his knowledge and it will cease to trouble him.

If we confine ourselves to the *Ethics*, this reply is irreproachable. But Spinoza's handling of the problem does not allay the worry that the philosopher's joy and resilience is bought at an unacknowledged cost. To see what the cost might be, we need to move away from Spinoza's philosophical system to a worldview in which there is space to examine it. For Spinoza himself, any such outlook is bound to fall within the purview of imagination and thus fall short of understanding. But that is precisely the problem; a Spinozist conception of philosophical knowledge excludes the possibility that understanding has affective costs. To explore this idea further I shall draw on two novels by J. M. Coetzee, *The Childhood of Jesus* and *The Schooldays of Jesus*. With Coetzee's help, we may be able to consider afresh whether the process of self-transformation deprives the Spinozist philosopher of affective relationships with ordinary, imaginative people, and in doing so exposes him to a significant form of sadness.

IV

The main protagonists of Coetzee's two fictions are recent immigrants to a Spanish-speaking country where people are encouraged to let go of their old attachments and be 'washed clean of old ties'.[11] On the boat that brings him there, a man called Simón takes charge of a young boy, David, who has become separated from his mother. Simón is set on finding the missing mother, but when he

---

[11] Coetzee 2013, 24.

arrives he first has to get a job and a place to live. In the process he meets a number of people, and although most of them are perfectly friendly and helpful, he finds them bloodless. 'Everyone I meet is so decent, so kindly, so well intentioned. No one swears or gets angry. No one gets drunk. No one even raises his voice. You live on a diet of bread and water and bean paste and you claim to be filled. How can that be, humanly speaking?'[12] Simón misses good food, but he also misses sexual passion. 'Benevolence, I must tell you, is what we keep encountering here. Everyone wishes us well, everyone is ready to be kind to us. We are positively borne along on a cloud of goodwill. But it all remains a bit abstract. Can goodwill by itself satisfy our needs? Is it not in our nature to crave something more tangible?'[13] However, his efforts to get his point across are rebuffed. Benevolence *is* enough, his friend Ana tells him; the storms of passion he longs for only produce 'frustration, doubt and heartsore', and the something-more that he wants is an illusion.[14] Reflecting on his new life, Simón wonders if he might learn to be satisfied by friendship and 'emerge as a new, perfected man', but he is not persuaded.[15] 'What he wants to say, *for his part*, is that life here is too placid for his taste, too lacking in ups and downs, in drama and tension—is too much, in fact, like the music on the radio.'[16]

As far as Simón can tell, the people he encounters are incurious and lack intellectual ambition. They are not philosophers as Spinoza understands them, but they nevertheless illustrate a problem that is liable to afflict the relationships between philosophers and ordinary individuals. Like Spinozist philosophers, they are unable to respond to Simón's passionate desires in a way that satisfies him, and their failure to do so is a source of pain, made worse by their unshakeable conviction that the objects of his desires are illusory. Living in the ambit of a philosopher would be similar. A philosophically insightful person who understood the inadequacy of Simón's ideas would not be able to enter into his storms of passion and would be unable to satisfy them on his terms. Despite the philosopher's pedagogical aspiration to increase joyfulness, he would be a force for sadness.

This conclusion may seem peripheral to our problem; the issue, after all, is not whether philosophers are liable to cause sadness in others, but whether sadness is integral to their own pursuit of knowledge. But the two issues are linked, and in his portrayal of David's relationship with Simón, Coetzee shows how this is so.

Simón quickly becomes attached to David, although the boy is frustratingly reserved and unaffectionate. 'Perhaps the truth is', Simón concedes, 'I am the one who needs him.'[17] He continues his search for David's mother, and when he encounters Inès, a childless woman about whom he knows next to nothing, he is convinced he has found her. Inès accepts the role he presses on her, and over time the three of them come to form a makeshift family. They are bound together by

---

[12] Coetzee 2013, 37.   [13] Coetzee 2013, 66–7.   [14] Coetzee 2013, 68, 75.
[15] Coetzee 2013, 68.   [16] Coetzee 2013, 76.   [17] Coetzee 2013, 113.

David, although as the boy often tells people, 'Simón is not my father' and 'Inès is not my mother'. He is, he says, 'nobody's son'.[18]

David, as many characters in the novels remark, is an exceptional child. He is intelligent, but his teachers are convinced that he has learning difficulties and want to send him to a special school; he is restless and does not make friends with other children; he is sensitive to atmosphere, but rarely expresses affection for Inès or Simón. Simón keeps trying to get David to acknowledge his quasi-paternal authority and absorb his beliefs, but is moved to desperation by the child's way-wardness. When, for instance, Simón has carefully explained that one must work so as not to take from others, he asks David if he wants to be the kind of person who gives or the kind who takes. 'The kind who takes', comes the reply.[19] In the face of the boy's relentless stream of questions, Simón tries to produce 'correct, patient, educative' replies, but comes to feel that doing so is futile. 'Where is there any evidence', he wonders, 'that the child absorbs his guidance or even hears what he says?' Every now and then his patience gives out. 'Think of it this way, he says. We are tramping through the desert, you Inès and I. You tell me you are thirsty and I offer you a glass of water. Instead of drinking the water you pour it into the sand. You say you thirst for answers. *Why this? Why that?* I, because I am patient, because I love you, offer you an answer each time, which you pour away into the sand. Today, at last, I am tired of offering you water.'[20]

This tension is at first exacerbated when David is enrolled in an academy of dance run on Platonist lines. Through dance, the Academy teaches children to see beyond mathematical rules such as addition and subtraction to the stars—the realm of the numbers themselves—and to bring their souls into accord with the underlying movement of the universe.[21] David excels at this activity; but he longs for Simón to see what he sees when he dances ('Did you see seven?') and help him understand it. He wants Simón to accompany him in the process of enlighten-ment on which he finds himself embarked, and is upset when Simón is unable to do so. 'You say you love me, but you don't love me. You just pretend.'[22] The gulf between David and Simón is painful to them both. Each is committed to an intel-lectual outlook that the other cannot grasp, and suffers from their inability to share it. Each wants a love that the other cannot give, and suffers from the lack of it.

Coetzee's account of Simón's dissatisfaction with the benevolent individuals around him has already cast a preliminary light on the sadness that ordinary people experience in the face of philosophical understanding, but his description of Simón's relationship with David illuminates it more sharply. Because Simón loves David, David's inability to requite his feeling is a deeply painful emotional loss. This time, however, David's answering frustration with Simón gestures at the reciprocal sadness suffered by the philosopher. Most of the people David knows

---

[18] Coetzee 2013, 38.   [19] Coetzee 2013, 36.   [20] Coetzee 2013, 51.
[21] Coetzee 2016, 68.   [22] Coetzee 2016, 51.

find his claims to knowledge mysterious and some of his actions unfathomable. They are not sure whether he is a damaged child who cannot develop ordinary attachments, or an exceptional one who is in the process of understanding a rare and elusive truth. David himself does not know what to make of his insights— this is partly why he needs Simon's help. But even if he did know—even if he were in the position of a philosopher who cannot doubt his own intuitions—his inability to share them would carry a double burden of sadness. In part, the philosopher's sadness lies in knowing that he is unable to give ordinary people what they want by way of affective exchange and is almost bound to disappoint them; and in part it lies in knowing that they are unable to share the joy he derives from understanding. For ordinary people, the satisfactions that matter most to the philosopher are a closed book.

In the second of his two novels, Coetzee broaches the question of whether, and how, the estrangement between Simón and David might be overcome. David's outlook does not allow for compromise. While he shows flickers of concern for Simón, he is incapable of subordinating his ideas and affects to paternal authority, and cannot ameliorate his own feelings of loss by cultivating the affects Simón would like him to feel. Simón, by contrast, comes to acknowledge that David cannot love him as he wants to be loved, and recognizes that the only way to get closer to him is on the boy's terms. At one level, this remains a source of sadness to Simón; he is by no means unequivocally committed to becoming 'a new perfected man'. But he also feels the charismatic pull of David's insight and wants to try to share it. Eventually, he goes to the school to learn to dance, and the novel ends—perhaps too easily—with his first lesson. 'It is cool in the studio; he is conscious of the high space above his head. Mercedes [his teacher] recedes: there is only the music. Arms extended, eyes closed, he shuffles in a slow circle. Over the horizon the first star begins to rise.'[23]

Simón's efforts to dance are born, perhaps, out of a mixture of desire and resignation; desire to know whatever it is that David knows, and the resigned acknowledgement that this is the only way to gain his love. In their mutual struggle to be recognized and loved on their own terms, David has won. But the triumph of the child is at the same time the triumph of the philosopher who insists, with whatever humility, on the superiority of his way of life. He knows with unparalleled certainty that his insights are true and his way of life more empowering than any other, and is confident in demanding that others should learn to share it. When Simón begins to dance, he begins to philosophize.

Throughout the philosophical tradition, accounts of the intense joyfulness that philosophy generates have been carefully crafted into a picture of a way of life that more than makes up for other affective losses. For philosophers such as Spinoza,

---

[23] Coetzee 2016, 260.

this image is ready and waiting. It furnishes what he describes as an exemplar to imitate; but it simultaneously creates a blind spot that cannot be seen or investigated within his ethical system. What becomes invisible are the affective losses secreted in the gulf between an ordinary and a philosophical existence. As the philosopher becomes more like God and ruptures his affective bonds with those he leaves behind, he creates sadness in himself and others. His sadness may be slight by comparison with the joys he embraces, but it is integral to the project of understanding.

V

I began by asking whether the joy purportedly experienced by the Spinozist philosopher is, as Spinoza claims, unmarred by sadness, and I have argued that it is not. As the philosopher develops his understanding, he become increasingly estranged from affective relationships with what I have been calling ordinary people; and this, I have suggested is a source of sadness or affective loss. The more the philosopher loses the power to enter into the imaginative affects that are the stuff of everyday life, the more emotionally isolated he becomes. Perhaps this is why Spinoza sets such store by the joy philosophers gain from one another. The members of a community of wise men, he claims, are able to rejoice in their mutual understanding and reciprocate one another's active affects. But this resolution of the problem does not sit easily with his emphasis on the political role of philosophy. The task of the state, as he conceives it, is not just to allow philosophers to enjoy their understanding, but to enable as many people as possible to share it. If a state is to flourish, philosophical understanding must be a public good. This latter strand in Spinoza's thinking suggests that the loss I have been trying to articulate is not only a disempowering source of sadness to philosophers, but to the state as well. Spinoza's political philosophy gives him a reason to acknowledge the sadness which is integral to the pursuit of understanding, but which he chooses in the *Ethics* to suppress.

13

Fortitude

Living in the Light of Our Knowledge

I

The difficulty of acting on what we know is all too familiar.[1] You know that you are getting flu, but you ignore the warning signs, keep working, and end up spending days in bed. Nation states know that they are destroying the planet, but continue to haggle about who is responsible and what should be done. In these cases, as in so many others, we are not completely in the dark. We know what is likely to happen and also have a good idea of how to avoid the damage. Yet we fail to act. Philosophers, psychologists, and social theorists have offered many explanations of why this should be the case; but our reluctance or inability to put our understanding to work can also be viewed as a moral limitation. When we turn away from uncomfortable truths, cling to our prejudices or allow ourselves to be persuaded by opinions we know to be dubious, we fall short of virtue.

Many seventeenth-century writers draw attention to this weakness. Itemizing some of our failings in the opening discourse of their *Logic*, for example, Antoine Arnauld and Pierre Nicole protest against our willingness to be satisfied by bad reasons, to let ourselves be carried away by appearances, to insist stubbornly on nonsense, and to make bold decisions about things we do not understand.[2] These errors, they imply, do not just flow from blameless ignorance, but are manifestations of culpable mental habits such as laziness, obstinacy, and overconfidence. When, for example, we wilfully defend opinions tainted by self-interest, or knowingly ground policy decisions on slender evidence, we fall short of standards that are simultaneously epistemic and moral.[3] In failing to live up to what we know, we fail to live well.

[1] I am particularly grateful to Lisa Shapiro for her response to an earlier draft of this essay. I am also indebted to Aurelia Armstrong, Deborah Brown, Alexander Douglas, Simona Forti, Francis Gilbert, Timothy Harrison, MM McKenzie, Christopher Kutz, Jonathan Lear, Stephen Nadler, Calvin Normore, Yi-Ping Ong, Robert Pippin, Miriam van Reijen, Piet Steenbakkers, Robert Stern, Nadia Urbinati and Rosemary Wagner for a wealth of comments and suggestions about fortitude.
[2] Arnauld and Nicole 1996, 5–6.   [3] See Frankfurt 2005.

Spinoza on Learning to Live Together. Susan James, Oxford University Press (2020). © Susan James.
DOI: 10.1093/oso/9780198713074.001.0001

In at least some areas of contemporary life, we have lost touch with this virtue.[4] Our susceptibility to fake news, our unwillingness to confront outlooks that disturb us, and our incuriousness about the practical effects of legislation are arguably manifestations of a failure to put our understanding to work, which in turn has profound effects on our way of life. Yet there seems to be relatively little determination to address this weakness. Here, I suggest, our seventeenth-century predecessors may be able to help us, if not by showing us what to do, at least by enabling us to articulate the virtues we need. I ask in particular what we may be able to learn from Spinoza, who characterizes the power to put our knowledge to work as fortitude (*fortitudo*) or strength of mind (*fortitudo animi*). The quality we need, in his view, is the fortitude to understand what we know and to draw conclusions; and for Spinoza, the conclusions in question are actions. Fortitude, as he construes it, is the power to act as our understanding dictates.

II

Spinoza construes our everyday failures to act on what we know as manifestations of a kind of thinking and an associated way of life that he describes as imagination or imagining. Insofar as we work with the inadequate ideas we derive from the way external things affect us, we are liable to make mistakes about what is good for us and pursue self-destructive courses of action. Worse still, some of our dispositions tend to prevent us from correcting these failings, and even exacerbate them. For example, our desire to represent ourselves as individuals who know what's what and are in control encourages us to believe that we are more capable than we are, and to misconstrue the causal powers of things around us. Instead of creating the securely satisfying ways of life that Spinoza describes as joyful, we render ourselves vulnerable to disempowering forms of sadness, such as anger, envy, and hatred.

The most effective way to overcome these difficulties, Spinoza argues, is to cultivate the power to reason or understand. By gradually supplementing our muddled or inadequate grasp of the world with more adequate ideas of the way things affect us, and thereby acquiring more adequate ideas of ourselves, we increase our power to live in an empowering and joyful fashion. Moreover, since understanding is the key to this achievement, there is nothing we have better reason to pursue. 'What we strive for from reason', Spinoza concludes, 'is nothing but understanding; nor does the mind, insofar as it uses reason, judge anything useful to it except what leads to understanding' (E IVp26; II/227).

---

[4] Lindquist 1997, for example, describes the quality we lack as the courage to understand what we know and draw conclusions, p. 2.

One of the benefits of understanding is that it makes the mind more powerful. This is partly because, as its understanding grows, the mind gains more adequate ideas, and thus a fuller grasp of the causal structure of the world. By acquiring a better knowledge of the relations between things, we get a better knowledge of the things themselves. But it is also because we become able to play a more active role in the exercise and pursuit of understanding.[5] As our ideas become more adequate, the connections between them become more transparent and we become better placed to assess our own efforts to reason. Instead of acting uncritically on the basis of the somewhat arbitrary sequences of ideas that constitute imagining, we put ourselves in a position to direct and evaluate our own thought processes.

This is clearly an important intellectual transition, but it also has an affective dimension. Like all increases in our power, the exercise of understanding is manifested in joyful affects. But in this case the satisfaction we gain is what Spinoza calls an active affect. Instead of responding joyfully, but passively, to the way an external thing affects us, we rejoice in the exercise of our active power of reasoning. The consciousness that we are in control of our understanding, and thus of our own empowerment, gives us a particular kind of satisfaction, and the more we exercise our understanding the more the satisfaction grows.[6]

In Spinoza's view, this is a feature of all understanding. Regardless of *what* we understand, the activity itself enhances our joyfulness and reinforces our desire to understand more. But some areas of understanding are particularly salient in relation to our empowerment and well-being. As we gain more adequate ideas of the processes through which our own passive affects arise, and learn how their destructive manifestations can be offset, we put ourselves in a better position to avoid sadness. We empower ourselves twice over, first by taking joy in understanding, and again by taking joy in using our understanding to make ourselves more securely joyful. Rather than simply enjoying our intellectual acumen, we put our understanding into practice so that it informs our way of life.

In the ideal case, our understanding and actions would be perfectly aligned and we would invariably act as our understanding dictates. But as Spinoza repeatedly emphasizes, this condition is virtually impossible for any human being to achieve. We often see what it would be best to do (what understanding dictates) yet fail to do it, and no one 'has such a powerful and unimpaired mind that he is not sometimes broken down and apt to be overcome' (TP VI.3). Learning how to suit our actions to our most adequate ideas is therefore a further power we need to develop and a further aspect of understanding we need to cultivate.[7]

---

[5] For a helpful table of the active affects see Lebuffe 2009, 204–5.
[6] Jaquet 2003 describes fortitude as the 'active joyful *conatus*', p. 20. See also Bove 2004, 117–25, 209–26.
[7] On fluctuating affects as a threat to fortitude see Laux 1993, 223–6; Stolze 2014, 569.

III

Spinoza describes the power to act on our understanding as fortitude. In the words of the *Ethics*, 'all actions that follow from affects related to the mind insofar as it understands, I relate to fortitude' (E IIIp59s; II/188). Since the actions in question follow from affects that are aspects of understanding, fortitude is clearly an active affect, a joyful determination to exercise understanding that is part of understanding itself. Here Spinoza tacitly enters into an ancient debate, conveniently rehearsed by Aquinas, about whether fortitude is a general or a particular virtue.[8] Ideally, Spinoza implies, it is a general one. We act as our understanding dictates in everything we do, whether we are solving a mathematical problem or having dinner with a friend. But fortitude also has a more particular focus. Spinoza's primary concern is not, for example, with the strength of mind that enables us to live in the light of our knowledge of triangles or stars, although insights such as these are not irrelevant. Instead, the core of fortitude lies in understanding how to cultivate in ourselves the power to act on our understanding. Fortitude therefore consists in a particular form of self-understanding, which is in turn manifested in two more specific virtues.

The first of these subordinate virtues is what Spinoza calls *animositas*, 'the desire by which one strives, solely from the dictate of reason, to preserve one's being (E IIIp59s; II/188). *Animositas*, Spinoza explains, is the determination to look after oneself, for example by staying sober, avoiding sexual excess, and sticking to a good diet (E III, Dftn. of the Affects, XLVIII; II/203). But these specific aspirations blend into a broader attentiveness to the complexity of our physical needs and a desire to sustain our overall health (E IVp60: II/256). Without a degree of physical strength and resilience we shall be unable to exercise fortitude.

At the same time, Spinoza's conception of the parallelism between body and mind implies that the capacity to look after our bodies is one aspect of a broader power to preserve ourselves by attending to our psychic in addition to our physical well-being. When we take care of our physical health by eating well, for example, we simultaneously cultivate our psychic health by avoiding the feelings of lethargy and liverishness that come from eating badly. It is therefore interesting to ask why Spinoza's examples of *animositas* focus so firmly on the body.

In foregrounding the body, I suggest, Spinoza concedes something to a classical conception of fortitude: the view that it is above all a virtue of the warrior who trains himself to endure physical hardship.[9] But we should not allow ourselves to be carried away by this allusion. While Spinoza allows that cultivating and exercising the physical strength needed in battle is one way of expressing *animositas*,

---

[8] Aquinas 1947, II.ii.123, Article 2.
[9] Aquinas 1947 attributes the view that fortitude is primarily displayed in battle to Aristotle (*Nicomachean Ethics* 1115a30–35). II.ii.123, Article 5.

he stresses that we also express it by avoiding conflict. Knowing how to avoid disempowerment is at least if not more important than knowing how to overcome it, so that a man who defuses tension may display greater *animositas* than one who fights his way out of a corner (E IVp69; II/262). In fact, as the *Political Treatise* emphasizes, those with true strength of mind will not promote war, but maintain and restore peace (TP V.4; III/296).

The centrality accorded to *animositas* is therefore not an indication that Spinoza regards fortitude as a predominantly military virtue. But it does reflect his view that we are fundamentally embodied creatures whose mental and physical well-being go hand in hand. To live as understanding recommends, we must not only learn to overcome a range of debilitating vices such as gluttony or drunkenness, but also learn how to avoid more systemic hardships such as poverty, famine, and war. By implication, then, *animositas* has a political dimension.

Alongside *animositas*, fortitude also incorporates a second affect that Spinoza describes as *generositas*, 'the desire by which each one strives, solely from the dictate of reason, to aid other men and join them to him in friendship' (E IIIp59s; II/188). This aspect of the analysis is grounded on the recognition that we cannot practise fortitude on our own. We need the help of other people, and therefore need to form cooperative or friendly relations that will help the project along. In the ideal case, the friendships that flow from understanding are entirely equitable bonds, in which friends guide each other 'considerately, kindly and with the greatest steadfastness of mind' (E IVp37s1; II/236). Whether the relationships in question are personal ties, agreements between citizens or alliances between states, they are equally beneficial and satisfying to everyone concerned. In practice, of course, friendships are not completely stable and harmonious, and can only aspire to this model of perfection; but insofar as we manage to cultivate *generositas*, we strive to resist sadness by uniting with others in a fashion that sustains collectively joyful ways of life (E IV App XII; II/269).

Spinoza's distinction between *animositas*, an individually oriented aspect of *fortitudo*, and *generositas*, its socially oriented counterpart, picks up a division between love of self and love of others that was familiar in early-modern Dutch culture. (Grotius, for example, cites a string of authorities who distinguish them.[10]) But in fortitude the two are linked together so closely that they become inseparable. We exercise *animositas* when we act on our understanding in order to further our individual well-being; but of all the things we need to understand about ourselves, one of the most vital is that well-being lies beyond our individual grasp. To practise *animositas* successfully we have to cultivate it in cooperation

---

[10] 'Generally speaking, good and evil things are divided into two classes. The first and more important group consists of those which directly concern the body itself....The second group has to do with things existing outside of ourselves, but nevertheless beneficial or injurious, painful or pleasing to us' (Grotius 2006, 22). On the Stoic antecedents of this view see Miller 2015, 105–7.

with other people, that is to say, we need to exercise *generositas*. Each capacity therefore blends into the other. Rather than having two distinct aspects, fortitude amounts to the stable and consistent power to live in the light of our understanding by looking after ourselves and cultivating friendship. This is the complex virtue that we have to learn to practise if we are to progress towards a truly joyful way of life.

IV

I am not aware of any other writer who presents fortitude as the unification of *animositas* and *generositas*, but whether or not Spinoza's analysis is original, it implicitly challenges at least three competing conceptions of what fortitude amounts to. One of these, as we have seen, is the view that fortitude is a military virtue. When Aquinas discusses this sense of the term, he endorses Aristotle's claim that fortitude is primarily a matter of the way one faces death in battle.[11] But he also cites Cicero's contrary opinion that, since the greatest fortitude is about the greatest things, and some civil affairs are more important and glorious than war, the greatest fortitude can be displayed in civil contexts.[12] Perhaps this is also the view that Rembrandt represents in his painting of Minerva, completed in 1635 and copied the following year by his pupil, Ferdinand Bol.[13] Minerva, the Roman equivalent of Athena, was associated with the strategic aspects of war and is traditionally shown wearing armour. But she is also the goddess of wisdom, and in this guise uses her strategic skills to uphold peace. A helpful account of her qualities can be found, for example, in Cesare Ripa's *Iconologia*, where the figure of Fortezza is shown holding a spear and a sprig of oak, and carrying a shield embossed with images of a boar and a lion.[14] As the accompanying description explains, she is armed like Athena, and her proper role is to suffer setbacks courageously. Her spear and the boar on her shield represent her bodily strength, while the sprig of oak and the lion indicate her strength of mind.

While the goddess's military attributes are certainly present in Rembrandt's painting, they are less prominent than the accoutrements of peace. With her hair flowing down over her shoulders and a laurel wreath on her head, Minerva sits reading a large book. Her helmet and shield are piled up behind her, but although they are within reach, her laurel wreath tells us that she is already victorious and

---

[11] Aquinas *1947*, II.ii.123, Article 5.   [12] Ibid.

[13] Rembrandt, *Minerva in her Study*, 1635. Oil on canvas, Leiden Collection; Ferdinand Bol, *Minerva in Her Study*, c. 1636, pen and brush in grey ink and black chalk, Rijksprentenkabinet, Rijksmuseum, Amsterdam. Bol later painted a closely related subject, *Portrait of Margarita Trip as Minerva instructing her sister Anna Maria Trip*, 1663, oil on canvas Rijksmuseum, Amsterdam.

[14] The first illustrated edition of Cesare Ripa's *Iconologia* was published in 1603 (Ripa 1603). The work became extremely popular throughout Europe, and a Dutch edition appeared in 1644 (Ripa 1644).

has no need to use them. She is free to devote herself to learning, represented both by the book in her hands, and by others on a shelf in the background.[15] The cultivation of the civil arts takes priority over physical force. The steadfastness in the face of setbacks that Ripa attributes to Athena likewise takes a peaceful form and is strengthened by the pursuit of understanding. Spinoza's conception of fortitude echoes this interpretation. Following in the footsteps of a Dutch humanist tradition that looked to Cicero and other classical authors for inspiration, he portrays fortitude as a predominantly civil virtue and marginalizes its military connotations.

A second conception of fortitude aligns it with the endurance of suffering. Aquinas, for example, discusses the view that, because it is more difficult to 'stand immovable in the midst of dangers than to attack them', steadfastness is the mark of the greatest fortitude.[16] 'The principal act of fortitude is to endure, not only certain things that are apprehended by the soul such as loss of life...but also things relating to the body such as wounds and blows'.[17] While Spinoza agrees that the capacity to confront death calmly is a mark of fortitude, he firmly repudiates a Christian conception of fortitude as passive endurance. Fortitude in this sense was often associated with martyrs who, as Calvin puts it, display their love of God by eagerly confronting death.[18] But Spinoza's philosophy has no space for such an outlook. There is no reward for passive suffering, whether on earth or in the afterlife, and to succumb to it is a failure of understanding. Rather, we display the greatest fortitude when we use our rational knowledge to live as positively as we can by resisting all forms of saddening disempowerment. Here Spinoza adds a conception of fortitude as passive suffering to the list of Christian virtues he rejects. Like humility, he implies, it 'is not a virtue nor does it arise from reason' (E IVp53; II/249). On the contrary, it displays a lack of power to combat the saddening effects of external things.

A third entrenched interpretation of fortitude also attracts Spinoza's criticism. 'One of the ways we fail to be rational', Aquinas had written, 'is because the will is disinclined to do what reason demands on account of some difficulty. To overcome this we need strength of mind.'[19] Spinoza can hardly dismiss this view outright; after all, he too views fortitude as the power to conform to the dictates of reason. But he is utterly at odds with Aquinas's claim that what prevents us from being rational, or from acting on our understanding, is a disinclination of the will. To attribute our failure to exercise fortitude to the will, he argues, is to misconstrue the nature of the mind by supposing that we can will ourselves to exercise fortitude. In truth, however, this is not a power we possess. We can only exhibit fortitude by

---

[15] In an earlier picture, Rembrandt painted a similar scene. Minerva sits surrounded by books, a globe and a lute, and her arms hang from a peg on the wall. *Minerva in Her Study*, c. 1631, oil on panel, Gemä ldegalerie, Berlin.

[16] Aquinas 1947, II.ii.123, Article 6.   [17] Aquinas 1947, II.ii.123, Art. 8.

[18] Calvin 1960, Book I, ch. viii, p. 13.   [19] Aquinas 1947, II.ii.123, Article 1.

exhibiting *animositas* and *generositas*, and these powers are functions of our understanding.[20]

Spinoza's insistence that we cannot simply will ourselves to exercise fortitude is also implicit in his account of *generositas*. Some commentators have tried to align his analysis of this virtue with Descartes' discussion of *générosité* in *Les passions de l'âme*, and there are certainly affinities between the two.[21] Each is the power to act resiliently on our clear and distinct ideas of what is best for us, and many of the specific traits that Descartes includes in *générosité* are echoed in Spinoza's account of *generositas*. For example, individuals who possess either of these virtues render each his due,[22] treat other people considerately and graciously,[23] and are able to control debilitating passions such as anger, envy, and hatred. If we concentrate on these similarities, it may seem that Spinoza simply takes over Descartes' account of *générosité* and incorporates it into his analysis of fortitude. But any such interpretation would fail to acknowledge a deep ontological gulf between the two philosophers. For Descartes, *générosité* is a power of the will. The man who possesses it 'knows that nothing truly belongs to him but his freedom to dispose his volitions, and that he ought to be praised and blamed for no other reason than using this freedom well or badly'.[24] For Spinoza, by contrast, no such power exists. *Generositas* and the fortitude to which it contributes are powers that we exercise through reasoning or understanding.

The three negative comparisons I have offered help us to see what Spinoza is opposing. Here, as elsewhere in his philosophy, he runs the risk of outraging his contemporaries by hijacking a current term and giving it a specific and in some ways a contentious sense. But the comparisons also help us see what he is trying to get across. The cultivation of fortitude, he aims to show, is partly a matter of individual self-discipline.[25] To make headway, we have to understand enough about the value of looking after ourselves and cooperating with others to be motivated to develop our capacities for *animositas* and *generositas*, and because each person is different, there are many ways in which this can be achieved. To some extent, our pursuit of fortitude is up to us, and it is therefore tempting to believe, as many of Spinoza's contemporaries did, that we have the power to exercise fortitude at will. For Spinoza, however, this is a leading example of our imaginative disposition to invest in our inadequate ideas and represent ourselves as more powerful than we are. By imagining that we can will ourselves to exercise fortitude when it matters, and by rejoicing in this self-image, we prevent ourselves from recognizing that fortitude depends on a range of antecedent causes. To practise it consistently we must already have made progress with *animositas* and *generositas*, and these are

---

[20] On Spinoza's analysis of *akrasia* see Lin 2006, 395–414; Montag 1999, 26–61.
[21] See Jacquet 2003, 17–18.   [22] Descartes 1985, Part III, articles 156 and 164.
[23] Descartes 1985, Part III, Article 156.   [24] Descartes 1985, Part III, Article 153.
[25] This aspect of fortitude, prominent at TP 1.6; III/275, is emphasized, for example, by Macherey 1995, 386, and Smith 2003, 200–1.

social as well as individual virtues. To cultivate them is to cultivate a social ethos, and here Spinoza's argument shifts from an individual into a political key.

V

Since no one has the power consistently to exercise fortitude on their own, cultivating it must be a collective project. The more adequately we understand ourselves, the more fully we appreciate that the most effective way to develop and sustain our power to act as our understanding dictates is to mobilize the power embodied in political associations. The more we are guided by reason, Spinoza contends, the more we desire to live in accordance with the common decision of the state (TP III.6; III/286) Fortitude therefore manifests itself in a desire to uphold the political communities in which we find ourselves, while maintaining the conditions in which this desire can thrive is one of the most important functions of government.

Some of Spinoza's most programmatic explications of the point of political life accordingly emphasize the need to encourage *generositas*. In general, he argues, our passive affects militate against cooperation. Lacking much understanding, and acting on our largely inadequate interpretations of the world, most of us are at least intermittently aggressive and self-destructive, and need political institutions that will contain our antisocial dispositions. By mobilizing affects such as fear, pride, or ambition, laws and social conventions help to bring it about that we are able to live somewhat as we would if our understanding were greater than it is, and where this strategy succeeds, individuals do not need to possess much fortitude. Rather than relying on their citizens to practise *animositas* and *generositas*, states employ other strategies to enhance their subjects' power to cooperate. They try to bring it about, for example, that fear of punishment is stronger than the satisfaction of disobeying the law, and that people are rewarded for treating one another considerately.

As Spinoza frequently points out, however, this approach is made precarious when the fortitude embodied in political institutions is challenged by citizens who view the established terms of cooperation as obstacles to the realization of their individual desires. To maintain the habit of fortitude by manipulating people's ever changing passive affects would require exceptional vigilance (*vigilantia*) and skill (*ars*), and since these qualities are usually in short supply, states cannot rely on them (E IVApp. XIII; II/269). As well as using political institutions to short-circuit the need for individual fortitude, they must also use institutions to create it. They must help citizens to understand the value of *animositas* and *generositas*, and promote circumstances in which they can put these virtues into practice. States, in short, have a vital role to play in the project of transforming our ways of life through understanding.

Spinoza's interpretation of the relationship between cultivating understanding and cultivating fortitude, and his analysis of the two elements of this virtue, reflect his own political situation and offer an unusually deep exploration of the virtues on which a successful republic depends. Moving beyond the standard demand that republican citizens should identify their interest with the common good and seek their own well-being in the well-being of the state, he examines the powers and states of mind that this political stance assumes. A republic, he suggests, must encourage a self-reflexiveness in our desires that brings them to rest on the satisfactions we derive from looking after ourselves in community with others, summed up in the virtue of fortitude. Somehow, states must enable us to affirm these aspirations with enough force and constancy to ensure that they guide our lives, both by offsetting our destructive passions and by helping us to cultivate cooperative forms of joyfulness.[26] But how are states supposed to achieve this, and what resources are they meant to deploy?

The responses we find in Spinoza's work are not as rich as one might wish, though his silence is partly justified by the fact that there is, as he sees it, no political recipe for cultivating fortitude.[27] Since the patterns of affect and levels of understanding that predominate in a community are the fruit of its history and material circumstances, a practice that strengthens fortitude in one state may fail in another. Among the fruits of understanding on which we have to learn to act is the insight that, just as each individual has to find out how best to develop their fortitude, so too does each state at every stage of its history.[28] To this extent, cultivating fortitude is a culturally specific project. At the same time, however, there are some general things to be said about it, and Spinoza offers some preliminary suggestions.

One of his lines of thought draws on the widespread early-modern conviction that some of the dispositions constituting *animositas* and *generositas* can be instilled with the help of maxims. To prepare yourself to do the right thing in a demanding situation, you employ the technique of imagining it in advance. The ideas you work with are bound to be inadequate—you do not know whether the imagined situation will arise, what the circumstances will be, or how you will be affected. However, by trying to envisage the obstacles you may have to face, along with the satisfaction of overcoming them, you can give yourself a model to imitate and strengthen your determination to live up to it. If and when the situation arises, you will know what to do and will have rehearsed the steps you need to

---

[26] See Gatens 2011, 23; Balibar 2018, 211–22.

[27] In the *TIE* Spinoza mentions the relevance of 'philosophia moralis', education, and medicine, and adds that 'mechanics is in no way to be despised'. But he gives pride of place to the process of healing and purifying the intellect 'so that it understands things successfully, without error and as well as possible' (TIE 15–16; II/9). On education see Merç on and Armstrong 2011; Leo 2015; Armstrong 2018; Gilbert 2017.

[28] On Spinoza's use of the Old Testament to illuminate the character of fortitude see Green 2013, 208–12.

take. Pedagogical practices of this type provided ready-made interpretations of what understanding reveals and thus what fortitude requires. For example, on the assumption that understanding recommends us to return hate with love, as Spinoza believes it does, the corresponding rule, 'Return hate with love', pinpoints an aspect of the way fortitude is expressed. But to make sure that 'we have this rule of reason ready when it is needed', Spinoza explains, 'we ought to think about and meditate frequently on the common wrongs of men, and how they may best be warded off by *generositas*. For if we join the image of this wrong to an imagination of this maxim, it will always be ready for us when a wrong is done to us' (E Vp10s; II/287–8).[29]

The success of this kind of training partly depends on repetition. Through repeated meditation on exemplary instances, one literally makes the idea of a pattern of action more present to the mind by ensuring that it recurs in one's train of thought. But it is also significant that maxims enter into a common way of life, in which we hold one another to the standards they set. Rather than having to work out from scratch what fortitude demands and what is involved in exercising it, existing practices embody answers to these questions. The maxim Spinoza picks out, 'Return hate with love', is of a piece with his view that fortitude is manifested in the determination to uphold peace, and in choosing it he is implicitly avoiding the many more warlike maxims that abounded in early-modern culture. His example speaks to the role of *generositas* as a defining feature of fortitude, just as other maxims will speak to his conception of *animositas* as the power to maintain one's individual well-being.

The importance of this latter virtue is also implicit in Spinoza's account of the rational habits that help people to sustain their health. The wise man, he tells us, has various pastimes: 'he restores himself with pleasant food and drink, with scents, with the beauty of green plants, with decoration, music, sports the theatre and other things of this kind' (E IVp45s; II/244–5). When a community makes these empowering pleasures available, whether by cultivating the arts, creating a beautiful environment, or providing decent food, it creates a way of life in which looking after oneself becomes the norm. By strolling in a park, sharing a pleasant meal or going to see a play, the inhabitants of a state exercise *animositas* within the domain of the everyday. Their material environment and its resources make a vital contribution to their fortitude.[30]

A state's success in creating shared ways of life therefore gives some indication of how far, and how well, it is succeeding in nurturing fortitude. But as well as upholding existing forms of community, Spinoza emphasizes the need for states to enable their members to broaden their understanding, thereby learning to exercise fortitude in unfamiliar ways. As he argues in the *Ethics*, we develop our

---

[29] See Stolze 2014, 573–4; Marshall 2013, 155–8.   [30] See Lord 2018; Rawes 2012.

capacity to live in the light of our understanding, and test our ability to do what reason dictates, by dealing with a wide variety of people and situations. Whenever possible, communities should therefore encourage their members to seek out difference, and treat their encounters with it as opportunities to unite *animositas* with *generositas*. Learning how to look after oneself in unfamiliar conditions, and how to cooperate with people whose desires differ from one's own, are central aspects of fortitude, and a virtuous state will strive to provide conditions in which we can develop these capacities safely.

This aspiration is perhaps most clearly reflected in Spinoza's defence of religious and philosophical pluralism. Because states have to work with the levels of understanding that they and their citizens possess, and can only go as fast as these ideas permit, they need to sustain a range of imaginative resources that will help individuals of different temperaments to live cooperatively. By refraining from imposing more than minimal doctrinal requirements, and permitting many forms of worship, a state allows people to develop their understanding by a multiplicity of routes, and to cultivate their fortitude by diverse means. But fortitude is also developed within explicitly political practices, above all within democratic institutions that give many classes of people a voice in government. If a democracy is to function well, it must be alert to the embodied traits that go to make effective citizens who can play their part in the state. It must practise and cultivate *animositas*. At the same time, political representatives must know how to take account of diverse and conflicting desires and outlooks, and be committed to accommodating them within a shared way of life. They must exercise *generositas*. Democratic deliberation, as Spinoza construes it, can help these processes along by requiring citizens to confront opinions and ways of life at odds with their own.

Maxims, the material fabric of social life, and the constitutional forms of political society are therefore relevant to a community's ability to cultivate *animositas* and *generositas*. Each plays a part in sustaining circumstances in which its members can develop the determination to exercise their understanding through thick and thin. But how would this conception of fortitude or strength of mind have been received by Spinoza's first readers? As we have seen, his analysis conflicts with some of the other interpretations of fortitude in play in seventeenth-century Dutch society. At the same time, however, it echoes certain aspects of a broadly Augustinian conception of fortitude that remained central to Dutch Protestantism. Although Spinoza rejects any hint of the idea that fortitude consists in passively enduring suffering, he is not completely out of sympathy with Augustine's claim that fortitude is 'the love that bears all things for the sake of the beloved', namely God.[31] For Augustine, suffering is one of the means through which God teaches us to understand ourselves. If we are to become more virtuous we must learn

---

[31] Augustine, *De moribus ecclesiae catholicae*, ch. xv. Quoted in Aquinas 1947, II.ii.123, Article 2; Article 4.

from our setbacks by striving to understand our 'cut and bleeding souls'.[32] Spinoza's theological outlook is of course quite unlike Augustine's; he denies, for example, that God takes an interest in human beings or acts with their ends in mind, and therefore cannot endow suffering with a divine purpose. But he nevertheless shares the view that, as we come to understand the causes of our suffering or sadness, and in doing so increase our understanding of God, circumstances that were once intensely painful become more bearable and may even be incorporated into a joyful outlook.

The power to endure sadness is thus an aspect of Spinozist fortitude that Augustinians among his readers might have recognized. It resonates not only in Spinoza's philosophy, but also in his politics, where his individual and collective heroes are steadfast citizens whose understanding urges them to uphold the law in all circumstances. The citizens of the Dutch Republic, for example, should exercise *generositas* by respecting legal forms of religious pluralism; the Roman general, Manlius Torquatus, was a model of *generositas* when he condemned his son to death in accordance with military law; and however strongly citizens disagree with a piece of legislation, they should act as it demands. People who refuse to obey the civil law, Spinoza argues, are like young men who, rather than submitting to the irksome authority of their parents, run off and join the army. They impetuously exchange a minor inconvenience for a real danger, and risk creating a situation in which the rule of law is damaged or destroyed. Fortitude is therefore not manifested in acts of lawlessness or resistance; on the contrary, it is displayed in the most heroic proportions by people who manage to keep cooperative exchange alive and find ways of avoiding or resolving conflict. Fortitude, in short, is the power to hang in there, keep on talking, and nurture the strength to try again.

VI

As our knowledge grows, the *Ethics* contends, we converge on a set of truths about the metaphysical structure of being and become increasingly determined to live as these truths dictate. But alongside this grand conception of fortitude, Spinoza proposes a more modest one. Our political lives are guided by our limited understanding of the forms of organization that will empower us most effectively and of the practices that can best enhance them. And since our efforts to develop our fortitude can only be based on such understanding as we have, they will often be misguided. Some of our schemes for increasing our bodily strength will fail; some of our efforts to cooperate will come to grief. For all that, we are never

---

[32] Augustine, *Confessions*, III. iv. 8; quoted in Brown 1967, 169.

without some level of understanding and some determination to put it to work. On however small a scale, we can continue to exercise fortitude.

In this modest form, fortitude gives meaning to our collective lives by articulating one of the values that unifies a disparate range of practices that may appear to have nothing in common. Why, after all, do we teach critical thinking in schools, encourage one another to exercise, or train ourselves in peaceful forms of protest? Part of the reason, Spinoza suggests, is that activities such as these are small steps in the project of building fortitude. This description need not be self-conscious; as we have seen, we sometimes follow the rules and conventions in which fortitude is embodied without putting it to ourselves that this is what we are doing. But once we recognize that we are working to develop fortitude, our activities appear in a new light. A teacher, for example, may find it helpful to view what he is doing as trying to increase the fortitude of adolescents with low self-esteem.[33] A mediator, who already practises fortitude, may find it helpful to examine her approach in Spinozist terms. By acknowledging such activities as small steps in the cultivation of fortitude, we empower ourselves to consider how far they complement one another and what they can achieve. We put ourselves in a position to ask how effectively we are exercising fortitude and how we might do better.

Because we no longer live in Spinoza's world of nascent nation states, our cultivation of fortitude is bound to take new forms. We have different imaginative blind spots and are implicated in different kinds of power. The political actors Spinoza envisaged mainly belonged to a male, patrician class, whose institutions reflected their culture and values. Although he acknowledges the existence and political significance of difference, the differences he has in mind are by our standards relatively limited and the power relations between groups unsatisfyingly lopsided. Men dominate women, the educated strata of society dominate the uneducated ones, and the strains of intersectionality are barely present. Insofar as Spinoza's interpretation of fortitude is shaped by this political context, we are unlikely to find it useful. The question for us is whether we can draw on his analysis to develop a less harmonious, more cacophonous kind of fortitude.[34]

Spinoza undoubtedly offers us some leads. His emphasis on *animositas* speaks to the situation of oppressed or deprived groups whose power to look after themselves has been diminished, whether for want of material resources or because their form of life has been damaged or destroyed.[35] And despite his general reticence on the subject of pedagogy, he does touch briefly on its role in promoting fortitude. But there are also problems that Spinoza does not address. One of these

---

[33] Gilbert 2017.
[34] See Stolze 2014, 561–80; Stolze 2007, 338–9; Gatens 2014, 31–3; Sharp 2007, 748–52; Ginsborg and Labate (2019), 83–94.
[35] On Spinoza's account of the strategies open to oppressed groups see Sangiacomo, 2019, 6.5.

arises from his portrayal of the state as the arena in which *animositas* and *generositas* are created and sustained. While he discusses the positive role that states can play in upholding these values, he does not fully acknowledge the ways that states can undermine them. Rather than acting as a force for fortitude, states can damage the conditions on which it depends, whether by instituting policies that block *animositas*, or undercutting *generositas*. In these circumstances, fortitude will have to take new forms that may go beyond the possibilities envisaged in Spinoza's texts.

A second area of difficulty concerns the role of *generositas*. When Spinoza talks about the difficulties of building friendships between diverse groups of people, he tends to focus on the relationships between individuals with different levels of understanding. Those with greater understanding, he implies, are in a position to handle their dealings with people who are less wise, and entice them into friendly relationships. Where this strategy is successful, the terms of friendship are determined by the wiser parties, who employ their knowledge to avoid conflict and encourage understanding. But this way of building *generositas* does not address the problem of building empowering relationships between oppressed groups and their oppressors, and fails to grapple with a prevalent form of conflict. To ameliorate oppression, we need to develop forms of fortitude that empower the oppressed to act on their understanding of how they are disadvantaged and what values they are denied, and at the same time empower their oppressors to hear them and act on what they learn.

At this point, however, Spinoza's notion of *generositas* is put under tremendous strain. For the oppressed, such cooperative relationships as they are able to build with their oppressors may fail to do justice to their understanding of their situation, and thus represent a failure of fortitude. For their oppressors, the terms of cooperation that the oppressed demand may seem to amount to a failure of understanding. In such circumstances, cooperative friendships are notoriously difficult to build; but while Spinoza concedes this point, his unqualified commitment to *generositas* may also begin to seem out of place. Perhaps refusing friendship is the only way for the oppressed to stake their claims. Perhaps incommensurable differences between the understanding of the oppressed and their oppressors stand in the way of friendship or cooperation between them. To take these possibilities seriously, we may need to adapt Spinoza's conception of *generositas*. In many circumstances, as he argues, we express fortitude by building cooperative or friendly relationships. But this may not always be possible. Fortitude in the face of oppression may sometimes be a matter of learning how to endure conflict, without being able to resolve it into anything approaching friendliness or cooperation with one's oppressors, and simultaneously learning how to contain the sadness that such disempowerment produces.

Just as Spinoza's conception of fortitude departs from his contemporaries' understandings of the term, so the forms of fortitude I am pointing to may go beyond his interpretation; and just as some of Spinoza's contemporaries would have rejected his account of fortitude out of hand, so he might baulk at the suggestion that it may need to be revised. Perhaps he would. However, although some of the problems I have touched on lie outside the immediate scope of Spinoza's political theorizing, they are not alien to his outlook. As I have tried to suggest, they are continuous with his analysis of fortitude and with his philosophically ambitious spirit.

Bibliography

Althusser, Louis (1976), *Essays in Self-Criticism* (London: New Left Books).

Aquinas, Thomas (1947), *Summa Theologiae*, ed. and trans. the Dominican Fathers. Digital version available at https://dhspriory.org/thomas/summa (Cincinnati: RCL Benziger Brothers).

Armstrong, Aurelia (2009), 'Natural and Unnatural Communities: Spinoza beyond Hobbes', *British Journal for the History of Philosophy* 17/2: 279–305.

Armstrong, Aurelia (2018), 'Affective Therapy: Spinoza's Approach to Self-cultivation', in M. Dennis and S. Werkhoven (eds), *Ethics and Self-cultivation: Historical and Contemporary Perspectives* (New York: Routledge), pp. 30–46.

Arnauld, Antoine and Nicole, Pierre (1996), *Logic or the Art of Thinking*, trans. and ed. J. V. Buroker (Cambridge: Cambridge University Press).

Augustine (1998), *The City of God*, trans. and ed. R. W. Dyson (Cambridge: Cambridge University Press).

Bacon, Francis (1996), 'Of Superstition', in B. Vickers (ed.), *Francis Bacon* (Oxford: Oxford University Press).

Balibar, Étienne (1994), *Masses, Classes, Ideas. Studies on Politics and Philosophy Before and After Marx* (London: Routledge).

Balibar, Étienne (1998), *Spinoza and Politics*, trans. P. Snowden (London: Verso).

Balibar, Étienne (2018), 'Individualité et transindividualité chez Spinoza', in *Spinoza politique. Le transindividuel* (Paris: Presses Universitaires de France), pp. 199–244.

Barbone, Steven (1999), 'Power in the *Tractatus theologico-politicus*', in P. Bagley (ed.), *Piety, Peace, and the Freedom to Philosophize. The New Synthese Historical Library* (Texts and Studies in the History of Philosophy) vol. 47 (Dordrecht: Springer), pp. 91–109.

Beard, Mary, North, John, and Price, Simon (1998), *Religions of Rome, vol. 1: A History* (Cambridge: Cambridge University Press).

Belaief, Gail (1971), *Spinoza's Philosophy of Law* (The Hague: Mouton).

Bennett, Jane (2010), *Vibrant Matter: A Political Ecology of Things* (Durham, NC: Duke University Press).

Bennett, Jonathan (2003), 'Spinoza on Belief and Error', in *Learning from Six Philosophers*, vol. 1 (Oxford: Oxford University Press), pp. 186–206.

Bijlsma, Rudmer (2015), 'Spinoza, Hume, and the Fate of the Natural Law Tradition', *International Journal of Philosophy and Theology* 76: 267–83.

Bijlsma, Rudmer (2017), 'The Philosopher, The Ordinary Believer, and Their Piety: Spinoza's Philosophical Religion', *Intellectual History Review*, 27/4: 515–41.

Black, Robert (2001), *Humanism and Education in Medieval and Renaissance Italy: Tradition and Innovation in Latin Schools from the Twelfth to the Fifteenth Century* (Cambridge: Cambridge University Press).

Blom, Hans (1995), *Morality and Causality in Politics: The Rise of Naturalism in Dutch Seventeenth-Century Thought* (The Hague: Gegevens Koninklijke Bibliotheek).

Bove, Laurent(2004), 'Hilaritas and aquiscientia in se ipso' in Y. Yovel and G. Segal (eds.), *Spinoza on Reason and the Free Man. Spinoza by 2000 – the Jerusalem Conference (Ethica IV)*. (New York: Little Room Press).

Boxhornius, Marcus Zuerius (1657), *Institutiones politicae* (Amsterdam: n.p.).

Brown, Peter (1967), *Augustine of Hippo. A Biography* (London: Faber & Faber).

Burgersdijk, Franco (1686), *Idea politica*, ed. G. Hornius (Leiden: Felix Lopes de Haro).

Calvin, Jean (1960), *Institutes of the Christian Religion*, ed. J. T. McNeil. (Louisville, KY: Westminster John Knox Press).

Carr, Spencer (1987), 'Spinoza's Distinction between Rational and Intuitive Knowledge', *Philosophical Review* 87/2: 241–52.

Charlton, Kenneth (1965), *Education in Renaissance England* (London: Routledge).

Cicero, Marcus Tullius (1913), *On Duties (De Officiis)*, trans. W. Miller (Cambridge, MA: Harvard University Press, Loeb Classical Library).

Cicero, Marcus Tullius (1933), *On the Nature of Gods (De Natura Deorum)*, trans. H. Rackham (Cambridge, MA: Harvard University Press, Loeb Classical Library).

Cicero, Marcus Tullius (1968), *On Invention (De Inventione)*, trans. H. M. Hubbell (Cambridge, MA: Harvard University Press, Loeb Classical Library).

Coetzee, John Maxwell (2013), *The Childhood of Jesus* (London: Harvill Secker).

Coetzee, John Maxwell (2016), *The Schooldays of Jesus* (London: Harvill Secker).

Cunaeus, Petrus (1617), *De republica Hebraeorum*.

Cunaeus, Petrus (1653), *Of the Commonwealth of the Hebrews*, trans. C. Barksdale (London: William Lee).

Curley, Edwin (1973a), 'Experience in Spinoza's Theory of Knowledge', in M. Grene (ed.), *Spinoza: A Collection of Critical Essays* (Garden City, NY: Anchor Books), pp. 25–59.

Curley, Edwin (1973b), 'Spinoza's Moral Philosophy', in M. Grene (ed.), *Spinoza: A Collection of Critical Essays* (Garden City, NY: Anchor Books), pp. 354–63.

Curley, Edwin (1991), 'The State of Nature and Its Law in Hobbes and Spinoza', *Philosophical Topics* 19: 97–117.

Curley, Edwin (1999), 'Kissinger, Spinoza and Genghis Khan', D. Garrett (ed.), *The Cambridge Companion to Spinoza* (Cambridge: Cambridge University Press), pp. 315–42.

Dancy, Jonathan (2004), *Ethics without Principles* (Oxford: Oxford University Press).

De Deugd, Cornelis (1966), *The Significance of Spinoza's First Kind of Knowledge* (Assen: Van Gorcum).

De la Court, Johan (1662), *Consideratien van Staat*, 4th edition (Amsterdam: n.p.).

De la Court, Pieter (1972), *The True Interest and Political Maxims of the Republic of Holland* (New York: Arno Press).

Deleuze, Gilles (1988), *Spinoza: Practical Philosophy*, trans. R. Hurley (San Francisco: City Lights).

Deleuze, Gilles (1990), *Expressionism in Philosophy: Spinoza*, trans. M. Joughin (New York: Zone Books).

Deleuze, Gilles (1997), 'Spinoza and the Three "Ethics"', trans. D. Smith and M. Greco, in W. Montag and T. Stolze (eds), *The New Spinoza*, (Minneapolis: The University of Minnesota Press), pp. 21–36.

Della Rocca, Michael (2003a), 'A Rationalist Manifesto: Spinoza and the Principle of Sufficient Reason', *Philosophical Topics* 31: 75–93.

Della Rocca, Michael (2003b), 'The Power of an Idea. Spinoza's Critique of Pure Will', *Nous* 37/2: 200–31.

Della Rocca, Michael (2008), *Spinoza* (New York: Routledge).

Den Uyl, Douglas (1983), *Power, State and Freedom: An Interpretation of Spinoza's Political Philosophy* (Van Gorcum: Assen).

Descartes, René (1985), *The Passions of the Soul*, trans. J. Cottingham et al., in *The Philosophical Writings of Descartes, vol. 1* (Cambridge: Cambridge University Press), pp. 325–404.

Douglas, A X., (2015), Spinoza and Dutch Cartesianism (Oxford: Oxford University Press).

Erastus, Thomas (1589), *Explicatio gravissimae quaestionis utrum excommunicatio, quatenus religionem intelligentes et amplexantes, a sacramentuorum usu, propter admissum facinus arcet, mandato nitatur divino, an excogitata sit ab hominibus* (London: n.p.).

Foucault, Michel (1986), *The History of Sexuality*, vol. 3: *The Care of the Self*, trans. R. Hurley (London: Penguin Books).

Fraenkel, Carlos (2012) *Philosophical Religions from Plato to Spinoza: Reason, Religion, and Autonomy* (Cambridge: Cambridge University Press).

Fraenkel, Carlos (2013), 'Spinoza's Philosophy of Religion', in M. Della Rocca (ed.), *The Oxford Handbook of Spinoza* (Oxford: Oxford University Press), pp. 377–407.

Frankfurt, Harry (2005), *Bullshit* (Princeton, NJ: Princeton University Press).

Friend, Stacie (2015), 'Fiction and Emotion', in A. Kind (ed.), *The Routledge Handbook of Philosophy of Imagination* (London: Routledge), pp. 217–29.

Frijhoff, Willem, and Spies, Marijke, with the collaboration of W. Van Bunge and N. Veldhorst, (2004), *Dutch Culture in European Perspective: 1650, Hard-Won Unity* (Assen: Van Gorcum).

Garrett, Aaron (2003), 'Spinoza as Natural Lawyer', *Cardozo Law Review* 25/2: 101–16.

Garrett, Aaron (2012), 'Knowing the Essence of the State in Spinoza's *Tractatus Theologico-Politicus*', *European Journal of Philosophy* 20: 50–73.

Garrett, Don (2008), 'Representation and Consciousness: Spinoza's Naturalistic Theory of the Imagination', in C. Huenemann (ed.), *Interpreting Spinoza* (Cambridge: Cambridge University Press), pp. 4–25.

Garrett, Don (2009a), 'Spinoza's Theory of Scientia Intuitiva', in T. Sorell, G. A. J. Rogers, and J. Kraye (eds), *Scientia in Early Modern Philosophy: Studies in History and Philosophy of Science (24)* (Dordrecht: Springer), pp. 99–116.

Garrett, Don (2009b), 'Spinoza on the Essence of the Human Body and the Part of the Mind that is Eternal', in O. Koistinen (ed.), *The Cambridge Companion to Spinoza's Ethics*, (Cambridge: Cambridge University Press), pp. 284–302.

Garver, Eugene (2006), 'Spinoza and the Discovery of Morality', *History of Philosophy Quarterly* 23/4: 357–74.

Gatens, Moira (1996), *Imaginary Bodies: Ethics, Power and Corporeality* (London: Routledge).

Gatens, Moira (2000), 'Feminism as Password: Re-thinking the "Possible" with Spinoza and Deleuze', *Hypatia* 15/2: 59–75.

Gatens, Moira (2009a), 'The Politics of Imagination', in M. Gatens (ed.), *Feminist Interpretations of Benedict Spinoza*, (University Park, PA: University of Pennsylvania Press), pp. 189–209.

Gatens, Moira (2009b), 'Spinoza's Disturbing Thesis: Power Norms and Fiction in the *Tractatus Theologico-Politicus*', *History of Political Thought*, 30/3: 455–68.

Gatens, Moira (2011), *Spinoza's Hard Path to Freedom* (Assen: Van Gorcum).

Gatens, Moira (2012), 'Compelling Fictions: Spinoza and George Eliot on Imagination and Belief', *European Journal of Philosophy* 20: 74–90.

Gatens, Moira (2014), 'Affective Transitions and Spinoza's Art of Joyful Deliberation', in M. L. Angerer, B. Bösel, and M. Ott (eds), *Timing of Affect. Epistemologies, Aesthetics, Politics* (Zürich: Diaphanes).

Gatens, Moira (2015), 'Spinoza on Goodness and Beauty and the Prophet and the Artist', *European Journal of Philosophy* 23/1: 1–16.

Gatens, Moira and Lloyd, Genevieve (1999), *Collective Imaginings. Spinoza Past and Present* (London: Routledge).

Gilbert, Francis (2017), *Spinoza and the Joy of Learning* (London: FGI Press).

Ginsborg, Paul and Labate, Sergio (2019), *Passion and Politics* (Cambridge: Polity Press).

Grafton, Anthony and Jardine, Lisa (1986), *From Humanism to the Humanities: Education and the Liberal Arts in Fifteenth- and Sixteenth-Century Europe* (London, Duckworth).

Green, Alex (2013), 'Spinoza on the Ethics of Courage', *Modern Judaism* 33/2: 199–225.

Grey, John (forthcoming). 'The Metaphysics of Natural Right in Spinoza', *Oxford Studies in Early Modern Philosophy, Volume 10* (Oxford: Oxford University Press).

Grotius, Hugo (1984), '*De republica emendanda*,' ed. A. Eyffinger et al., *Grotiana* , vol. 5.1

Grotius, Hugo (2005), *The Rights of War and Peace*, with an introduction by R. Tuck, ed. J. Barbeyrac (Indianapolis: Liberty Fund).

Grotius, Hugo (2006), *Commentary on the Law of Prize and Booty*, ed. and with an introduction by M. J. van Ittersum (Indianapolis: Liberty Fund).

Hadot, Pierre (1995), *Philosophy as a Way of Life*, ed. Arnold I. Davidson (Oxford: Blackwell).

Hammill, Graham (2012), *The Mosaic Constitution. Political Theology and Imagination from Machiavelli to Milton* (Chicago: Chicago University Press).

Hampshire, Stuart (2005), *Spinoza and Spinozism* (Oxford: Oxford University Press).

Hardt, Michael, and Negri, Antonio (2000) *Empire* (Cambridge, MA: Harvard University Press).

Harrington, James (1992), *The Commonwealth of Oceana*, ed. J. G. A. Pocock (Cambridge: Cambridge University Press).

Hobbes, Thomas (1991), *Leviathan*, ed. R. Tuck (Cambridge: Cambridge University Press).

Hobbes, Thomas (1994a), *Leviathan*, ed. E. Curley (Indianapolis: Hackett).

Hobbes, Thomas (1994b), *The Elements of Law, Natural and Politic*, ed. J. C. A. Gaskin (Oxford: Oxford University Press).

Hobbes, Thomas (1998), *On the Citizen*, ed. R. Tuck (Cambridge: Cambridge University Press).

Hoekstra, Kinch (2006), 'A Lion in the House: Hobbes and Democracy', in A. Brett, J. Tully, and H. Hamilton-Bleakley (eds), *Rethinking the Foundations of Modern Political Thought* (Cambridge: Cambridge University Press), pp. 191–218.

Hooker, Richard (1989), *Of the Laws of Ecclesiastical Polity*, ed. A. S. McGrade (Cambridge: Cambridge University Press).

Howie, Gillian (2002), *Deleuze and Spinoza: Aura of Expressionism* (Basingstoke: Palgrave Macmillan).

Hutto, Daniel (2007), (ed.), *Narrative and Understanding Persons* (Cambridge: Cambridge University Press).

Israel, Jonathan (1995), *The Dutch Republic: its Rise, Greatness and Fall 1477–1806* (Oxford: Oxford University Press).

Israel, Jonathan (2001), *Radical Enlightenment: Philosophy and the Making of Modernity 1650–1750* (Oxford: Oxford University Press).

Jacquet, Chantal (2003), 'La fortitude cachée', in C. Jacquet, P. Sévérac, and A. Shumy (eds), *Fortitude et Servitude* (Paris: Éditions Kimé), pp. 15–25.

James, Susan (2012), *Spinoza on Philosophy, Religion, and Politics: The Theologico-Political Treatise* (Oxford: Oxford University Press).

Josephus (1926), *The Life. Against Apion*, ed. and trans. H. St. J. Thackeray (Cambridge, MA: Harvard University Press, Loeb Classical Library).

Josephus (1930–65), *Jewish Antiquities,* 8 vols, ed and trans. H. St. J. Thackeray and L. Feldman (Cambridge, MA: Harvard University Press, Loeb Classical Library).

Klever, Wim (1991), 'A New Source for Spinozism: Franciscus van den Enden', *Journal of the History of Philosophy* 29: 613–31.

Laerke, Mogens (2012), 'Leibniz on Spinoza's Political Philosophy', in D. Garber and D. Rutherford (eds), *Oxford Studies in Early Modern Philosophy, Volume 6* (Oxford: Oxford University Press), pp. 105–34.

Laux, Henri (1993), *Imagination et religion chez Spinoza: La potentia dans l'histoire*. (Paris: Vrin).

Lebuffe, Michael (2009), 'The Anatomy of the Passions', in O. Koistinen (ed.), *The Cambridge Companion to Spinoza's Ethics* (Cambridge: Cambridge University Press).

Lenz, Martin (2013), 'Spinoza on the Normativity of Ideas', in M. Lenz and A. Waldo (eds), *Contemporary Perspectives on Early Modern Philosophy: Nature and Norms in Thought* (Dordrecht: Springer), pp. 37–50.

Leo, Russ (2015), 'Spinoza's Calvin: Reformed Theology in the *Korte Verhandeling van God, de Mensch en Deszelfs Welstand*', in Y. Melamed (ed.), *The Young Spinoza*, (Oxford: Oxford University Press), pp. 144–159.

Levene, Nancy (2004), *Spinoza's Revelation: Religion, Democracy, and Reason* (Cambridge: Cambridge University Press).

Lin, Martin (2006), 'Spinoza's Account of Akrasia', *Journal of the History of Philosophy* 44/3: 395–414.

Lindquist, Sven (1997), '*Exterminate All the Brutes*'. *One Man's Odyssey into the Heart of Darkness and the Origins of European Genocide*, trans. J. Tate (Cambridge: Granta Books).

Livy, Titus (1926), *History of Rome* vol. IV, trans. B. O. Foster. Loeb Classical Library (Cambridge, Mass.; Harvard University Press).

Lord, Beth (2018), 'Ratio as the Basis of Spinoza's Concept of Equality', in B. Lord (ed.), *Spinoza's Philosophy of Ratio*. (Edinburgh: Edinburgh University Press), pp. 61–73.

Macherey, Pierre (1995), *Introduction à l'Éthique de Spinoza. 3e partie: La vie affective* (Paris: Presses Universitaires de France).

Machiavelli, Niccolò (1996), *Discourses on Livy*, trans. H. C. Mansfield and N. Tarcov (Chicago: University of Chicago Press).

MacIntyre, Alasdair (1981), *After Virtue* (Notre Dame: University of Notre Dame Press).

Malcolm, Noel (2002), 'Hobbes and Spinoza', in *Aspects of Hobbes* (Oxford: Oxford University Press), pp. 27–52.

Malinowski-Charles, Sylvaine (2003), 'The Circle of Knowledge: Notes on Reason and Intuition in Spinoza', in D. Garber and S. Nadler (eds), *Oxford Studies in Early Modern Philosophy, Volume 1* (Oxford: Clarendon Press), pp. 139–63.

Marshall, Eugene (2013), *The Spiritual Automaton. Spinoza's Science of the Mind* (Oxford: Oxford University Press).

Matheron, Alexandre (1969), *Individu et communauté chez Spinoza* (Paris: Minuit).

Matheron, Alexandre (1984), 'Spinoza et le problematique juridique de Grotius', *Philosophie* 4: 69–89.

Matheron, Alexandre (1985), 'Le "droit du plus fort": Hobbes contra Spinoza', *Revue philosophiqe de la France et de l'etranger* 110: 149–76.

Matheron, Alexandre (1994), 'L'indignation et le conatus de l'état spinoziste', in M. R. D'Allonnes and H. Rizk (eds), *Spinoza: puissance et ontologie* (Paris: Editions Kimé).

Matheron, Alexandre (1997), 'Spinoza and Hobbes', in W. Montag and T. Stolze (eds), *The New Spinoza*, (Minneapolis: The University of Minnesota Press), pp. 207–16.

Menn, Stephen (1998), *Descartes and Augustine* (Cambridge: Cambridge University Press).

Merçon, Juliana and Armstrong, Aurelia (2011), 'Transindividuality and Philosophical Enquiry in Schools: A Spinozist Perspective', in N. Vansieleghem and D. Kennedy (eds), *Philosophy for Children in Transition: Problems and Prospects* (Hoboken, NJ: John Wiley & Sons), pp. 82–96.

Miller, Jon (2015), *Spinoza and the Stoics* (Cambridge: Cambridge University Press).

Mommsen, Theodore and Krueger, Paul (eds) (1985), *Digest of Justinian*, trans. A. Watson, 4 vols (Philadelphia: University of Pennsylvania Press).

Montag, Warren (1999), *Bodies, Masses, Power: Spinoza and His Contemporaries* (London: Verso).

Nadler, Steven (1999), *Spinoza. A Life* (Cambridge: Cambridge University Press).

Negri, Antonio (1982), *L'Anomalie Sauvage: puissance et pouvoir chez Spinoza* (Paris: Presses Universitaires de France).

Negri, Antonio (1997), 'Reliqua Desiderantur: A Conjecture for a Definition of Democracy in the Final Spinoza', in W. Montag and T. Stolze (eds), *The New Spinoza*, (Minneapolis: The University of Minnesota Press), pp. 219–47.

Nelson, Eric (2010), *The Hebrew Republic: Jewish Sources and the Transformation of European Political Thought* (Cambridge, MA: Harvard University Press).

Nobbs, Douglas (1938), *Theocracy and Toleration. A Study of the Disputes in Dutch Calvinism from 1600 to 1650* (Cambridge: Cambridge University Press).

O'Neill, Joseph (2008), *Netherland* (New York: Harper Collins).

Pettit, Philip (1997), *Republicanism. A Theory of Freedom and Government* (Oxford: Oxford University Press).

Pfersmann, Otto (2003), 'Law's Normativity in Spinoza's Naturalism', *Cardozo Law Review* 25/2: 643–56.

Plato (1997), *Plato: Complete Works*, ed. J. M. Cooper (Indianapolis: Hackett).

Plato (2016), *Timaeus*, trans. and ed. P. Kalkavage, 2nd edition (Indianapolis: Hackett).

Proietti, Omero (1985), 'Adulescens luxu perditus: classici latini nell'opera di Spinoza', *Rivista di Filosofia Neo-Scolastica* 2: 210–57.

Prokhovnik, Raia (2004), *Spinoza and Dutch Republicanism* (Basingstoke: Palgrave Macmillan).

Radford, Colin (1975), 'How Can We Be Moved by the Fate of Anna Karenina?', in *Proceedings of the Aristotelian Society, Supplementary Volume* 49: pp. 67–80.

Ravven, Heidi M. (2003), 'Spinozistic Approaches to Evolutionary Naturalism: Spinoza's Anticipation of Contemporary Affective Neuroscience', *Politics and the Life Sciences* 22: 70–4.

Ripa, Cesare (1603), *Iconologia* (Rome).

Ripa, Cesare (1644), *Iconologia of uytbeeldingen des Verstands*,   trans. Dirck Pietersz (Amsterdam: Pers).

Rosenthal, Michael (1999), 'Toleration and the Right to Resist in Spinoza's *Theological-Political Treatise*: The Problem of Christ's Disciples', in P. Bagley (ed.), *Piety, Peace, and the Freedom to Philosophize* (Dordrecht: Kluwer), pp. 111–32.

Rosenthal, Michael (2001), 'Tolerance as a Virtue in Spinoza's Ethics', *Journal of the History of Philosophy* 39/4: 535–57.

Rosenthal, Michael (2003), 'Spinoza's Republican Argument for Toleration', *Journal of Political Philosophy* 11/3: 320–37.

Rowen, Herbert (1978), *John De Witt: Grand Pensionary of Holland 1625–1672* (Princeton, NJ: Princeton University Press).

Rutherford, Donald (2010), 'Spinoza's Conception of Law: Metaphysics and Ethics', in Y. Melamed and M. Rosenthal (eds), *Spinoza's Theological-Political Treatise: A Critical Guide* (Cambridge: Cambridge University Press), pp. 143–67.

Sangiacomo, Andrea (2019), *Spinoza on Reason, Passions, and the Supreme Good* (Oxford: Oxford University Press).

Santos Campos, Andre (2012), *Spinoza's Revolution in Natural Law* (London: Palgrave Macmillan).

Schaff, Philip (2007), *The Creeds of Christendom: The Evangelical Protestant Creeds* (New York: Cosimo Books).

Schliesser, Eric (2011), 'Angels and Philosophers: With a New Interpretation of Spinoza's Common Notions', Proceedings of the Aristotelian Society, new series, vol. CXI, pp. 497–18.

Schmitt, Carl (1996), *Leviathan in the State Theory of Thomas Hobbes: Meaning and Failure of a Political Symbol*, trans. G. Schwab and E. Hilfstein (Westport, CT: Greenwood Press).

Scott, Jonathan (2002), 'Classical Republicanism in Seventeenth-Century England and the Netherlands', in M. Van Gelderen and Q. Skinner (eds), *Republicanism: A Shared European Heritage, Vol. 1, Republicanism and Constitutionalism in Early Modern Europe* (Cambridge: Cambridge University Press), pp. 61–84.

Sedley, David (1999), 'The Ideal of Godlikeness', in G. Fine (ed.), *Plato 2: Ethics, Politics, Religion, and the Soul* (Oxford: Oxford University Press), pp. 309–28.

Seneca (1971), *Epistulae Morales*, ed. E. H. Warmington, Loeb Classical Library (Cambridge, Mass., Haarvard University Press).

Sharp, Hasana (2007), 'The Force of Ideas in Spinoza', *Political Theory* 35.6, 732–55.

Shklar, Judith (1989), 'The Liberalism of Fear' in Nancy Rosenblum ed. *Liberalism and the Moral Life* (Cambridge, Mass.: Harvard University Press).

Skinner, Quentin (1998), *Liberty before Liberalism* (Cambridge: Cambridge University Press).

Smith, Stephen B. (2003), *Spinoza's Book of Life: Freedom and Redemption in the 'Ethics'* (New Haven, CT: Yale University Press).

Spinoza (1925), *Spinoza Opera*, 4 vols (vol. 5, 1987), ed. C. Gebhardt. (Hildesheim: Carl Winter).

Spinoza(1985) 'Descartes' "Principles of Philosophy"', in *The Collected Works of Spinoza, Vol. I*, ed. and trans. E. Curley (Princeton, NJ: Princeton University Press), pp. 224–346.

Spinoza (1985) 'Ethics' in *The Collected Works of Spinoza, Vol. I*, ed. and trans. E. Curley (Princeton, NJ: Princeton University Press), pp. 408–617.

Spinoza(1985) Letters August 1661–August 1663, in *The Collected Works of Spinoza, Vol. I*, ed. and trans. E. Curley (Princeton, NJ: Princeton University Press), pp. 163–218.

Spinoza(1985) Letters July 1664–September 1665, in *The Collected Works of Spinoza, Vol. I*, ed. and trans. E. Curley (Princeton, NJ: Princeton University Press), pp. 352–97.

Spinoza (1985) 'Short Treatise on God, Man and his Wellbeing', in *The Collected Works of Spinoza, Vol. I*, ed. and trans. E. Curley (Princeton, NJ: Princeton University Press), pp. 53–156.

Spinoza (1985), 'Treatise on the Emendation of the Intellect' in *The Collected Works of Spinoza, Vol. I*, ed. and trans. E. Curley (Princeton, NJ: Princeton University Press), pp. 7–45.

Spinoza (2016), Letters, September 1665—September 1669, in *The Collected Works of Spinoza, Vol. II*, ed. and trans. E. Curley (Princeton, NJ: Princeton University Press), pp. 10–44.

Spinoza (2016), Letters January 1671–Late 1676, in 'Theologico-Political Treatise' in *The Collected Works of Spinoza, Vol. II*, ed. and trans. E. Curley (Princeton, NJ: Princeton University Press), pp. 374–488.

Spinoza (2016), 'Political Treatise' in *The Collected Works of Spinoza, Vol. II*, ed. and trans. E. Curley (Princeton, NJ: Princeton University Press), pp. 503–604.

Spinoza(2016), 'Theologico-Political Treatise' in *The Collected Works of Spinoza, Vol. II*, ed. and trans. E. Curley (Princeton, NJ: Princeton University Press), pp. 65–364.

Steinberg, Diane (2005), 'Belief, Affirmation and the Doctrine of Conatus', *Southern Journal of Philosophy* 43: 147–58.

Steinberg, Justin (2009), 'Spinoza on Civil Liberation', *Journal of the History of Philosophy* 47/1: 35–58.

Steinberg, Justin (2014), 'Following a Recta Ratio Vivendi: The Practical Utility of Spinoza's Dictates of Reason' in *The Ethics of Spinoza's Ethics*, Matthew Kisner and Andrew Youpa eds., Oxford: Oxford University Press, 178–96.

Steinberg, Justin (2017), 'Two Puzzles Concerning Spinoza's Conception of Belief', *European Journal of Philosophy* 26: 261–82.

Steinberg, Justin (2018), *Spinoza's Political Psychology: The Taming of Fortune and Fear* (Cambridge: Cambridge University Press).

Stolze, Ted (2007), 'Spinoza on the Glory of Politics', in R. Caporali, V. Morfino, and S. Visentin (eds), *Spinoza: Individuo e moltitudine* (Cesena: Società Editrice 'Il Ponte Vecchio'), pp. 327–40.

Stolze, Ted (2014), 'An Ethics for Marxism: Spinoza on Fortitude', *Rethinking Marxism: A Journal of Economics, Culture and Society* 26: 561–80.

Strauss, Leo (1965), *Spinoza's Critique of Religion*, trans. E. M. Sinclair (New York: Schocken Books).

Strauss, Leo (1988), 'How to Study Spinoza's Theologico-Political Treatise?', in *Persecution and the Art of Writing* (Chicago: Chicago University Press).

Strauss, Leo (1995), *Philosophy and Law* (Albany: State University of New York Press).

Tacitus (1931), *Annals*, trans. C. H. Moore and J. Jackson (Cambridge, MA: Harvard University Press, Loeb Classical Library).

Tuck, Richard (2006), 'Hobbes and Democracy', in A. Brett, J. Tully, and H. Hamilton-Bleakley (eds), *Rethinking the Foundations of Modern Political Thought* (Cambridge: Cambridge University Press), pp. 171–90.

van Bunge, Wiep (1989), 'On the Early Dutch Reception of the Tractatus Theologico-Politicus', *Studia Spinozana* 5: 225–51.

van Gelderen, Martin (2007), 'The Low Countries: The Quest for Concord', in G. Burgess, H. Lloyd, and S. Hodson (eds), *European Political Thought 1450–1700: Religion, Law and Philosophy* (New Haven, CT: Yale University Press), pp. 376–415.

Vatter, Miguel (2004), 'Strauss and Schmitt as Readers of Hobbes and Spinoza', *New Centennial Review* 4/3: 186–91.

Verbeek, Theo (1992), *Descartes and the Dutch: Early Reactions to Cartesian Philosophy, 1637–1650* (Carbondale, IL: Southern Illinois University Press).

Verbeek, Theo (1993), 'Tradition and Novelty: Descartes and Some Cartesians', in T. Sorell (ed.), *The Rise of Modern Philosophy: The Tension between the New and Traditional Philosophies from Machiavelli to Leibniz* (Oxford: Oxford University Press).

Verbeek, Theo (1999), 'Spinoza and Cartesianism', in A. Coudert (ed.), *Judaeo-Christian Intellectual Culture in the Seventeenth Century: A Celebration of the Library of Narcissus Marsh (1638–1713)* (Dordrecht: Kluwer Academic).

Verbeek, Theo (2003), *Spinoza's Theologico-Political Treatise: Exploring 'The Will of God'* (Aldershot: Ashgate).

Verbeek, Theo (2007), 'Spinoza on Natural Rights', *Intellectual History Review* 17/3: 257–75.

Vinciguerra, Lorenzo (2005), *Spinoza et le signe: La Genèse de l'imagination* (Paris: Vrin).

von Friedeburg, Robert (2005), 'The Problems of Passions and of Love of Fatherland in Protestant Thought: Melanchthon to Althusius, 1520s to 1620s', *Cultural and Social History* 2: 81–98.

Wansink, H. (1981), *Politieke wetenschappen aan de Leidse universiteit, 1575–1650* (Utrecht: n.p.).

Winnicott, Donald (1971), *Playing and Reality* (London: Tavistock Publications; reprinted London: Routledge, 1991).

Index

For the benefit of digital users, indexed terms that span two pages (e.g., 52–53) may, on occasion, appear on only one of those pages.